DE   '98

D1058512

THE EDUCATION OF A SENATOR

Everett McKinley Dirksen, c. 1930. (Courtesy of the Dirksen
Congressional Center, Pekin, Illinois)

THE
EDUCATION OF A SENATOR

Everett McKinley Dirksen

Foreword by
Howard H. Baker Jr.

Introduction by
Frank H. Mackaman

UNIVERSITY OF ILLINOIS PRESS

URBANA AND CHICAGO

Publication of this book was supported by a grant from the
Everett McKinley Dirksen Endowment Fund

© 1998 by the Everett McKinley Dirksen Congressional
Leadership Research Center
Manufactured in the United States of America
C 5 4 3 2 1

This book is printed on acid-free paper.

Library of Congress Cataloging-in-Publication Data
Dirksen, Everett McKinley.
The education of a senator / Everett McKinley Dirksen ;
foreword by Howard H. Baker Jr. ; introduction by
Frank H. Mackaman.
p.   cm.
Includes bibliographical references and index.
ISBN 0-252-02414-1 (alk. paper)
1. Dirksen, Everett McKinley. 2. Legislators—
United States—Biography. 3. United States. Congress.
Senate—Biography. 4. United States—Politics and
government—1945–1989. I. Title.
E748.D557A3   1998
328.73′092—dc21
[B]   97-46696
CIP

CONTENTS

FOREWORD

Howard H. Baker Jr.

I had a unique privilege in my life, and that was to serve as minority leader and then four years as majority leader of the United States Senate. A few years after retiring from the Senate in 1985, I saw Senate leadership from yet another vantage point, as chief of staff to President Ronald Reagan. My respect for the office of Senate leader has only grown over the years—and so has my appreciation for what my father-in-law, Everett McKinley Dirksen, accomplished as minority leader in the 1960s.

I sometimes wonder if my fellow Americans—or perhaps even my former colleagues and friends in the Senate—really understand the role of that body's leaders. What I have called the "office of Senate leader," comprised of both the majority and minority leaders, is an institution in and of itself. It must speak for the Senate, must see that the body functions, must ensure that it produces a result. The power of the office of Senate leader is extraordinary; its relevance to the formulation of public policy, indispensable. Tradition, circumstance, and a few singular individuals have invented and shaped the office. Make no mistake about it, Everett Dirksen was one of the most singular in a distinguished group.

What accounted for Senator Dirksen's success? You will learn from reading this memoir of his faith, hard work, and preparation for public service. But speaking as one who observed him closely as a member of his family and who served with him in the Senate from 1967 until his death in September 1969, I recall three bedrock qualities. First, Everett Dirksen had a real concern for his colleagues. He had a great affection for, and respect for, senators on both sides of the aisle. A leader in the Senate cannot lead as a drill sergeant leads because there is so much more individuality involved, so much less party discipline. You don't really *lead* in the classical sense. You urge. You create a previous inclination to *follow* on the part of your colleagues.

Dirksen excelled at that. He was genuinely concerned for every single member of the Republican party in the Senate. He wanted to know what their requirements were, what their constituents demanded of them, what they had the liberty to do. He tried to honor their obligations. He was at once patient and persistent; only rarely did he lean on people. He cajoled, persuaded—he called it "gentle discussion," like using oil to make sure that the bearings never got hot. No one ever doubted that Everett Dirksen was sincerely interested in every member of the Senate. That was his single greatest quality as leader.

Senator Dirksen coupled that with an unbounded affection for the institutions of government and an unbridled faith in the people. These are not contradictory notions. On the one hand, he was loyal to the processes of democracy embodied in the federal government—all three branches. Although he was himself a man of the Congress, he held the presidency in great esteem, sometimes at a substantial personal cost. His defense of Lyndon Johnson late into the Vietnam War, for example, did not endear him to many of his colleagues. But Dirksen understood that governing required respect, even in the heat of disagreement. He respected his adversaries, including presidents from the other party, and commanded their respect as well.

Dirksen knew, too, that America's story was one of progress. Coming from the nation's heartland, from the land of Lincoln, he felt instinctively the brilliance of the people in their ability to surmount difficulties, as individuals and as a society. It may sound out of fashion today, but Everett Dirksen's faith in people made him an optimist. "Life is a matter of development or decay," he would say. "You can either grow or you can retrogress. . . . The challenge will make you grow, if you are willing to assert a leadership and look on the challenge as something to be met and disposed of." Meeting and disposing of challenges comprised the essence of Dirksen's career in the House and Senate.

Lastly, Dirksen had another practical attribute in a profession sometimes rent by orthodoxy and inflexibility: virtually every idea he held, he held tentatively. The world would be better off if more people did that these days. He understood with exceptional clarity that a great and diverse people do not speak with a single voice and that adherence to rigid ideology leaves little room for compromise and response to change. I remember that the journalist Neil MacNeil, his biographer and good friend, opened his book on Dirksen with the senator's own words: "I am not a moralist. I am a legislator." As leader, Dirksen did what had to be done to conduct the nation's business. His was the politics of the possible, not of the promise.

The Education of a Senator speaks to the experience of one remarkable individual who became a Senate leader. But is there more to it than that? Are there lessons to be drawn from Dirksen's story? Whatever else might be said about his brand of leadership, the simple fact is that it worked. He made his troops in the Senate more effective than their numbers. Without Dirksen's leadership, we would not have had the Nuclear Test Ban Treaty of 1963, nor a series of civil rights bills beginning with the landmark 1964 act. Equally important, especially to him, were the laws that, by the dint of hard work, he kept off the books. The Senate minority leader carries the obligation to serve as the responsible opposition, and at times that office is the last line of defense to stop the worst from happening.

Whether or not a different leader might have enjoyed more success is unknowable. Whether or not a Dirksen would have comparable success today is also unknowable. Congressional leadership, both House and Senate, operates in a context, not a vacuum. The context is a rich, ever-changing amalgam of public expectations, the relative strength of political parties, the control of the other body and the White House, the nature of Congress itself, the array of tools available to leaders, the willingness of others to follow, the issues agenda, what historians like to call the "tenor of the times," and so on.

What worked in Dirksen's time at the helm of the Senate, or in my time, might not work so well now. But that does not gainsay the quality and effectiveness of Everett Dirksen's leadership of the Republicans in our most challenging decade since World War II.

INTRODUCTION

Frank H. Mackaman

Everett Dirksen spent much of the last three weeks before his unexpected death in September 1969 working on this book. Following the mid-August recess of the Ninety-first Congress, Dirksen had retired to his home to rest up for scheduled lung surgery. At "Heart's Desire" in Virginia, he tended his gardens, prepared for the resumption of the legislative session, and put the finishing touches on his autobiography. Dirksen's thoughts had turned increasingly to the deterioration of the nation's civic life. Appalled by the country's social and political turmoil, manifested in race riots and demonstrations against the war in Vietnam, he worried that young people seemed to be turning their backs on their American heritage. He sought to bring them, in his words, "back into the stream of tradition,"[1] and he hoped that the telling of his life story would help reestablish the virtue of public service.

The Education of a Senator was the result. In it Dirksen described the three primary ingredients in his career: preparation, ambition, and opportunity. He recounted the story as only Dirksen could, with anecdotes, observations about people met along the way, lessons learned. The memoir's style is vintage Dirksen, too, written as if he were telling a story to his grandchildren, filled with those marvelous words and phrases he seemed to summon up at will. As Dirksen himself put it: "I make no pretense in this narrative of maintaining any kind of strict chronology," preferring instead to skip around, relying on his memory—he did not keep a diary or a strict accounting of his activities. Neither is there evidence that Dirksen employed a researcher or consulted historical studies during the preparation of the manuscript. In other words, *The Education of a Senator* was distinctly a personal story, not a political or legislative history, not a scholarly treatise. Dirksen carried the account only through his election to the Senate in 1950, apparently planning to write a second volume dealing with his years in the Senate. It is not possible to know what he would have said, but the story of his life is not complete without reference to his remarkable career there. This introduction will fill out that story and provide context for Dirksen's own account of his life before the Senate.

The manuscript lay unpublished in a recently unsealed portion of the Dirksen Papers housed at the research center named for him in his hometown. The idea of publishing it emerged at the time of the centennial observance of the senator's birth on January 4, 1896.

"The Carefree Halcyon Days"

Dirksen's affection for his family and his community was as plain as could be. It was a theme in his autobiography and at the root of his outlook on life and politics. Dirksen was the son of immigrant parents, part of a big colony of their countrymen who had settled in Pekin, Illinois, in the mid-1800s. The Deutschlanders were frugal, industrious, civic-minded, and Republican. Everett McKinley Dirksen had an older brother, Benjamin Harrison; an identical twin, Thomas Reed; and two half brothers.

Although his father, Johann, died before Everett was ten, the family foundation remained unshakeable. His mother, Antje, took up vegetable gardening and livestock raising to keep the family together. The boys helped out at an early age. A neighbor recalled the three Dirksen youngsters going barefoot around the neighborhood, carrying pails of milk to the family's customers.[2] Later Dirksen would say that "there was a certain ruggedness about life, and a certain ruggedness in living that life."[3] His memoir suggests an upbringing long on earnest determination, hard work, uncompromising principles, and stern discipline fairly meted. He described the family home and routine, the importance of the Reformed Church in their lives, and his pals in the neighborhood "gang." Everett particularly prized the family's plot of land. The Dirksens kept a half-dozen cows, a half-dozen pigs, 150 chickens, and a horse. They raised berries, turnips, lettuce, onions, and radishes. Dirksen called it "one acre and liberty."

Roman L. Hruska, later Dirksen's best friend in the Senate, once recalled that Dirksen "was fortunate in being born near the center of our Nation in a rural environment where initiative and hard work were complemented by both failures and successes, and to parents who had faith in man's abilities through Divine guidance."[4]

Schooling paved the way for Everett Dirksen to move beyond the neighborhood and his community. His brothers dropped out before attending high school, but Everett rose to the challenge with relish. School came easily to him. Here he cultivated friendships, practiced leadership in student groups, indulged his passion for the theatrical, and acquired a knowledge of the world beyond Pekin, largely because he was a voracious reader. In hindsight, all these experiences were essential to his preparation for politics and public service, although the ambition was by no means clear at this early age. Dirksen graduated as class salutatorian, taking the class motto as his theme for the graduation address: "Ad Astra per Aspera"—"through difficulties to the heights." One wonders how the audience responded; next to Dirksen's picture in the yearbook appeared the appellation, "bigworditis." A classmate once said that Dirksen "must have swallowed a dictionary."[5]

Dirksen found employment in a corn refining company upon graduation, working eleven hours each day for one week and thirteen hours each day for the second week for fifty-four dollars per month. His industry paid off in a promotion to assistant chemist. What spare time he had went to amateur theater. When his mother suggested that he take a vacation to visit his half brother in Minnesota, young Everett seized the moment. After returning home to discuss his plans, he enrolled in the University of Minnesota in the fall of 1914. He worked to earn the money to stay there, tasted of politics for the first time in the presidential campaign of 1916, and engaged in spirited campus discussions about the war raging in Europe. Later, Dirksen would trace his political aspiration to his days on campus "when we sat around in the Student Union, [as] the budding politicians discussed the various things they hoped to accomplish in life." On January 4, 1917, his twenty-first birthday, Dirksen was inducted into the army.

Off to War and Home Again

World War I proved every bit as essential to his preparation for politics as had his upbringing and schooling. The war took him outside the Middle West and outside the United States. He encountered Jim Crow laws for the first time while training at Camp Jackson in South Carolina. In France, he became a horse officer at Camp Coëtquidan, then was assigned to the Nineteenth Balloon Company at Toul. Europe fascinated him, and he traveled widely after the armistice. But inducements to remain fell on deaf ears. After eighteen months of overseas duty, Dirksen wanted desperately to return home.

He took with him, he wrote in his memoir, a conviction: "I was not sure that I wanted to return to school and complete my law course, but I did know that I wanted to do something to end the madness of conflict and the insane business of arbitrating the differences of men and nations with poison gas and high explosive shells." He believed that false pride and a hypernationalism had bred the conflict. Further, he was optimistic that "if these problems could be approached with proper humility and a realization of the ghastliness of conflict, settlements might be more easily contrived. In any event, the answer now was becoming simpler for me. I must go into politics."

Despite Dirksen's preparation for politics and his budding ambition, the right opportunity did not present itself immediately. He returned home in October 1919 but admitted to "floundering" for some time. Expecting a hero's welcome, he was barely noticed. Dirksen wrote that he was "unhappy and bewildered." Dirksen did not mope around for long, though. He fell into a routine rooted in his upbringing: religion, theater, home, and work. "Life meant work," he recalled, "for only in work could one be happy and really content." He tried various endeavors from washing-machine manufacture to dredge-boat operator with mixed success. Finally, he joined his brothers in a wholesale bakery, a job that required Dirksen to travel throughout central Illinois delivering bread to grocery stores.

Dirksen filled in at the pulpit of his church for several months, too, brushing up on the Bible and honing his use of the language. The returning veteran indulged his theatrical passion as well, composing more than one hundred works (plays, short stories, and five novels) between 1919 and 1926. Although none paid the bills, "I began to make plans to pursue a theatrical existence, which I confided to my widowed mother," Dirksen recollected. "But she had a typical old-country, small-town, puritanistic view of the stage as a wicked domain. She demanded that I assure her right there that I would not essay it as a career. I gave her that assurance, but that, of course, did not destroy the urge. I *had* to appear before people." Dirksen looked up Clarence Ropp, a chum from school, to find an outlet for their "common urge for self-expression." They collaborated on a production for Pekin's centennial in 1924, an event noted more for bringing Dirksen together with the future Mrs. Dirksen than for the quality of the show. Meeting Louella Carver was fortuitous, for Dirksen's mother died during this period in his life. Everett and Louella were married in 1927. Their only child, Danice Joy, was born on February 10, 1929.

Upon his return to Pekin after the war, Dirksen did something else that proved crucial to his career. He joined the American Legion. Perhaps he merely sought the friendship of those who had served in the armed services.

Or it may have been an early demonstration of Dirksen's political acumen. As it happened, the American Legion was organized into districts that coincided with the boundaries of congressional districts. Dirksen plunged into legion activities, becoming district commander in 1926. He refined his speaking skills on that circuit and slowly, carefully began to build the network of contacts that would assure him a place in Congress.

But Dirksen's first political opportunity developed in Pekin. In the 1927 elections to the town's nonpartisan city council, a huge turnout selected Dirksen first among eight candidates vying for four seats. His record suggests that Dirksen saw government action positively, appreciating that it had a place in people's lives. He favored the development of city services, from parking meters to bus transportation to ornamental lighting. He supported the city's purchase of the local waterworks and public funding in the amount of $100,000 for the construction of a bridge across the Illinois River. He was appointed to the local committee of the governor's Commission on Unemployment Relief, which was responsible for preparing measures for future emergencies.[6]

Dirksen enjoyed the attention and worked hard at his job, admitting to the "great lure" of service. "It is exhilarating when something is accomplished," he noted, ". . . and finally there is some recognition, no matter how humble the office." He admitted to having an ego: "There is usually enough written in the local press to satisfy what egotism one may possess. I was no exception to this. I regarded myself as a normal human being with normal tastes and weaknesses, and with that feeling of delight that goes along with hearing yourself referred to as 'The Honorable Everett McKinley Dirksen, Commissioner of Finance of the city of Pekin.' It sounded pretty good to me, I admit." But as much as Dirksen enjoyed the life of public servant, he grew tired of the endless stream of petty complaints on the local level. As his ambition grew, he looked to a larger stage.

To the U.S. House

Restless and emboldened, in 1929 Everett McKinley Dirksen announced his decision to forsake Pekin politics for the national arena and a seat in the U.S. House of Representatives. He said that his aspiration was similar to the "flu" in that "everybody gets it at some time or another." The incumbent, William Edgar Hull of Peoria, had unseated an incumbent himself in 1922. Wealthy and well connected, Hull seemed to have every advantage going into the race. But he did not possess Dirksen's vigor and voice. The challenger poured his energy into the race, losing thirty pounds in the bargain. The outcome seemed in doubt well into election night. But Dirksen had misjudged the opportunity. "Dirksen Loses in a Brilliant Race" read the next day's headline in the *Pekin Daily Times.*

Undeterred, Dirksen announced immediately after the election that he intended to seek the seat in 1932, and he began campaigning. Two years of grueling work paid off in an upset of Hull in the Republican primary, when Dirksen won 52 percent of the votes. In the general election campaign, he dismissed the doctrine of party regularity, questioned high taxes, deplored farm and home foreclosures, and claimed that the country's problems were moral and ethical as well as economic. This time he won, and with a plurality that matched Franklin D. Roosevelt's in his district (some twenty-three thousand). Dirksen staked out his independence early. He would not take the Republican pledge. "With unemployment increasing, . . . banks popping . . . and . . . business stagnant, what could one say," he explained to his neighbors following the election, "in behalf of Herbert Hoover and against Franklin D. Roosevelt? . . . How could one apologize for Republican leadership when the nation was bleeding from the wounds of depression?"[7]

Dirksen knew his district intimately and was inextricably bound to it. Years of selling bread to area groceries, his American Legion activity, and two congressional campaigns put him in close touch with his constituents. Even after he left for Washington, Dirksen remained a Pekinite. "All the major decisions of my life have been made here," he reflected. "This is my native city, where the family taproot goes deep, and it will ever be."[8] The Sixteenth Congressional District stretched across six counties in north-central Illinois, partly rural, partly urban, with some coal mines, a corn-hog economy, considerable soybean production, and the city of Peoria its manufacturing and commercial hub. Located across the river and about eight miles north of Pekin, Peoria boasted a population of over 100,000, was a major producer of whiskey and industrial alcohol, and served as a transportation hub for fourteen railroads, as well as the Illinois Waterway's River and Rail Terminal.[9] Taken as a whole, the sixteenth district encompassed a variety of economic and social activity. Its people suffered mightily during the Depression, but they, as Dirksen with them, kept their skepticism about government-sponsored programs.

In the present memoir, Dirksen described the experience of a thirty-six-year-old freshman congressman setting up his office, getting to know the ropes. It was not an unalloyed pleasure. First, he faced the fact that the Republicans were outnumbered in the House 313 to 117. It disappointed him that his colleagues lacked the historical presence he had expected to find—they seemed too much like himself. In his first vote, he opposed Roosevelt, setting off a torrent of mail chastising Dirksen. "When it was all put together, I was a rather unhappy freshman congressman," Dirksen remembered. "The gloating of the New Dealers did not ease my pain or anguish." And what he called the "radical design of the legislation which had been pummeled through Congress" seemed alien to his conservative nature. He felt relief when that first historic session adjourned on June 15, 1933.

Although he opposed the Democrats in his vote against the so-called Economy Act, Dirksen actually supported many New Deal measures. In the early New Deal days, Dirksen voted for the Agricultural Adjustment Act, the Federal Emergency Relief Act, the Home Owners' Loan Act, the National Industrial Recovery Act, the National Labor Relations Act, the Social Security Act, and the Guffy-Snyder Coal Act. Twenty years later, Dirksen explained his support in these words: "Those days of 1932 and 1933 were troublous and beset with difficulty. Insofar as conviction permitted, one was expected to adjourn all partisanship and participate in the common enterprise of lifting the Nation from its despondency."[10]

As the Depression wore on, Dirksen continued to exercise his independence from the standard Republican position, even receiving support from the American Federation of Labor and the Railroad Brotherhoods. In 1938 he campaigned on a record of support for New Deal farm legislation during his service on the House Appropriations Committee's Agriculture Subcommittee. He opposed strip mining on the grounds that it created environmental damage and job losses for shaft miners. He also seemed amenable to the Capper Bill, a federal health insurance scheme providing for an employer-employee contributory system, with federal matching grants of 25 percent for the states.[11]

Yet, Dirksen gradually distanced himself from the New Deal. The mounting national debt troubled him, mostly because it reflected the growing intrusion of government into the ordinary affairs of citizens, and it represented the ceding of congressional authority to the president. Dirksen deplored both developments. Furthermore, Dirksen did not believe that the New Deal was very effective at what he thought was its primary purpose: recovery. In recounting those days of the mid- and late 1930s, he wrote that "the New Deal was long on reform, much longer on relief, yet very short on actual recovery and restoration of normal conditions."

The historian Elliot Rosen reminds us that Dirksen's misgivings reflected those of Main Street. Many a midwesterner desired the benefits afforded by the New Deal without the tendency toward omnicompetent government that seemed integral to the Tennessee Valley Authority, the Agricultural Adjustment Administration, the Resettlement Administration, and Roosevelt's proposals for government reorganization.[12] Dirksen began to draw the line more plainly after 1937. He played a primary role in the 1939 debate over the Townsend Plan, which called for a tax on every commercial transaction to guarantee every person a minimum income at age sixty-five. Dirksen led the opposition and succeeded in defeating the bill. Dirksen described the episode in his memoir, but he did not recall a letter he wrote to Louella immediately following the vote. In it, he described an epiphany:

> In my case, it was a good deal more than a speech and a vote. For such a long time, I have perhaps done as other politicians have done. Never wanted to offend any considerable segment of the voters. But the trouble is that such a course sooner or later developes [sic] a fear-complex which[,] if left to continue, must inevitably destroy that sense of conviction that a student of public problems should have. I am afraid that on other occasions, I have approved of or supported proposals which were broadly demanded by this group or that group, which I knew down deep to be wrong. And so there came a time—there had to come a time—when I must emancipate myself from those fears and determine, irrespective of the cost, to do that which every impulse of conscience dictated that I should do. It was like going thro [sic] a mental crisis. There is the temptation to say nothing or to sit back and shirk the duty which heart and conscience imposed. And so I did. I believe I shall find now that if my own estimate of a proposal is that it is wrong, it will take more than the mere endorsement of an organization with votes to persuade me to change my mind. Thus Mother darling, as the years move on, values become more fundamental and one sets greater store by the fact that he has a conscience with which he must live, long after the transitory things are gone.[13]

Among the many thousands of pages he wrote, this letter is one of the most reflective Everett Dirksen ever composed. It spoke to his evolution as a politician and legislator. It marked his support of Edmund Burke's notion that legislators must exercise independent judgment even at the risk of unpopularity. Dirksen loathed what he later called the "ghastly cowardice" of all men in public life who "cannot bear the thought of losing office."[14]

As his time in Washington lengthened, Dirksen acquired a commanding knowledge about the House that he used skillfully to influence the legislative process. He paid heed to the advice of the pragmatic, moderate assistant minority leader, Massachusetts's Joseph Martin, who counseled Dirksen, "Perfect yourself in committee work, and in due course you'll start up the ladder. Study the rules. Those who know the rules know how to operate under the rules." Dirksen took this advice to heart, spending countless hours reading the House rule book and the multivolume edition of Asher Hinds's *Precedents of the House of Representatives.*[15] "I suppose I could describe my congressional existence over the years as a diligent effort to remain abreast of every legislative proposal which was submitted to Congress," Dirksen recalled, "to answer the mail as expeditiously as possible, to process the complaints, and to do the errands requested by constituents at home." Preparation, a hallmark of Dirksen's career, stood him in good stead as he rose in the ranks of the House Republicans. As his memoir made clear, however, Dirksen complemented his book knowledge with practical information, meaning that he observed people, tried to understand what motivated them, and marveled in the pulling and hauling that is politics.

By 1940 the New Deal was struggling with its promises and its lack of performance. After eight years of Democratic rule, opposition was building to Roosevelt and his program. "One thing is absolutely certain and that is that we discovered that there were no royal roads to a solution" to the Depression, Dirksen opined. He shared in the growing disillusionment, although he opposed the dismantling of the New Deal and, as he put it, the stirring up of dead dreams within his party. He also developed a powerful sense of limits, believing that government, and particularly the executive branch, needed to be restrained.

Within a year, though, the nation's attention turned to the war in Europe. Dirksen, generally an isolationist as befitted a representative of the sixteenth district, anguished over the position of the United States in the conflict. In Dirksen's first eight years in the House, he had voted against reciprocal trade, against U.S. participation in the International Labor Organization, against lend-lease. Then in September 1941, he delivered a speech in the House that signaled a profound metamorphosis. He called for a "moratorium on hate" and said that he was satisfied "now that the President means to keep us out of war if he can." He abandoned his isolationist opposition to the draft and aid to Great Britain in favor of a strong internationalism.

Although Dirksen had changed his mind repeatedly since arriving in the House, this foreign policy reversal, just months before the attack on Pearl Harbor, captured more attention from the public and foreshadowed a career of introspective, considered policy reversals. Critics called it, variously, political opportunism, inconsistency, or spinelessness. Over the years, Dirksen fashioned a series of responses to those charges, often citing Abraham Lincoln: "The dogmas of the quiet past are inadequate to the stormy present.

The occasion is piled high with difficulty and we must rise with the occasion. As our case is new, so we must think anew and act anew, we must first disenthrall ourselves and then we shall save the Union."[16]

Dirksen did not devote much attention to the war years in his autobiography. But he did emphasize how much power flowed to the White House as a result of the conflict, accentuating the trend toward centralization in government that so bothered him. For Dirksen it boiled down to this: "Will the American system of living, which rests upon the morals of individualism, become the victim of a pious collectivism and will freedom be just a word or a way of life?"[17]

By the end of World War II, Dirksen had risen to a prominent position within the national Republican party. In 1944 he conducted a brief campaign for the presidency, in the hope of securing a vice-presidential bid. His effort failed, but he used the accumulated campaign funds to take a four-month trip to Africa, the Middle East, India, and Europe, arriving in Paris on May 7, the day before victory in Europe was declared. The trip had a huge influence on Dirksen's thinking. In small notebooks Dirksen used to record his thoughts almost daily, he wrote nearly 260 pages of notes about that trip—a remarkable testimony to the methodical way he approached his work. What follows is a sample of the dialogue he carried on with himself:

How can one earnestly ponder the present forces without getting that uneasy feeling that maybe after all it is One Total World to which we move—a world in which the total idealogy [sic] of Russia, Germany and others is gaining the upper hand and that our palaver about freedom and the sacrifices of pulsing young lives is just another sham and mockery. . . . that unless we do a sharp about face and forsake this doctrine of [planning], we are headed for the very serfdom that has taken millions of young men from their homes to die in the fevered infested marshes of the tropics and on the icy fields of the western front. What a tragedy this would be. Tragedy. That's scarcely the word. It would be the greatest catastrophe yet visited upon mankind because it would mean frustration and the death of the most promising civilization that has ever sprung up on earth.[18]

When Dirksen returned from his twenty-one-nation trip, his conversion to internationalism seemed complete and permanent. He voted *for* U.S. participation in the International Monetary Fund and the International Bank, supported President Truman's policies in Iran, Turkey, and Greece, and even envisioned the "development of a United States of Europe." He hailed the Marshall Plan and talked enthusiastically of making it a $19 billion program, much larger than it eventually became.

On the domestic side, Dirksen supported Harry Truman selectively. He voted for the Employment Act of 1946, an extension of selective service, the Federal Employee Loyalty Act, the Atomic Energy Act, and civil rights legislation. On the other hand, deficit spending concerned Dirksen very much, and he voted repeatedly to cut Truman's domestic spending.[19]

An August 1946 poll of House members by *Pageant* magazine rated Dirksen as that body's most effective speaker and its second-ablest member. When the Republicans took control of the House in 1947 for the first time in sixteen years, Dirksen became chairman of the District of Columbia Committee and the Appropriations Subcommittee on Agriculture.[20]

Leaving Public Life

Then apparent tragedy struck. After delivering a speech at Bradley University in Peoria, Dirksen made the short trip home. But when he arrived, the lights seemed dimmed. He saw "cobwebs" in his eyes. Despite rest, the affliction continued upon Dirksen's return to Washington, and he began a long series of medical consultations in 1946 and 1947. These culminated in a defining moment, which Dirksen described in detail in his autobiography, when he rejected his physician's advice to remove his right eye, a decision he reached during prayer. Instead, Dirksen resolved to let "the Great Physician" take care of his eyesight and to retire from the House to give his eyes a rest.

Dirksen could not get politics out of his blood, however. He even had second thoughts about retiring, though he did not change his mind. "You can believe me that the decision not to seek renomination for Congress was not an easy one and was dictated only by consideration for my family and my physical welfare," he wrote to his political adviser in Chicago. "I'm confident that with an adequate amount of rest this condition can be overcome. I consider it as an interlude in my public career and expect to render many more years of service as soon as I have regained my energy."[21] He answered a call from Thomas Dewey's campaign managers to help in the 1948 election. Dirksen's assignment was to travel with vice-presidential candidate Earl Warren and add some spark to his stump speaking. Dirksen tried, but Warren ignored him.

The Adlai Stevenson–Paul Douglas victory in Illinois in 1948 decimated the Republicans. Dirksen began to receive entreaties from those who wanted someone to run against Scott Lucas, the Democratic leader in the Senate, in 1950. As Dirksen told it, no one seriously thought Dirksen could win. He was not sure either, and he pondered the possibility for weeks. Then the miracle he had prayed for happened; he learned that his eye ailment was not malignant, and that it would eventually clear up. The news created the opportunity that all his preparation and ambition had groomed him for—the race for the U.S. Senate. In Dirksen's words: "Why does one do it? How does one do it? How [to] summon enough energy to do it on a statewide basis? If a man devoted an equal amount of time, energy, and concentration to any business or profession, I felt he would be bound to succeed, but there was a lure, a fascination in politics that had appeal to certain people and I knew I had placed myself in that category."

Success, according to Dirksen, would require three elements: a clear-cut image with the voters for the Republican party; mass exposure of the candidate; and energized party workers who would stay on their toes through election day. Success would also call for a high degree of political dexterity. Dirksen was an ambitious midwestern Republican. Because he was ambitious, he could not dedicate himself completely to Illinois GOP conservatism and ignore the occasionally conflicting views of the national party. But because he was a midwestern Republican, he could not wholly forsake isolationists and follow the rising star of "modern" Republicanism. He was caught between the two Republican poles, and it had become, over the years, an increasingly awkward perch.

In the 1930s, for instance, it had been perfectly safe to be an isolationist conservative from downstate Illinois. But as the national party swung liberal (behind Wendell Willkie and Thomas Dewey) and his own ambitions expanded, Dirksen saw the focus of power swinging away from him, and he went with the pendulum, risking the wrath of the *Chicago Tribune*. When Dewey lost in 1948, however, Dirksen saw it was time to re-embrace Illinois Republicanism. Gearing up for a statewide run in 1950, Dirksen felt he had no choice.[22]

The entire Dirksen family—the Three Musketeers, as Everett called them—dove into his first statewide campaign, a 21-month, 1,500-speech, 250,000-mile ordeal. Dirksen lambasted the "failure" of the Truman administration's foreign policy, calling it "expensive, inconsistent and ineffective." He labeled the European Recovery program "Operation Rat-hole." He attacked the Yalta agreement and the Truman administration's handling of communists and corruption in government. In Dirksen's mind, the race was not against Scott Lucas, who merely "carries the banner and takes instructions." No, for Dirksen "the real issue is the Fair Deal Program which is taking us down that very same road which threw Britain into the very arms of Socialism and liquidated those liberties for which Jefferson so steadfastly stood."[23]

If boundless energy and long hours guaranteed victory, Dirksen would have been a cinch to win. But the opposition did not roll over. Scott Lucas had his staff analyze Dirksen's voting record in the House. The result was a two-volume document, "The Diary of a Chameleon," which concluded that Dirksen "has literally stood for nothing."[24] The *Chicago Sun-Times* took the theme public, accusing Dirksen of switching his position on military preparedness 31 times, on isolationism 62 times, and on farm policy 70 times during his years in Congress.

Dirksen could not deny the charge in principle. His record was not consistent. On the matter of defense spending, for example, one would have been hard put to categorize Dirksen. Early in his House days, Dirksen had argued that military spending must be curtailed for the economy's sake and because "great force and such large armaments . . . will be the inspiration for another war." By 1936 he had changed his mind to the extent of saying that "a large Navy is not a cause for war any more than a police force is a cause of crime." By 1937 he had reversed himself again and demanded that no money be spent on naval supplies for maneuvers more than three hundred miles off the continental U.S. shoreline. In 1937 and 1938 he backed the Ludlow Amendment, which would have required a national referendum before a declaration of war. In 1939 he voted against the fortification of Guam and the construction of 1,283 war planes. But by 1940 he was saying, "Thank God there is a national defense program under way." He then voted against the draft act.[25]

Other newspapers picked up the *Sun-Times* story in 1950. Shrewdly, Dirksen fended off the criticism by embracing change, not repudiating it. In the tradition of Illinois Republicans, he relied on Lincoln for support, citing his remark about the "dogmas of the quiet past." Dirksen added his own words, too: "You sort of walk the middle of the road. You try to be a rational being. I've learned that nothing is white or black—there are too many shadings in life. In a society such as ours you can't plow just that one furrow. You have to re-examine your premises in the light of changing conditions."[26] Try as he might to blunt the charge, however, it became the staple of every subsequent election to resurrect the *Sun-Times* story analyzing Dirksen's "flip-flops."

On election eve, Dirksen sensed victory—correctly. The indefatigable campaigner from Pekin beat Lucas by 294,000 votes, carrying 82 of 102 counties with 54.1 percent of the vote. "To the voters of Illinois, I am humbly grateful for the fidelity and vigor with which they rallied to the American ideal in an hour of jeopardy," Dirksen said in acknowledging the win. "With their own eyes they could see the Socialist pattern which was being readied for our country. They saw the ugly head of Communism within the citadel of government. They knew full well, the burden of taxes which a squandering administration had placed upon them. They saw the ineptness of a leadership which has taken us to the brink of our fourth war in thirty-three years. They've had enough [of] this and have accepted the pledges of the Republican Party to take this country on the road to sanity, safety, strength and solvency."[27]

The Education of a Senator ended with the fulfillment of Everett Dirksen's ambition to serve in the United States Senate. After thanking the people who were his special friends (none of whom had made their life's work politics), Dirksen expressed his concern for the lack of respect accorded to political work and public service, quoting in its entirety the letter he would send to those seeking his advice about a career in politics. It is worth reading today.

Back to Washington

Of course, Dirksen's career did not end with that election in 1950. In fact, it only really began, in the sense of the national impact this baker boy from Pekin would eventually have. From January 3, 1951, when he took the oath of office for the Senate, until his death in Walter Reed Hospital on September 7, 1969, Everett McKinley Dirksen established a career that brought him national fame and an apparently complete fulfillment of his political ambitions. He was reelected easily in 1956, again in 1962, and with a still-comfortable margin in 1968. His influence as Republican whip and later as minority leader grew steadily throughout his long tenure of office both in his own party and with the Democratic administrations of President John Kennedy and President Lyndon Johnson. Few senators in our history have known and enjoyed such power; few have managed to keep on good terms with so many colleagues and government officials of all political stripes; few have gained such widespread recognition as a public figure.

The Washington to which the Dirksens returned at the end of 1950 had not changed outwardly. Many of the new senator's friends in the capital city were still there, and he knew the legislative ropes from his terms in the House. But the political climate had become decidedly more conservative. The Korean War and troublesome, persistent economic problems had roused a feeling of discontent with the administration of Harry Truman. Dirksen believed that the president was leading the nation to welfare statism, that government controls and the regulatory bureaucracy had stifled economic freedom, and that Dirksen's job as the newly minted senator from Illinois was to check those dangerous trends.[28]

To no one's surprise, the new senator allied himself with the conservative elements in the Eighty-second Congress. He was already a friend and to some extent a disciple of Bob Taft, "Mr. Republican" and leader of the conservatives. In an unusual gesture of confidence toward a freshman senator, Taft appointed Dirksen chairman of the Republican Senatorial Campaign Committee. It was the bottom rung of the leadership ladder, but it was essential preparation for what followed.

Astutely, though, Dirksen hedged his bets, much as he had done throughout his House career. He retained the friendship and esteem of many who considered Taft too conservative, exerting his independence at key moments. Dirksen himself admitted on "Meet the Press" in 1951 that he and Taft had disagreed on the five most important votes in the Senate that term. But Dirksen pointed out that they had agreed on the fundamental principle: "the preservation of our free economic system within the framework of a free government."[29] This ability to adapt himself to people and circumstances, to do his homework thoroughly on any pending legislation, and to bide his time became characteristic during Dirksen's first few years the Senate. Gradually he won the favor of his colleagues by his willingness to do party chores and to help raise money and make speeches in their reelection campaigns.

Dirksen burst on the national scene at the 1952 Republican convention. He was an active supporter of Taft for president and had been mentioned as a possible vice-presidential nominee. Then millions of Americans saw him on television fighting against Dwight Eisenhower and shaking an accusing finger at Eisenhower's floor lieutenant, Thomas Dewey. "We followed you before and you took us down the road to defeat," Dirksen bellowed. This to a man he had supported vigorously in 1944 and 1948. The frankness of his speech disturbed many supporters of the Eisenhower ticket. No speech he ever made created more of a stir than this one. It was one of only a handful in his entire career that he composed, word for word, in advance. A loyal party man, Dirksen campaigned wholeheartedly for Ike and the ticket even after Taft's defeat, giving speeches in two dozen states. But it took some time for the rift with the new president to heal. Neil MacNeil, a Dirksen biographer, termed the early 1950s "The Black Years" because of Dirksen's stridency and hard-edged conservatism.

In public, Dirksen himself chose not to focus on the split in the Republican ranks. Instead, he emphasized the challenge the new team faced in overcoming the New Deal and Fair Deal legacies. He delivered the Republican response to Harry Truman's last State of the Union message, where he made that strategy clear. He began by describing the Democrats' legacy: "excessive and outrageous taxation," "staggering national debt," "prodigious waste of public money," and "disastrous inflation." Dirksen said the Republicans' first priority would be devising a fresh approach to world economic stability as the basis for security and peace. The new administration must tackle, he said, "the job of arresting the moral deterioration of government and of establishing honesty, integrity, and trust in public service."[30]

The Taft wing and the Eisenhower wing of the Republican party had different ideas about how best to set the nation back on course. For the most part, Dirksen cast his lot with Bob Taft. For example, he joined with isolationist Republicans, including Joseph McCarthy, to oppose Eisenhower's nomination of Charles "Chip" Bohlen as ambassador to Russia. The junior senator from Illinois also backed the Bricker Amendment, designed to limit the president's treaty-making powers. Dirksen opposed Ike's spending plans, urging deeper cuts in the budget in areas such as foreign aid. More controversial was Dirksen's decision to back McCarthy's hunt for "Reds" in government. Dirksen exclaimed in early 1953 that Republicans "have to eliminate Communists and their fellow travelers from government. It will have to expose those who seek to destroy America's free institutions."[31] Although his rhetoric mimicked the excesses of the times, Dirksen actually tried to persuade McCarthy to cut short his probe, but failing that he backed the senator from Wisconsin to the very end. In the first years of the new Republican administration, Dirksen proved to be a thorn in Ike's side.

But the senator's public comments during this period also suggested a philosophical, as opposed to political, basis for his dramatic, flamboyant posturing against Eisenhower's early initiatives. In April 1953, for example, Dirksen addressed a commission investigating intergovernmental relationships. He sounded a theme that recurred throughout his career: the threat of an expanding federal government. When his remarks were published later, he chose this as the title: "Big Government—The Road to Tyranny." He singled out the intrusion of government into so many aspects of life as the primary difference between 1932 and 1953. It amazed him that people had ceded so much authority to Washington. He worried that the "concentration of power" threatened "individual liberty and freedom as we have known it." Dirksen called for a return to, as he called it, "the plain channel."[32] It did not particularly matter to him whether the government was run by Republicans or Democrats if the effect was to disenfranchise the citizenry through centralization. His experience with the New Deal had convinced him that the concentration of power on the national level was inconsistent with the principles of American democracy.

Bob Taft died on July 31, 1953. For Dirksen, this did not have an immediate political impact. He continued to oppose the administration and associate with the conservative side of the party. But Taft's successor as Republican leader in the Senate, William Knowland of California, proved inept, contributing to a growing strain between the White House and Senate Republicans. Eventually Dirksen saw the opportunity this situation afforded him. In 1955 he began to mend fences with the Eisenhower administration. Political circumstances in Illinois, such as the death of the power behind the *Chicago Tribune,* Colonel Robert McCormick, on April 1, made it possible. President Eisenhower, frustrated legislatively in his first term, turned equally to Dirksen for support. It was a marriage of convenience that would pay big dividends for the senator from Illinois. The following year Dirksen led a campaign to enact the administration's civil rights bill. Throughout 1956, Dirksen supported the president, frequently at the risk of his standing with his party's conservative Senate hierarchy. The future now lay with the Eisenhower wing of the party. In terms of percentages, Dirksen supported Ike 75 percent in 1955, 85 percent in 1956, and 95 percent in 1957.[33] Dirksen's reputation soared, and power and influence within the Senate came with it.

To win reelection in 1956, Dirksen used his new alliance with Ike to good effect. On September 22, 1955, Eisenhower agreed to let Dirksen make public a letter of glowing endorsement at a fund-raising dinner in Chicago: "Especially in the past three years, I have come to know and appreciate the great value to our country of Senator Dirksen's labors in his influential position. Since 1952 Everett and I have not, of course, agreed on every public issue, but never have I had the occasion to doubt that sincerity and conviction have motivated every vote he has cast."[34]

Dirksen's speech to the National Federation of Republican Women during his reelection campaign showed how far he had moved toward Ike and how much more modulated his arguments had become—the hard edge of Taft conservatism and McCarthy-style zealotry had softened. "It is not the length of one's days but the worth of one's days that matters," he began. "It is the impress of character and leadership on one's own generation which matters. It is the legacy which one leaves to the future which matters." One can almost hear the phrases rolling off Dirksen's tongue, for history and legacy were subjects dear to his heart. "There is a need for faith and hope in a fretful world. There is a need for peace of mind and courage. There is a need for standards and ideals by which to live. There is a need for moral and spiritual leadership in public affairs." Then Dirksen, the candidate, closed his remarks by associating himself with Eisenhower, attributing to Ike's leadership a new sense of decency and honor and an energized conscience within the country: "He has helped us to rediscover the well-springs of our strength and greatness. Such has been the worth of his days."[35]

Dirksen's new-found fidelity to Ike baffled some. A newspaper called Dirksen "the strangest figure in this bizarre election." This former protégé of the *Chicago Tribune* and spokesman for the isolationist faction of the Republican party was basing his entire campaign upon his close ties to Eisenhower. "It's a hell of a switch to keep in mind," a faithful supporter said.[36]

But change did not perturb Dirksen. He did not fear it as a campaign issue. "I long ago learned that formula of vegetate or decay, grow or die. And government is not unlike that. I think its [*sic*] just like individuals; you simply have to grow; you have to feed on new things; re-orient your thinking; keep abreast of what goes on; because the world is certainly not a static place where things suddenly stand still. It's a dynamic thing and is constantly moving forward and so you've got to be abreast of change."[37] Dirksen won in 1956, traveling two hundred miles per day in the last ten weeks of the campaign.

Eisenhower's second term in the White House turned out to be one of the most constructive and satisfying periods of Dirksen's life. Ike found him far easier to deal with than Bill Knowland, who continued as the titular leader of the Republicans in the Senate. Often in situations calling for parliamentary skill and aplomb, Dirksen showed himself to be Knowland's superior. He developed a leadership style based, as his biographers have chronicled, on mastery of details, cordiality, concern for the principles espoused by his colleagues, and the ability to persuade without being obnoxious.[38] In 1957 Dirksen became the Republican whip in the Senate.

Dirksen as Senate Leader

As Dirksen emerged as a leader in the Senate, reporters paid more attention to him, and in their interviews Dirksen revealed himself in more nuanced detail. He possessed a coherent, conservative political philosophy, one that he held to even as he changed positions on specific issues. He fashioned this philosophy from four principles: faith in the individual, optimism, skepticism about an active government, and the importance of adapting to change. About the worth and promise of the individual, Dirksen felt especially keen. He believed that the hope of society reposed in the individual, in his integrity, his dignity, his peace of mind, "and the power that he can wield in the area where he lives and serves." The individual, within the context of his community, living and working one day at a time, represented for Dirksen "the last and best and noblest hope of mankind."[39]

After the disastrous congressional elections of 1958, in which the Democrats considerably increased their majorities in both houses of Congress, it became clear that Dirksen was in line for the post of minority leader, left vacant on the retirement of Knowland. There was considerable opposition from the liberal Republicans, but Dirksen enjoyed some advantages. First, the small number of Republicans in the Senate made it easier for the new leader to pass out good committee assignments, essentially buying off potential opponents. For example, he ducked a potential split between conservatives and moderate-liberals in the party by backing the liberal Thomas Kuchel of California to the post of assistant minority leader. Dirksen also gave up his own seats on the prestigious Appropriations Committee and the Labor and Public Works Committee to younger members, engendering loyalty among the junior senators of his party. His years of preparation, in this case as chairman of the Senate Republican Campaign Committee, paid off, too.

Second, the soon-to-be minority leader enjoyed a warm, personal, and respectful professional relationship with his counterpart for the Democrats, Majority Leader Lyndon Johnson. Finally, President Eisenhower, tired of working with Knowland and grateful to Dirksen for assisting behind the scenes, embraced him. Dirksen was named leader by a caucus vote of 20 to 14 and began his long tenure in the important post, destined to last until his death.

In his leadership role, he was to become the uncrowned king of the Senate, a situation made all the more remarkable in that Dirksen played his leadership cards with the deck always stacked heavily against him; only in his last few months as minority leader did Dirksen have more than forty Republicans serving with him in the Senate. Despite continuing Democratic majorities, he managed by adroitly combining the conservative elements of both parties and by employing his substantial knowledge about Senate rules and procedures. Dirksen explained his philosophy of leadership, with its emphasis on making the legislative process work, this way: "The Senate is a public institution; it must work; it's a two-way street; and that requires the efforts of both parties. One party cannot do it on its own because if the opposition, or minority party, wanted to be completely obstructionist, you could tie up the Senate in a minute, even with a handful of people."[40] By cajoling, by gentle pressure, by using his remarkable memory and his gift of repartee, the senator took over power in his own painless way. As he was wont to say, "The oil can is mightier than the sword."

By virtue of his almost twenty-five years in Congress, Dirksen had a rich understanding of how things worked. He appreciated that leading such a temperamental body as the Senate was a subtle business. He brought to it an instinct for self-effacement rare for a public figure; ambitious, yes, but self-centered, no. He accepted those gritty little debts and commitments that are part and parcel of political life. And he was willing to put in the time, hours upon hours, to master the substance and the process. Dirksen had little faith in obstructionism for the sake of obstructionism—of opposition to Democratic proposals simply because they may have implemented the majority party's goals. He found such an attitude both unrealistic and self-defeating. In many cases, in his view, the minority simply abstained from participation in the great problems of the day if it took so stubborn a partisan stand.[41]

Dirksen's unwillingness to follow the Knowland model of leadership did not mean that he followed a passive course. Dirksen was an activist leader, partly because that was the only way to exert influence when outnumbered two-to-one. He worked unceasingly to unite his party. He placed a great deal of importance on communicating with his colleagues at regular briefings and at social occasions that he would arrange. In contrast to the stodgy Knowland, Dirksen went out of his way to cultivate the press, with good results, for the most part.

According to one biographer, by the time Dirksen settled into his duties as leader, he had undergone a political and personal reorientation. "The role of leadership and responsibility transformed Dirksen," Neil MacNeil wrote. "His frustrated ambitions were satisfied, and he played the game of politics with renewed zest."[42] He had abandoned his aspirations for the presidency and channeled his ambition along a new course in the Senate. He came to view the Senate as an end in itself. The nature of his ambition had changed.

In August 1959, *U.S. News and World Report* could report on Dirksen's success. The story reasoned that President Eisenhower had gained the upper hand with the Democratic Congress largely because of the unpublicized activities of Dirksen and his counterpart in the House, Charles Halleck. The article talked about the "revolution" in the relationship between the White House and the Hill. "Under the Dirksen-Halleck regime, members of the congressional group return to the Capitol with the feeling that they know and understand what the President wants, that they and the President are in agreement on legislative issues. This is considered to be a new and important contribution to Republican vigor."[43]

It seemed almost effortless, the way Dirksen drew the press to him. William Barry Furlong, in *Harper's* in December 1959, wrote a detailed feature entitled "The Senate's Wizard of Ooze: Dirksen of Illinois." Furlong's piece became the archetype for stories about Dirksen. In an apparent effort to mimic Dirksen, the article employed such embellishments as these: "Everett McKinley Dirksen is a moist, able, unctuous individual who has achieved influence through the use of what a newspaperman has described as 'tonsils marinated in honey,' plus a remarkable flexibility"; "his every scene is overplayed and rich in rhetoric. His face set in spaniel-like sadness, his stance that of the dramatically beleaguered"; "at times, he clearly gets carried away by the opulence of his own oratory." Furlong called Dirksen a "virtuoso of the switch," citing another famous story about Dirksen attributed to an unnamed newspaperman: "He delivered the best speech in favor of foreign aid and the best speech against foreign aid that I ever heard." Yet the author also wrote that "what is usually overlooked in the flummery is that Dirksen is a skilled parliamentarian, a wily legislator, an effective if oleaginous floor speaker, and an able advocate of whatever cause he is currently pleading."

Such articles marked the ascendancy of Dirksen and his distinctiveness. Here obviously was a man who enjoyed his job, cultivated good relations with the press and his colleagues, was able to poke fun at himself and battle the Democrats with high good humor, without pettiness or undue partisanship. At a moment of declining Republican fortunes, his ability stood out and won him national acclaim. Even his eccentricities, such as the deliberately tousled hair and the "ham" quality noted by observers, friendly and otherwise, made him conspicuous.

Dirksen could point to several legislative achievements as his first leadership term ended. He had taken the lead in getting Eisenhower's defense budget approved, secured the enactment of the Landrum-Griffin Labor Management Reform Act, supported amendments to Social Security to increase health benefits for the aged, and pushed through a public housing bill acceptable to the administration.[44]

A great deal of hard work lay behind this attainment. He had little time for diversions or private life. Principally he relied on Mrs. Dirksen for advice and comfort, and he took his greatest pleasure in seeing his daughter and her husband, Howard H. Baker Jr., son of a congressman from Tennessee, and their children. Everett and Louella had purchased property near Sterling, Virginia, where they built a pleasant, modern house, all on one level, on a branch of the Potomac. The senator could relax there and indulge his passion for growing flowers and vegetables in a large garden. But moments of relaxation were few and far between.

In 1961 the conditions for Dirksen's leadership changed markedly, in a fashion that would happen only one more time, near the end of his life. As a result of the 1960 election, a Democrat replaced a Republican in the White House. Dirksen and John F. Kennedy had a personal history, but not an intimate one. The two men shared committee work on occasion. In 1959 they had spent a great deal of time working on the Landrum-Griffin Bill together, both in committee and as Senate conferees. Though they held fundamental political differences, they remained friendly.

But now Dirksen's role as Senate Republican leader required some adjustment. Once the faithful lieutenant to Ike, Dirksen achieved a new measure of independence and exposure as the highest elected Republican in the capital city. Although he continued to support the president in foreign policy, as witnessed in the 1961 Bay of Pigs disaster and the Cuban missile crisis, Dirksen worked to delay or change Kennedy's New Frontier at home. He once said that the 1962 State of the Union address resembled "a Sears Roebuck catalog with all the old prices marked up."[45] He used the media to great advantage. The senator and Representative Charles Halleck, the Republican House leader, had undertaken to make regular television appearances shortly after Kennedy became president in order to present the Republican side of things at a moment when all the publicity was going to the new masters. It proved a deft move, particularly for the more telegenic Dirksen. The "Ev and Charlie" show, as it was sometimes derisively called even by Republicans, soon became a staple of the night-time news. In fact, throughout the 1960s, no senator and no Senate leader received more press mentions than did Dirksen.[46]

In these appearances and on the stump, Dirksen rooted his opposition to the New Frontier in the familiar, conservative vernacular. He opposed government's interference with the economy as inevitably compromising personal freedoms. His remarks in Boston in February 1962 were vintage:

> Let government but dictate when to sow and reap and sell and juggle prices with loans or by surplus dumping; let government soak up surpluses with public funds; let government but manage public opinion by every modern device of communication; let government but prescribe under penalty how

businesses shall be operated and the whole system of production and distribution placed under prescribed controls, and socialism becomes complete without fanfare or struggle or bloodshed.[47]

It was on this basis that Dirksen fought the New Frontier. "I consider myself a conservative, probably not as conservative as some, not as moderately liberal or liberally moderate as others," Dirksen remarked on national television in March 1961, two months after the new administration had taken office. This deliberately vague statement of philosophy probably suited the Republican leader just fine. He understood that he could not lead without followers. "You see after all, a party leader has a job. There are viewpoints over here and viewpoints over here, but I think your first responsibility is to develop a degree of unity and cohesion in your party as best you can to make a good militant phalanx, and that I tried to do in the first two years of my leadership, and I am trying to do it again now, insofar as I can."[48] He was old fashioned but no anachronism.

In 1962, as Dirksen entered his fourth year in the back-breaking role of Senate Republican leader, he was greeted by conflicting appraisals. Fellow Republican senators, including most of the liberals who originally opposed his elevation to the job, now viewed him as irreplaceable. "If something would happen to Dirksen, we'd be in one hell of a fix," advised one GOP senator.[49] But prominent Republicans in the outside world viewed Dirksen as an unrelieved political liability. Party functionaries charged him with selling out to Kennedy on foreign policy. Conservatives claimed he temporized on matters of principle. Liberal Republicans regarded him as an obstructionist and stand-patter. And the image-conscious conservatives, liberals, and moderates alike unanimously viewed the sixty-six-year-old, tousled-haired Illinoisan as an old fogy who fit perfectly the caricature of the unappealing old-guard Republican.[50]

His liberal critics were in for a surprise. In 1962 Dirksen demonstrated his political sagacity by executing the first of three legislative reversals in three successive years that would seal his reputation as a leader and legislative craftsman. The first episode involved the Kennedy administration's effort to finance the United Nations. Kennedy requested authority to purchase United Nations bonds to make up deficits resulting largely from the refusal of the Soviet Union and France to pay peace-keeping assessments. Dirksen initially opposed the move. But on April 5, 1962, he rose on the Senate floor and admitted that he had done some soul-searching: "Mr. President, I will not charge my conscience with any act or deed which would contribute to the foundering of the United Nations, because I do not know how I would then be able to expiate that sin of commission to my grandchildren." The measure passed, 70 to 22, with Dirksen bringing along two Republicans for every one who voted against it. On August 22, colleagues from both sides of the aisle joined in an unusual, extemporaneous outpouring of tribute to the senator from Illinois.

Dirksen had taken his power to new heights, and the public recognized it immediately. The national media heaped attention on the minority leader. *Time* magazine featured him on the cover of its September 14, 1962, issue. The lead story concluded that "Dirksen has become one of the truly remarkable characters of the Senate," calling him the most effective GOP leader in memory. These accolades were especially well timed considering that Dirksen was up for reelection less than three months later. It was an election he won handily.

In the Eighty-eighth Congress, convened in 1963, the cooperation of Dirksen and his group of Republicans continued on foreign policy. The most sterling example involved the second legislative reversal by which Dirksen built his reputation. Like the United Nations bond issue, this one concerned foreign policy—a nuclear test ban treaty negotiated by the Kennedy administration. At the outset the minority leader condemned it, bolstered by forty thousand letters and by petitions containing ten thousand names backing his opposition. But in studying the treaty, Dirksen became convinced that his fears had been based on misunderstanding. He knew from his mail that millions probably shared the same misunderstanding. In handwritten notes to President Kennedy, he set forth questions on which senators wanted assurance. He asked the president to send a letter to Majority Leader Mike Mansfield and himself clarifying issues raised by critics. The president did so. On September 11, Dirksen rose again on the Senate floor, noting that his earlier opinions "did not stand up." He read the president's letter and then concluded: "Mr. President . . . this is a first single step. . . . But with consummate faith and some determination, this may be the step that can spell a grander destiny for our country and for the world. If there be risks, Mr. President, I am willing to assume them for my country." The treaty was approved 80 to 19, with 25 Republicans voting for it and 8 against. The Illinois chapter of Republican Women passed a resolution condemning Dirksen, and the *Chicago Tribune* asked, "Is Dirksen Going Soft?"[51]

If Dirksen's allegiance to the president on foreign policy caused him trouble, then he was careful to redress the balance on Kennedy's domestic agenda. He maneuvered skillfully and in cooperation with conservative

Democrats to defeat many key administration bills in the domestic field. Dirksen opposed the Kennedy civil rights legislation, mostly because of its public accommodations section, which he felt was unworkable and likely to lead to more rather than less racial conflict. By careful tactics and threats of a filibuster he was able to postpone final consideration of this bill.

The senator's conscientious attempts to perfect what he realized was a necessary piece of legislation were interrupted by the shocking events in Dallas. During the political moratorium that followed the assassination of John Kennedy, Dirksen offered his help and sympathy to the new president, his old and good colleague Lyndon Johnson. Their friendship was close and instinctive. "When I think the president is right, then I am in his corner," Dirksen told the press. "When I think he is wrong, I tell him so and I tell him in language I am sure he understands."[52] Their intimacy was so great and their relationship so informal that Johnson would often call his friend five or six times a day to chat, and at the end of the day would invite him to drop in at the White House for bourbon and branch water. "Dirksen could play politics as well as any man," Johnson wrote in his memoirs. "But I knew something else about him. When the nation's interest was at stake, he could climb the heights and take the long view without regard to party. I based a great deal of my strategy on this understanding of Dirksen's deep-rooted patriotism."[53]

In retrospect, two issues determined the relationship between the senator from Illinois and the president from Texas: civil rights and Vietnam. Only through the lens of these issues is it possible to understand Dirksen's career and leadership after November 1963. The first watershed related to civil rights. John Kennedy had submitted his proposal for civil rights legislation to Congress in June 1963, where it went to the House first for consideration.

In the past Dirksen had supported civil rights bills. According to his own records, he had personally introduced nineteen bills that dealt directly with civil rights and dozens more that addressed the problem indirectly. In all but two congressional sessions between 1932 and 1964, Dirksen had sponsored measures touching the entire range of civil rights issues including the poll tax, lynching, employment discrimination, voting rights, school desegregation, and housing.[54] He recognized, too, that social pressure to enact sweeping legislation had developed, erupting in violence in many cases. According to government statistics, there were nearly a thousand civil rights demonstrations in 209 cities in a three-month period beginning May 1963. Dirksen also knew that more Americans, especially northern whites, favored aggressive protection of minority rights. The National Opinion Research Center determined, for example, that the number who approved neighborhood integration had risen thirty points in twenty years to 72 percent in 1963.[55]

But the bill as it came from the House in February 1964 aroused great doubts in Dirksen. Consonant with his fear of government intrusion, Dirksen was particularly worried about Title II of the bill, which gave the federal government the power to enforce privately owned businesses against their will to serve black customers. He believed that such authority was an unconstitutional invasion of private property. He preferred voluntary compliance backed by state enforcement powers. The minority leader staked out his position in late March on the first day of debate in the Senate, attacking the bill and claiming, "They are remaking America and you won't like it." Grueling negotiations ensued, and Dirksen seized the leading part, working with Hubert Humphrey and Lyndon Johnson's White House and Justice Department staffs.

On April 16, Dirksen offered ten amendments that he believed would improve the bill, resolve his own questions, and provide a basis upon which other uncommitted senators could support the bill. He made it clear that he did not intend to weaken federal protection of minority rights: "I do not wish to save any pockets of prejudice for the future. I have an interest in what happens long after I have left this mundane sphere. I have a couple of grandchildren. I want them to grow up in a country of opportunity as completely free from hate and prejudice and bias as can be consummated by legislation, and a maximum amount of good will of the part of the lawmakers."[56]

The media recognized Dirksen's pivotal role. "His influence has never been so clear as in his handling of the hotly controversial civil rights bill," wrote James McCartney in the *Chicago Daily News.* "Dirksen today is at the peak of his power."[57] The *Chicago Tribune* reported that the Democratic majority, huge as it was, "would have been helpless without him."[58] More negotiations took place. In the Senate on May 26, Dirksen told the chair he was presenting an amendment in the nature of a substitute for the House bill, an amendment that had been shaped "on the anvil of controversy and discussion" with the Justice Department and the civil rights coalition. He hoped it would command enough support to make cloture possible and thus permit a vote.

By June, Dirksen estimated that he had heard from at least 100,000 people on the bill. Dirksen resented the pressure from black groups, who he felt had failed to recognize his progressive record on the issue, and he complained about it, giving hope to southern conservatives in the Senate who thought, momentarily, that Dirksen might side with them. But Dirksen stood tall. On June 10, cloture was invoked. Dirksen had succeeded. The Civil Rights Act of 1964 was signed into law shortly thereafter.

It was, perhaps, Dirksen's finest hour. Between February and June, he had gone through his greatest legislative reversal, the third in three years, and had managed to carry most of his Republican colleagues with him. In explaining to reporters why he was fighting for the bill he had violently attacked only two months before, the sage responded: "On the night Victor Hugo died, he wrote in his diary: 'Stronger than all the armies is an idea whose time has come.'"[59]

His work on the Civil Rights Act in 1964 marked him as a statesman. John Stennis, senator from Mississippi, summed up Dirksen's legislative legerdemain when he allowed that "the greatest thing to be said about his career is that he was a natural legislator. More than most of us, . . . he could really put the pieces of a measure together and then get a composite view of the thinking and ideas of the membership."[60] Lyndon Johnson added, "In this critical hour Senator Dirksen came through, as I had hoped he would. He knew his country's future was at stake. He knew what he could do to help. He knew what he had to do as a leader."[61]

As the 1964 presidential election approached, Dirksen made the nominating speech for the Republican candidate, Barry Goldwater, a close friend and a representative of the conservative Republican wing. Dirksen campaigned vigorously for him in the futile effort. The Johnson landslide and the resulting eclipse of Goldwater left Dirksen as the most prominent Republican in Washington, a position he thoroughly enjoyed for the next year or two.

As Dirksen began his fifteenth year in the Senate and approached the age of seventy, signs abounded that he had emerged as an elder statesman of sorts. He admitted that he had mellowed, citing the wisdom that comes with age. He had long ago recognized the virtue of patience, often likening free government to a waterlogged scow: "It doesn't move very fast, it doesn't move very far at one time, but it never sinks and maybe that is the reason we have a free government today." The old dredge-boat operator probably knew what he was talking about. When asked how he would sum up his philosophy of life, Dirksen replied: "Well, I want to be ready for change at all times. I think I fully subscribe to the definition of progress as the constant and intelligent and undramatic action of life on what is here." For him, the greatest hazard of public life was the danger of getting into a political rut, where life will pass you by. "I think over and over a person in public life has to take inventory, to see where he is at the moment, to take a look back to see from whence you came and then see where the high road goes and then if your thinking is not attuned to it you disenthrall yourself," Dirksen reflected. Such distance, he thought, would give someone "the right cast of mind and the right thoughts" to tackle the future.[62] "From Whence You Came" became a familiar title for Dirksen's remarks around the country.

In Congress, Dirksen sought to restore some ideological equilibrium to Republican positions on domestic and foreign policy issues. He used his influence to rid the party of extremist control. In matters of policy, it fell to him to band his small group of Republicans together to stem the Great Society juggernaut. In the first session of the Eighty-ninth Congress, in 1965, Johnson submitted 87 measures of which 84 were passed; in the second session, 97 of 113 were approved.[63]

In March, *Life* magazine published a detailed portrait of the "Grand Old King of the Senate." Reporter Paul O'Neil described Dirksen's homespun image before concluding that "none of this should suggest that he is a simple or unsophisticated man. He is pragmatic, unpredictable and shrewdly conciliatory; he is at once theatrical and introspective, hopeful and sardonic; he is widely read, and widely traveled, exquisitely aware of the nation's problems and tirelessly dedicated to both the Senate and the 'coun-tray.' "[64] Even his critics gave him a grudging respect. "There are a lot of Senators who are worse than they look," one colleague remarked. "Dirksen is the only one who is better than he looks."[65]

On many domestic issues, Dirksen continued the balancing act so central to his effectiveness, as he saw it: maintain a constructive relationship with the opposition and the loyalty of the Republican troops. He took issue with Medicare, for example: "I would be eligible," he said indignantly. "Why should I be allowed to use dollars the government is taking from some young factory worker in Cleveland in the promise of providing for his old age?"[66] The accumulation of Great Society spending programs appalled Dirksen. The taxpayers would have to come up with nearly $160 billion to fund them. Moreover, the programs brought with them an expanding federal bureaucracy and increasing centralization. To Dirksen, "the Great Society was a misguided attempt at creating an immediate, utopian 'blueprint for paradise.' "[67]

Even as he reached the height of his career and was being heralded for his statesmanship, however, Dirksen began to divert his energies into causes that many believed to be not only backward-looking but also futile. He sought constitutional amendments to permit voluntary prayer in public schools and to restore the principle of one man, one vote. On August 4, 1965, for example, Dirksen failed to win the two-thirds vote necessary for Senate approval of his proposed amendment to the Constitution, which would have permitted seats in one house of state legislatures to be apportioned on a basis other than that of population. He never gave up the battle, but the issue probably distracted him and compromised his leadership in the long run.

But the captivating Dirksen was still in command. The Capitol Hill Republican Club selected him as the Republican who did the most for his party in 1965. Dirksen tallied 1,426 points; Richard Nixon, 643; Gerald Ford, 561; and, John Lindsay, 543.

The task for Dirksen grew more difficult in 1966. Spiraling U.S. involvement in Vietnam and inflation were the dominant themes. Budgetary pressures to support Lyndon Johnson's "guns and butter" policies enlivened Republican opposition to domestic spending. Apprehension about the economy's performance came naturally to Dirksen. The overheated economy was the result of intrusive government activity on the domestic front, in Dirksen's view: "Somebody's got to pay the bill. And there is no free money that I have ever seen around any place in the last thirty years. I am afraid of these deeper intrusions."[68] When asked on television's "Issues and Answers" on July 3 about his greatest legislative accomplishment, Dirksen paused, then answered: "Well, if I had to put it in the large, probably it would be my endeavors to stop legislation that was not in the public interest. Because I have followed the old precept of Gibbon, the great historian, who said, 'Progress is made not so much by what goes on the statute book but rather by what is kept off and what is not put on.' "[69] In 1966 Dirksen led the opposition to civil rights measures aimed at housing policy and efforts by the Democrats to repeal section 14(b) of the Taft-Hartley Act. His efforts to amend the Constitution to permit prayer in public schools fell short in September 1966.

But Dirksen stood by his commander-in-chief on the more volatile issue of the war in Vietnam. "I've said to the President that I'm in his corner where our national security and interests are at stake," Dirksen announced. "Let's get the war over and done with and do what is necessary to bring peace over there."[70] No Democratic senator was so close to Johnson, and this was at least in part because Dirksen from the beginning had given his wholehearted support to Johnson's Vietnam policy. He continued to do so even after some of his Republican colleagues turned against escalation of the conflict. Between the end of 1965 and late 1966, U.S. troops increased from 181,000 to 389,000, deaths from 1,369 to 5,000.

His health declining, Dirksen finished out 1966 with his authority intact. Dirksen commanded Johnson's attention and allegiance. Congressional Democrats turned to him to find ways to pass or amend legislation. The

Republicans, some of them restlessly, still depended on Dirksen to promote their programs to the press and to the president. Dirksen's influence was an established fact, widely written about and acknowledged.[71]

What accounted for Dirksen's power in the mid-1960s? In hindsight it appears that several factors explained Dirksen's success. The lack of discipline in political parties, for example, permitted him to form alliances with conservative, southern Democrats and gave the other Democrats reason to seek his blessing. Once he cooperated with them, they were in his debt. That many senators, especially as the war in Vietnam dragged on, rebelled against what they perceived to be a cavalier president also gave Dirksen an opportunity. This diverse, undisciplined nature of the parties was complemented by Dirksen's own ideological flexibility, which permitted him to seize opportunities others might have avoided. Some analysts have suggested, for example, that Dirksen supported the 1964 Civil Rights Act at least partly to cement his power by putting Democrats in his debt and then backed Goldwater to maintain his influence on the Republican right.

It may have been, too, that the American people wanted an independent voice, especially in the face of an activist government. On domestic issues, Dirksen did not hesitate to challenge Lyndon Johnson's Great Society initiatives. Such a rivalry between president and Congress, Democrats and Republicans, served the media's interests as well. The press wanted to cover the opposition if only to escape White House control of the news. Furthermore, at least in the Senate, there was no one who by stature or temperament could counterbalance Dirksen. Mike Mansfield, the Democratic leader, lacked the inclination to bring his party to heel. He, in turn, suffered because Johnson handled the Great Society personally, not allowing others to establish an independent authority.

Add to this mix what Dirksen brought to the job: knowledge, institutional memory, shrewdness, timing, instinct, showmanship, and skillful use of language and media. Unlike many conservative Republicans, Dirksen tended to think in terms of people rather than symbols. He used stories of real people in real situations to make his points. "Home, Motherhood. Some of my colleagues smile when I speak on such subjects—perhaps they believe I am being evasive," Dirksen once said. "But these are basic. You can appeal to people only through things which motivate them strongly. If a man's home or his family are in jeopardy, he will stop at nothing to save them. Fear is the universal passion; even an infant understands the gesture of the upraised hand."[72]

The Power Wanes

Beginning around 1967, however, circumstances began to conspire against Dirksen. First was the matter of his deteriorating health. In the late 1950s, Dirksen had suffered a heart attack without knowing it. An enlarged and weakened heart caused him great physical distress over the final decade of his life. For a time the Senate Republican leader frequently checked in and out of Walter Reed Army Hospital, suffering from acute exhaustion as well as chronic emphysema and stomach disorders. In 1967 he said, "I've been trying for four years to get a vacation. If I don't get one pretty soon, some-thing is going to happen to me."[73] Shortly afterward, he was admitted to the hospital with infectious pneumonia so severe that it nearly killed him.[74] He also suffered a cracked vertebra from a violent fit of coughing, and he broke a hip falling out of bed in the hospital, which hobbled him on crutches for weeks. He smoked constantly. But Dirksen drove himself relentlessly. His only relief came at the eight-hundred-acre home on Broad Run, a small tributary of the Potomac. Much as he had at the beginning of the century, Dirksen found his solace in the land, away from "Tensionville," which is what he sometimes called the Capitol. As a home gardener, he was guided by two principles that seemed curiously to parallel his legislative life: he liked to have a little of everything and he liked to use all the space there was.[75]

Dirksen's alliance with Johnson on Vietnam began to hurt him, too. During the Ninetieth Congress (1967–68), the United States underwent two of the most trying years in the twentieth century. As a rising wave of rioting and looting swept over the nation's cities and the war in Vietnam continued to cost lives and dollars, two major political leaders, Martin Luther King Jr. and Robert Kennedy, were assassinated. The year 1967 was largely one of stalemate in Congress—the result of frustration with Vietnam and urban rioting and with the Democratic majority in the House diminished by the 1966 midterm elections. Johnson's proposals on an income-tax surcharge, civil rights, gun control, crime, and East-West trade went nowhere, although the Senate did ratify outer space and consular treaties with the Soviet Union. Congress's preoccupation turned to inflation, crime, and civil disorder in 1968. The session produced landmark housing and urban development bills and a strong civil rights law, prohibiting discrimination in most of the nation's housing.

Increasingly, as discontent over the war and the uncertain domestic situa-tion grew and Johnson lost his original popularity, Dirksen found himself in the odd position of having to defend the Democratic president against his own Republican colleagues especially with regard to the war. "All we want is for the communists to stop their aggression and let the South Vietnamese choose their own form of government," Dirksen stated simply.[76] Dirksen's support of Johnson, according to biographers, stemmed from three convictions: a sincere commitment to self-determination, an intense desire to see communist expansion checked, and a belief that once foreign policy was set by the president, the minority party had a duty to support it.[77]

Opposition to increased funding for the war and disagreements over military strategy became commonplace, however. Dirksen always rallied to the president's defense. "When you demean him," Dirksen said in the Senate, "you demean the prestige of this Republic." Criticism of Dirksen's friendship with Johnson mounted, and it was even rumored that Dirksen might have become a Democrat secretly.

The 1966 elections had given Dirksen three more Republican senators, but it was a mixed blessing. The Senate as a whole was generally less compliant with Johnson, more rambunctious. And Dirksen, faced with more troops to command, had no new weapons. Increasingly, talk turned to Dirksen's problems with the fractious junior Republicans and the likelihood that his power would be challenged. It was not a question of "if" but of "when." For the general public, though, Dirksen's popularity continued unabated. He had become something of a folk hero, and a particularly American one. His annual declarations on behalf of the marigold, his record contract with Capitol Records and the 1967 Grammy Award, an appearance on the "Johnny Carson Show," and a stint as grand marshal of the 1968 Tournament of Roses parade all contributed to his appeal.

As the Republican National Convention loomed in 1968, Dirksen remained an active force. He wanted to write the platform and made no bones about it. In spite of the opposition of the younger party men and women, he had the power and he intended to use it. The only question was whether or not he still had sufficient stamina at the age of seventy-one to play his role. "Age is a state of mind, and heart and will," Dirksen surmised. "Age is no factor."[78] Against the backdrop of Johnson's decision not to run for reelection, a decision that guaranteed a change in Dirksen's stature, Dirksen's role as chairman of the Platform Committee took on added significance. He had sought the post in hopes of using it to heal some of the differences in the Republican ranks and to unify the party. The platform as it emerged was not controversial, and it endorsed the Vietnam war, but in careful fashion.

Dirksen himself won reelection in 1968. In spite of bad health, Dirksen announced on February 17 that he would seek a fourth term. "The easy road would be to walk away and let the fire burn," his press release read. "But to retreat from an unfinished war or from unresolved and baffling problems would be alien to every conviction which I cherish."[79] Against a surprisingly resourceful challenger, William G. Clark, attorney general of Illinois, Dirksen scored his final electoral victory.

Perhaps from Dirksen's perspective, Richard Nixon's election in 1968 resembled John Kennedy's at the beginning of the decade. Both changed the basic calculus of Dirksen's leadership equation. Dirksen's influence and power diminished considerably upon the election of Richard Nixon. He was no longer the leader of the loyal opposition, the focus of Republican power. Instead he carried the new president's water on Capitol Hill, and he and the new president were not close. There were many fresh faces in the Senate, too. One of Dirksen's first tasks was to replace Senator Kuchel, who had been defeated, as Republican whip, Dirksen's top assistant. Dirksen favored another son of Middle America, Nebraska's Roman L. Hruska. But younger senators backed Hugh Scott, a liberal from Pennsylvania. Scott won, signaling the aging leader's diminishing influence. Columnist Jack Anderson said that Dirksen, "that delightful old political snake charmer, is losing his spell over his Republican charges."[80] Dirksen also lost his prized television forum when what had become the "Ev and Jerry Show" was canceled. The need for it had disappeared upon Nixon's arrival in the White House.

The sizable Democratic majorities in the House and Senate in 1969 hamstrung Nixon and Dirksen. They effectively prevented the new Republican administration from enacting a legislative program, resulting in a standoff. Nixon was the first president in more than a century to face in a first term a Congress dominated by the opposition in both houses.

It was hard for Dirksen to lead when there was no place to go. The victories were few and far between. After months of delay, on March 13 the Senate overwhelmingly consented to the ratification of the treaty to ban the spread of nuclear weapons, a bill Dirksen favored although his leadership was not essential. Nixon's only substantial win on Capitol Hill came in late summer. The administration had proposed to construct a system to defend U.S. missiles from Soviet attack, the Anti-Ballistic Missile system. On August 6, the Senate voted 50-50 on an amendment to the plan, effectively defeating the change and permitting the administration to proceed. The record for Dirksen's own legislative interests was not much better. He reintroduced his prayer amendment, cosponsored a bill to ban the interstate transportation of obscene material and another to increase federal penalties for drug trafficking, favored a study of voting rights violations, sought to protect federal employees' right-to-work activity, and pushed a measure to make his beloved marigold the national floral emblem. None succeeded.[81]

The minority leader's diminished effectiveness was not lost on the media. *U.S. News and World Report* devoted two pages of its May 19, 1969, issue to "Dirksen's New Role." His critics now felt freer to attack him, focusing on allegations, never proven, of unethical activities. The June 16, 1969, issue of *Newsweek* printed "The Other Ev Dirksen," alleging that Dirksen had profited financially from his relationships with Democratic presidents. It pointed to what it called his "extraordinary interest" in legislation affecting certain industries, notably drugs, chemicals, gas pipelines, and steel and lending institutions, and his frequent contact with members of federal regulatory agencies. Dirksen's opposition to legislation that would require public disclosure of income, or sources of income, by members of Congress also hurt him. Yet even these critics had to admit that these counts against Dirksen formed only a web of circumstantial evidence.

The first session of the Ninety-first Congress, the sixth longest in history, adjourned on December 23, 1969, with the lowest legislative output in thirty-six years. Most of what Congress finally did accomplish took place without the familiar leader of the Senate Republicans.

On August 12, just before the Senate recessed, the senator held a press conference in his office. He expressed the hope that when Congress met again action could be taken on a host of serious problems. The White House, he said, had assured him that priorities would be set and pressure brought to bear so that legislation would go through. After a brief run-in with a *Chicago Daily News* reporter who had been writing stories about Dirksen's financial interests, Dirksen resumed a relaxed and mildly optimistic mood. The senator chatted amiably with other reporters and joked with his staff. Everything seemed normal—yet it was not. He had just been told that he was seriously ill. The doctors had discovered a spot on his right lung and suspected cancer. An operation was necessary.

Surgery took place after he had rested for three weeks at "Heart's Desire" rummaging in his beloved garden and working on the memoir that forms the major portion of this book. The tumor proved to be malignant, but Dirksen's strong constitution and vigor brought him through the three-hour procedure, and his recuperation was rapid. Mrs. Dirksen and the Bakers found him alert and cheerful when they were first allowed to see him. The next day, however, he complained of pain, and it became necessary to replace the tube draining his lung. He rallied after this operation, but on the following day, September 7, his heart failed and the end came.

Mourning for the senator was national and of a personal quality, particularly among his colleagues in Congress and the government and his friends in Pekin. His body lay in state under the great dome of the Capitol, an honor accorded to only three members of the Senate before him. Richard Nixon and his cabinet, with the vice-president and many dignitaries, attended the funeral, after which the senator was buried in his hometown.

In his eulogy to the fallen leader, President Nixon recalled remarks Daniel Webster had made more than a century before in testimony to a political opponent: "Our great men are the common property of the country." That described Dirksen well. His public service spanned an era of enormous change, and he played a vital part in that change. Through six presidencies, as Nixon put it, "Everett Dirksen has had a hand in shaping almost every important law that affects our lives," and while he never became president, "his impact and influence on the Nation was greater than that of most Presidents in our history."[82]

Notes

1. Dirksen quoted in *Everett McKinley Dirksen: Late a Senator from Illinois. Memorial Addresses Delivered in Congress* (Washington, D.C.: Government Printing Office, 1970), pp. 45–46.

2. Ibid., p. 265.

3. This and all subsequent undocumented remarks by Dirksen in this introduction are from the present memoir.

4. Hruska quoted, *Everett McKinley Dirksen: Late a Senator from Illinois,* p. 64.

5. Ibid., p. 264.

6. Frank J. Fonsino, "Everett McKinley Dirksen: The Roots of an American Statesman," *Journal of the Illinois State Historical Society* (Spring 1983): 17–34.

7. Dirksen quoted in Elliot A. Rosen, "The Midwest Opposition to the New Deal," in *The New Deal Viewed from Fifty Years,* ed. Lawrence E. Gelfand and Robert J. Neymeyer (Iowa City, Iowa: Center for the Study of the Recent History of the U.S., 1984), p. 73.

8. Dirksen quoted in *Pekin Sesquicentennial* (Pekin: Pekin Chamber of Commerce, 1974), p. 180.

9. Rosen, "Midwest Opposition," p. 73.

10. Dirksen quoted in *The Reporter,* Oct. 28, 1952.

11. Rosen, "Midwest Opposition," p. 77.

12. Ibid.

13. Dirksen to Louella, ca. June 5, 1939, Dirksen Personal File, f. 17, Everett M. Dirksen Papers, Dirksen Congressional Center, Pekin, Illinois.

14. Dirksen quoted in *Life,* Mar. 26, 1965.

15. Senator Robert Byrd, *Congressional Record,* Oct. 10, 1986, p. S15876.

16. Dirksen, quoting Lincoln, CBS's "Washington Conversation," Mar. 5, 1961, transcript, Remarks and Releases, Dirksen Papers.

17. Dirksen, NBC radio, June 20, 1944, transcript, Remarks and Releases, Dirksen Papers. See also Edward L. Schapsmeier and Frederick H. Schapsmeier, *Dirksen of Illinois: Senatorial Statesman* (Urbana: University of Illinois Press, 1985), p. 39.

18. Dirksen writing in notebook 16, Notebooks, f. 66, pp. 18–19, Dirksen Papers.

19. Schapsmeier and Schapsmeier, *Dirksen of Illinois,* p. 45.

20. Senator Robert Byrd, *Congressional Record,* Oct. 10, 1986, p. S15877.

21. Dirksen to Harold Rainville, Jan. 10, 1948, Chicago Office File, f. 5457, Dirksen Papers. See also Dirksen to F. F. McNaughton, Jan. 8, 1948, F. F. McNaughton Collection, Dirksen Congressional Center; and Schapsmeier and Schapsmeier, *Dirksen of Illinois,* pp. 47–48.

22. William Barry Furlong, "The Senate's Wizard of Ooze: Dirksen of Illinois," *Harper's,* Dec. 1959.

23. Dirksen, speech to Illinois Federation of Republican Women's Clubs, Springfield, Illinois, May 17, 1950, transcript, Remarks and Releases, Dirksen Papers.

24. Quoted in Schapsmeier and Schapsmeier, *Dirksen of Illinois,* p. 58.

25. Furlong, "Senate's Wizard of Ooze."

26. Dirksen quoted in *Washington Daily News,* May 7, 1969.

27. Dirksen, statement upon his election, Nov. 7, 1950, typescript, Remarks and Releases, Dirksen Papers.

28. Schapsmeier and Schapsmeier, *Dirksen of Illinois,* p. 66.

29. Dirksen on NBC's "Meet the Press," Sept. 11, 1951, transcript, Remarks and Releases, Dirksen Papers.

30. Dirksen, reply to State of the Union message, Jan. 1953, transcript, Remarks and Releases, Dirksen Papers.

31. Ibid.

32. Dirksen, "Big Government—The Road to Tyranny," *American Economic Security* (May–June 1953).

33. Schapsmeier and Schapsmeier, *Dirksen of Illinois,* p. 97.

34. Quoted in Neil MacNeil, *Dirksen: Portrait of a Public Man* (New York: World, 1970), pp. 138–39.

35. Dirksen, speech to National Federation of Republican Women, Washington, D.C., Sept. 6, 1956, transcript, Remarks and Releases, Dirksen Papers.

36. Quoted in *The Reporter,* Nov. 1, 1956.

37. Radio broadcast, May 12, 1958, transcript, Remarks and Releases, Dirksen Papers.

38. Schapsmeier and Schapsmeier, *Dirksen of Illinois,* p. 113.

39. Dirksen, untitled remarks, 1958, typescript, Remarks and Releases, Dirksen Papers.

40. Quoted in Schapsmeier and Schapsmeier, *Dirksen of Illinois,* p. 151.

41. See Paul O'Neil, "Grand Old King of the Senate," *Life,* Mar. 26, 1965.

42. Neil MacNeil, biographical text written on occasion of first-day issue of Dirksen postage stamp, Jan. 4, 1981, Dirksen Information File.

43. "Winning Battles for Ike in a Democratic Congress," *U.S. News and World Report,* Aug. 10, 1959.

44. Schapsmeier and Schapsmeier, *Dirksen of Illinois,* p. 121.

45. Quoted in MacNeil, *Dirksen,* p. 195.

46. Burdett Loomis, "Everett McKinley Dirksen: The Consummate Minority Leader," in *First Among Equals: Outstanding Senate Leaders of the Twentieth Century,* ed. Richard A. Baker and Roger H. Davidson (Washington, D.C.: Congressional Quarterly Press, 1991), p. 251.

47. Remarks in Boston, Feb. 1, 1962, typescript, Remarks and Releases, Dirksen Papers.

48. Dirksen on CBS's "Washington Conversation," Mar. 5, 1961, transcript, Remarks and Releases, Dirksen Papers.

49. *Wall Street Journal,* Mar. 9, 1962.

50. Ibid.

51. MacNeil, first-day issue text.

52. Dirksen on CBS's "Face the Nation," Sept. 19, 1965, transcript, Remarks and Releases, Dirksen Papers.

53. Lyndon B. Johnson, *The Vantage Point: Perspectives of the Presidency, 1963–1969* (New York: Holt, Rinehart, and Winston, 1971), p. 158.

54. See Frank H. Mackaman and Marie S. White, *How a Bill Becomes Law: A Study of the Legislative Process and the 1964 Civil Rights Act* (Pekin, Ill.: Dirksen Congressional Center, 1979), p. 39.

55. Ibid., pp. 31–32.

56. Dirksen quoted, ibid., p. 40.

57. *Chicago Tribune,* June 8, 1964.

58. Ibid., May 31, 1964.

59. Dirksen, June 10, 1964, typescript, Remarks and Releases, Dirksen Papers.

60. *Everett McKinley Dirksen: Late a Senator from Illinois,* pp. 73–74.

61. Johnson, *Vantage Point,* p. 159.

62. WMAL interview, Feb. 7, 1965, transcript, Remarks and Releases, Dirksen Papers.

63. Schapsmeier and Schapsmeier, *Dirksen of Illinois,* pp. 170–74.

64. O'Neil, "Grand Old King." This lengthy article signaled Dirksen's emergence as a statesman.

65. *New York Times,* Mar. 14, 1965.

66. O'Neil, "Grand Old King."

67. Schapsmeier and Schapsmeier, *Dirksen of Illinois,* p. 176.

68. Dirksen, speech to Executives' Club in Chicago, published in *Executives' Club News,* Apr. 1965, Remarks and Releases, Dirksen Papers.

69. Dirksen on ABC's "Issues and Answers," July 3, 1966, transcript, Remarks and Releases, Dirksen Papers.

70. Interview with Dirksen, *U.S. News and World Report,* Jan. 1, 1966.

71. See, for example, Milton Viorst, "Honk, Honk, the Marigold," *Esquire,* Oct. 1966.

72. Quoted in *Life,* Mar. 26, 1965.

73. MacNeil, *Dirksen,* p. 307.

74. Senator Robert Byrd, *Congressional Record,* Oct. 10, 1986, p. S15879.

75. *Home Garden,* Nov. 1965, p. 65.

76. Quoted in Lloyd Shearer, "The Wizard of Ooze—72—and Still Oozing," *Parade,* Apr. 17, 1968.

77. Schapsmeier and Schapsmeier, *Dirksen of Illinois,* p. 200.

78. *Chicago Tribune,* Jan. 30, 1968.

79. Press release, Feb. 17, 1968, Remarks and Releases, Dirksen Papers.

80. Jack Anderson, *Chicago Daily News,* Aug. 11, 1969.

81. Schapsmeier and Schapsmeier, *Dirksen of Illinois,* pp. 224–27.

82. Richard M. Nixon quoted in *Everett McKinley Dirksen: Late a Senator from Illinois,* pp. 10–13.

Sources of Information about Everett McKinley Dirksen

Everett Dirksen has not attracted a large following among researchers, writers, and biographers. In *Senators of the United States: A Historical Bibliography* (Washington, D.C.: Government Printing Office, 1995), for example, Dirksen garners only sixteen citations, compared to sixty-six entries dealing with Lyndon Johnson's congressional career. Even the taciturn Senate majority leader during Dirksen's time, Mike Mansfield, rates eleven.

The literature about Everett Dirksen falls into five categories: contemporary press accounts, oral histories, scholarly journal articles and book chapters, dissertations, and book-length treatments. In addition, the late senator's papers are housed at the Everett McKinley Dirksen Congressional Leadership Research Center in Pekin, Illinois.

Among the contemporary journalistic treatments of Dirksen, six stand out. In April 1945, *Fortune* magazine published "Congressman: A Case History," describing how Congress worked and how it might be made to work better. The twelve-page spread, which was later reprinted for distribution, introduced Dirksen to a national audience, casting him as an effective, creative advocate of congressional reform.

As Dirksen climbed the Republican leadership ladder, he attracted more attention. William Barry Furlong wrote a lengthy feature for *Harper's* in December 1959. Entitled "The Senate's Wizard of Ooze: Dirksen of Illinois," the piece dealt with Dirksen's flexibility on the issues, his persona, and his usefulness to the White House. Furlong coined many of the phrases used by others to describe Dirksen. Three years later, Dirksen achieved a solo cover for *Time* magazine when the September 14, 1962, issue devoted nearly five pages to Dirksen's roots, leadership style, speechmaking, and legislative effectiveness.

Both the *New York Times Magazine* and *Life* printed feature-length studies of Dirksen in March 1965. Ben Bagdikian's "'The Oil Can Is Mightier Than the Sword'" and Paul O'Neil's "Grand Old King of the Senate" each captured Dirksen at the height of his power. Together, they provided a comprehensive, not altogether uncritical treatment of Dirksen the wily legislative craftsman and media star. In the October 1966 issue of *Esquire,* Milton Viorst explored the reasons why Dirksen had emerged as a modern-day hero in "Honk, Honk, the Marigold."

These are not the only press stories worth reading about Dirksen, but they contain information not available elsewhere and, when added to daily reporting of the period, give a reasonably full accounting of Dirksen's career. Clippings of these and other pertinent articles cited in the notes above are contained in the files at the Dirksen Congressional Center.

Interviews with Everett Dirksen provide another rich source of information about him and his views. Although he never conducted a formal oral history, Dirksen appeared on scores of radio and television interview shows, including such Sunday morning shows as "Issues and Answers" and "Meet the Press." Transcripts of these shows, many of them available in his papers, are all the more valuable because Dirksen rarely wrote full texts of his speeches and because video recording was not prevalent during his time. Interview transcripts survive as one of the best records of the man in his own words.

More formal oral-history interviews conducted with Dirksen's contemporaries exist at libraries and archival repositories throughout the country. The U.S. Senate Historical Office, for example, has more than a dozen taped and transcribed oral histories with senators and Senate staffers that contain references to the minority leader.

Among more scholarly studies in journals and book chapters, an essay written by the political scientist Burdett Loomis is the most recent example of a thoughtful, interpretive piece based primarily on secondary sources. His "Everett McKinley Dirksen: The Consummate Minority Leader" appeared as a chapter in *First Among Equals: Outstanding Senate Leaders of the Twentieth Century,* edited by Richard A. Baker and Roger H. Davidson (Washington, D.C.: Congressional Quarterly Press, 1991). The historian Frank Fonsino gives details of Dirksen's early life in an article entitled "Everett McKinley Dirksen: The Roots of an American Statesman," published in the *Journal of the Illinois State Historical Society* 22 (Spring 1983: 17–34). That journal also published an article by Edward L. Schapsmeier and Frederick H. Schapsmeier, the first scholars to make extensive use of the Dirksen papers. "Everett M. Dirksen of Pekin: Politician Par Excellence" was published in volume 76 (Spring 1983). The Schapsmeiers also wrote "Dirksen and Douglas of Illinois: The Pragmatist and the Professor as Contemporaries in the United States Senate," which appeared in *Illinois Historical Journal* 83 (Summer 1990), and "Senator Everett M. Dirksen and American Foreign Policy: From Isolationism to Cold War Interventionism," published in *Old Northwest* 7 (Winter 1981–82). Byron Hulsey's "Himself First, His Party Second, Lyndon Johnson Third: Everett Dirksen and the Vietnam War, 1967" (*Congress and the Presidency* 22 [Fall 1995]: 167–81) explores Dirksen's fascinating relationship with his former Senate colleague on the most disruptive issue of the day.

Two doctoral students have paid close attention to Dirksen. The titles of their dissertations are self-explanatory: Jean Torcom Cronin's "Minority Leadership in the United States Senate: The Role and Style of Everett Dirksen" (Johns Hopkins University, 1973) and Edward Keynes's "The Dirksen Amendment: A Study of Legislative Strategy, Tactics, and Public Policy" (University of Wisconsin, 1967). A third doctoral candidate, Byron Hulsey, University of Texas at Austin, is now writing a dissertation entitled "Everett Dirksen and the Modern Presidents: Truman, Eisenhower, Kennedy, and Johnson," which promises to shed new light on Dirksen's role in a twenty-year period of change, continuity, and conflict in the Republican party and national politics.

Books about Dirksen run the gamut from simple compilations to thoughtful biographies. Among the former is Annette Culler Penney's *Dirksen: The Golden Voice of the Senate* (Washington, D.C.: Acropolis Books, 1968), which mixes her brief analysis of Dirksen with famous Dirksenisms. The book contains candid photographs of the late senator, too. A year later, in 1969, Fred Bauer compiled *Ev: The Man and His Words* (Old Tappan, N.J.: Hewitt House), which combines the author's recollections and extensive examples of Dirksen's wit and wisdom.

Neil MacNeil, the chief congressional correspondent for *Time* magazine during Dirksen's years as minority leader, wrote the first and still the best Dirksen biography, *Dirksen: Portrait of a Public Man* (New York: World, 1970). MacNeil enjoyed a special relationship with his subject, gaining access to off-the-record meetings and privileged information. Beginning with the senator's boyhood, MacNeil follows the Dirksen trail to political eminence, placing the story in the context of political history and analyzing his impact on the national scene. *Dirksen: Portrait of a Public Man* provides the most thorough discussion of Dirksen's role in the legislative issues of the day.

The first biography informed by archival research in the senator's papers was written by two historians, Edward L. Schapsmeier and Frederick H. Schapsmeier. *Dirksen of Illinois: Senatorial Statesman* (Urbana: University of Illinois Press, 1985) contains a wealth of information drawn from Dirksen's notes, speeches, letters, and legislative files. The Schapsmeiers also visited archives containing the papers of Dirksen's colleagues and the presidents he served. Their book does not have the "insider" flavor of MacNeil's, but it succeeds in capturing the essence of Dirksen's character and leadership. *Dirksen of Illinois* contains chapter notes, too, guiding the reader to other sources, a feature lacking in the other book-length treatments.

Louella Carver Dirksen, the senator's widow, collaborated with Norma Lee Browning to write *The Honorable Mr. Marigold: My Life with Everett Dirksen* (Garden City, N.Y.: Doubleday, 1972). It is a self-described "special kind of love story—the love of a man for his country, for his family, and for God." More a book of memories than a biography, Mrs. Dirksen's work relies heavily on her husband's words, including excerpts from some fascinating letters he wrote to her during his years in the House of Representatives. It is largely uncritical, as one would expect, but *The Honorable Mr. Marigold* is must reading.

Finally, *Memorial Services Held in the Senate and the House of Representatives of the United States, Together with Tributes Presented in Eulogy of Everett McKinley Dirksen, Late a Senator from Illinois* contains remarks and reminiscences by nearly two hundred of Dirksen's colleagues in Congress. The volume, produced under the auspices of the Ninety-first Congress, First Session, 1969 (Washington, D.C.: Government Printing Office, 1970), also prints the eulogy delivered by President Richard M. Nixon and the family's response made by Senator Howard H. Baker Jr.

The richest source of information about Everett Dirksen remains largely unmined—his personal papers located at the Dirksen Congressional Center in Pekin, Illinois. The collection consists of about twelve hundred linear shelf feet of documents, photographs, films and tapes, books, and artifacts. Although the bulk of the material relates to Dirksen's career in the Senate, there are scattered references to the years leading up to 1950. Major file groups encompass campaigns and politics, public works, legislation, constituent correspondence, congressional leadership activity, remarks and press releases, and newspaper clippings. With only a few exceptions, the collection is processed and open to researchers.

THE EDUCATION OF A SENATOR

I dedicate this narrative account of a great political adventure to my beloved wife, Louella Dirksen, and my daughter, Joy Dirksen Baker, without whose constancy, devotion, love, and sacrifice this adventure could never have happened.

EVERETT McKINLEY DIRKSEN

I

THE HALCYON DAYS

"M R. DIRKSEN, YOU ARE the father of a pair of lusty twin boys, and Mrs. Dirksen is doing very well." So spoke Doctor William Schenk in the small hours of the morning on January 4, 1896—or at least it is probable that he said something like this. I was around, to be sure, as one of those twins but not very articulate, or at least not to the point where I could be understood or that I knew what was said.

"I have their names picked out." I assume Father said this to the doctor and perhaps he added, "You will recall, Doctor, that when my first son was born I named him Benjamin Harrison Dirksen. In keeping with that I shall name one of the twins Thomas Reed Dirksen after the noted Speaker of the House of Representatives in Washington and the other I shall name for McKinley; that is to say Everett McKinley Dirksen."

And that is how the adventure of life began. Of course the conversation between my father and the doctor is reconstructed entirely from what both he and Mother related about our advent into this world.

Now there is nothing very extraordinary about being born in the year 1896, though it's a very long time ago. Hundreds and thousands of people were born in that year all over the world. Nor is there any special significance in being born in January. There again thousands must have come into this world in the first month of the year. An astrologer might observe that being born in January makes one a winter child who tends to be introspective, sometimes moody, and of a saturnine nature. Nor is January 4 a particularly notable date on which to be born. This I know from the very simple fact that many people all over the country, on learning of my birthdate, have written to express the hope that if, perchance, I should happen to be in their section of the country at that time it might be possible for a joint birthday celebration.

Some things of importance did, however, happen in 1896. If I recall correctly, a French scientist discovered the radioactive quality of uranium. Succeeding scientists enlarged and built upon that discovery, and out of it came the fracture of the atom and the creation of a force that was powerful enough to bring an end to a world conflict. That development took a half century and the full implications of that force and its uses are not yet fully realized.

It was also the year when Idaho became the fourth state in the union to bestow the vote on women. How strange that it took such a long time to bring about the emancipation of women and restore the sex to the dignity and station that the creator must have intended. How strange it seems that this restriction was placed upon women in the early common law we inherited from England, and that it remained for so many years as if women did not bring an equal intelligence with men to the exercise of the right to vote.

It was also the year when William Jennings Bryan, who was born in Salem, Illinois, was unfurling his celebrated sixteen-to-one silver doctrine in all parts of the nation. Even if Bryan's silver ideas had no special appeal, his speeches did, especially the "Cross of Gold Speech," which every budding college orator sought to emulate. I should make it clear that I had nothing in common with Bryan except that we were both born in Illinois and, in fact, in the central area of the state. Nor was there a log cabin in my life, not that it makes any difference, but facts are facts and they should be properly observed.

My mother was a saint if ever there was a saint upon this earth. What a rigorous, full, and fruitful life she lived. She came from the old country when she was but a girl of seventeen with a ticket around her neck to indicate that on arrival at the port of New York, a decade after the Civil War, she was to be directed to the town of Pekin, Illinois.

Why did Mother come to the United States in the first place? The answer is quite easy. A number of others from the same general area in Germany had migrated to this country some years before, and they were quick to write to their friends in the ancestral land and tell them what a magnificent adventure it was to live in a free country. Both Mother and Father had lived under the rule of the German kaisers and knew full well that no matter how benevolent a kaiser might be, it was still an imperial dictatorship with all its paternalism and constricted freedom. So the fact that distant kinsmen and friends lived in a place called Pekin in the state of Illinois brought her here.

With us boys at her knee, she used to tell us of her journey to this land in a slow-moving vessel across the turbulent North Atlantic. It took many weeks, and it was not uncommon for passengers to develop scurvy and lose teeth as a result of this malady.

It did not take too long for Mother to become acclimated to the new land and to begin her ministration among neighbors and church associates. Was there illness in a family? Mother was there to minister to the afflicted person, to help with the meals, to see that the children were dressed and gotten off to school and that household chores were done. Was there a disastrous fire in the neighborhood? Mother was there to do what she could. Were there families for whom Christmas was but a bleak and uneventful day in the calendar? Mother was there to make certain that there would be a Christmas touch. This was her life—to minister to others who were in need. A son can only hope that some of this concern for fellow human beings may have come to him with mother's milk.

By occupation, Father was a decorator in a special field. It was in an age when spirited horses, buggies, and carriages were the vogue and the means of transportation. As much skill and care went into the manufacture of buggies and carriages as now goes into the modern, sleek, smooth-running motor cars, and not the least of the manufacturing business was the decoration of such vehicles with fine line striping brushes and other tools of the decorator's craft. Father was indeed an artist in this field, even as he was an artist as a penman. For years he served as the secretary of a workingman's society and his books were artistic beyond description.

Candor compels me to say that he drank a little too much but never to the point at which he actually became intoxicated or maudlin or mean. He had the grace and good nature of a patient martyr and if perchance Mother scolded a little too much, he would act hurt or injured. In fact, he did feel hurt on these occasions and subsided into complete silence.

When I was but five years of age, Father suffered an apoplectic stroke that completely paralyzed one side of his body. What a chore it was for Mother, with such aid as we could render, to nurse, dress, bathe, feed, and care for him as if he were a helpless child. But somehow we all managed in good spirit and lavished warm affection upon him until the day of his earthly demise.

At this point I should say a word about my twin brother. I suppose it may be truthfully said that in early life brothers of the same age rather cordially tolerate each other. Somewhat later in life they come a little closer together, and still later a deep affection ripens and they become deeply concerned about each other's well being. It was so in our case.

I did not mention in connection with the names which Father assigned to us that he was motivated in part by the fact that he was an avowed Republican, and perhaps his devotion to the party accounted for the fact that at a very tender age we were permitted to participate in a Republican rally. Perhaps I and my twin brother were four when a political parade and rally were held for a candidate for the United States Senate named Albert Hopkins. My older half-brother was one of the marshals of the parade and conspired with Father over Mother's protests that we be permitted to march in the parade and carry lanterns. It was quite an affair. The few streetlights that were available at that time made it necessary for every parade to provide its own illumination, and hence there was a plethora of lanterns and torches. I am quite sure that when it was all over and my own sense of excitement had subsided I said to my twin brother, "I want to be a senator." So it could well be that the ambition became rooted at a very early age.

In grade school years the pathways of both of my brothers and myself clearly led in opposite directions. They were lured by the thought of getting out of school at an early date and finding jobs so their earning powers might be put to immediate use. On the other hand, I might have been properly described as a bit bookish because I preferred to remain in school, and that is precisely what happened. In today's jargon I presume my brothers would have to be described as dropouts since my twin brother gave up his educational pursuits at the end of the sixth grade and my older brother at the end of the eighth. But notwithstanding this, they were diligent, hard working, devoted to church and family, and lived quiet but satisfying lives.

Church was a large part of our early lives. When Mother came from the old country one of the very first things she did was to enlist herself along with others in the building of a simple frame church where the Calvinist or Reformed faith could be pursued. When I say that she enlisted herself in this cause, it was not merely an effort to collect quarters, half dollars, and dollars for the building fund. She helped do the physical labor at the church site in whatever manner she could. Having consummated this task, she was not only regular in her attendance at midweek prayer meetings but also the church and Sunday school sessions on Sunday. If it was nothing more than the habit of attendance, it finally took me into the work of the Young People's Christian Endeavor Society on Sunday nights, and for three or four years I served as the president of the society. Among other things it was excellent training, since there was an assigned topic for each Sunday and I found that to sustain the interest of the members I had to prepare my remarks well in advance. It forced me to develop a kind of poise in standing before a group and presenting a subject in a logical and coherent way.

When I think of the teen-age gangs of today, with their fearsome names, I am reminded of the gangs of yesteryear, such as they were. Actually the term "gang" was in vogue three-quarters of a century ago but the resemblance to the modern gang ends right there. Our gang was made up of youngsters in the neighborhood of about the same age. Its activities for the most part were directed toward baseball, football, the ice sport then called "shinny," and various tag games at night. Sometimes the activity was varied, as when they all assembled for a trip into the woods to get walnuts, butternuts, and hazelnuts. Then too the gang took off from its regular activities in the crop season to pick strawberries, beans, cherries, and other fruit and truck crops in order to supplement their very slender means.

The activities of the gang did not extend into the late hours. In those days parents labored long and hard and were compelled to retire early in order to husband their energies. So when the hour of eight o'clock in the evening arrived, the gang disappeared and were soon at home and in bed.

Sometimes the gang could get into mischief. It was not the violent or malicious kind, but it was still mischief and in a way it sprang from the fact that a neighborhood group had to attach its loyalties to someone or something. In this case it happened to be the gang clubhouse or shanty. To a neighborhood group, a gang clubhouse or shanty becomes a social center and in fact becomes a rather dominant force in the life of the group. Of course, having a shanty meant that some parent had to give consent for its location, and then came the problem of finding old lumber, a stove, a lamp, some assorted furniture, and other items to give the shanty the aura of a clubhouse. Every member worked diligently at the project and in due course the shanty came into being. Its particular purpose was to provide a place to loaf, to indulge in heroic conversation, to boast about wonderful exploits, and over and above all else to think about food.

It was necessary to get one of the mothers to agree to cook an occasional dinner to be served in the shanty, but it was up to the members to find the necessary food. One member would offer potatoes, since his family had a garden and grew potatoes in quantity. Another would offer tomatoes, still another would offer pie, still another would offer bread. From a member whose family kept cows, the gang could expect butter and milk, but the proposed dinner still lacked that one article of diet around which the meal had to be built.

It took but little discussion to conclude that the ideal menu had to include chicken. Everybody liked chicken and virtually every gang member's family raised chickens. That made the problem quite simple. Each member would undertake to raid his own family's chicken coop and each boy would, therefore, donate a big, fat chicken. We were selective enough always to pick a rooster, since the hens laid eggs for the family larder and to be sold at the grocery store. Supplying chicken, therefore, was not a difficult operation to consummate nor was it much of a problem to clean and eviscerate the fowl and get it ready for dinner. To be sure, it sometimes took a bit of polite fabrication to explain how we came by the chicken. Usually, however, some days after dinner, parents of the members would compare notes and then the whole story was disclosed. Instead of being scolded, we were more often than not commended for raiding our own chicken roosts, thereby taking the taint of criminality from our action.

But in the shanty other mischief was concocted. There were many places that raised fruit and melons, and since it all looked so tantalizing from afar, it was easy enough to organize a foray on the orchards and melon patches. It seems that stealing melons and fruit was accepted as a part of our way of life, and the owners prepared for it. On a number of occasions a vigilant owner managed by means of shotgun shells loaded with salt and pepper to sting a few of our rather tender young gang associates. That usually brought to an end the melon and fruit-raiding expeditions.

I failed to mention that fishing was among our diversions in late spring and early summer. There were a number of available lakes near Pekin where pan fish, such as perch, bluegill, channel catfish, and bass, could be caught without much difficulty. That was in a day and time when we knew little or nothing about pollution, fishing licenses, and posted signs. Fish proved to be a very welcome diet supplement.

But let me tell you about our homelife. I was born in a humble frame house which stood on a rather small lot. Mother was quite unhappy because there was no place for a spacious garden, and she had a deeply ingrained garden instinct. Accordingly, we negotiated for the sale of our birthplace and for the purchase of property at the end of town which carried with it a full acre that could be devoted to fruit, berries, truck crops, and even corn to feed poultry, pigs, and cows. It was a much larger place. With our slender family income we managed to fix and furnish until I felt like a highborn prince in a majestic castle.

The parlor was indeed a showpiece. At least I thought so. On the floor was a red Brussels rug. How resplendent and beautiful it seemed. In the center of the parlor was a marble-topped table with a large Bible on it in which were recorded the family births, deaths, and marriages. It was an age of high infant mortality, and the page on which family deaths were recorded contained many entries. In the corner of the room there was a whatnot graced with an assortment of cheap bric-a-brac such as one wins at the contests conducted at county fairs.

There was a horsehair sofa. It was the kind one always associated with those early courting days when an ardent young swain would drive up to the home of his lady love, stable his horse, slick back his hair, and tremulously knock on the door and ask to see Mary. Generally his boots had been freshly greased and he looked stylish indeed. On such occasions the parlor was unlocked so that Mary and Jethro could sit at opposite ends of the sofa fairly overwhelmed with tender sentiments that sought expression. It was a reminder of the old anecdote about Jethro and his lady love on the sofa so inarticulate in his agony that finally he blurted, "Mary, how's you maw?—not that it matters much, but it makes a little conversation."

By the standards of yesteryear, I thought our living room was indeed palatial. Certainly it was for the humble neighborhood in which we lived.

In point of its importance, there was the huge glassware cabinet which seemed at least eight feet high and was filled with sparkling glassware and Mother's choicest china. In terms of money, it was probably quite inexpensive. In terms of today's antique values, some of it at least would be priceless. Then there was the full-length mirror where we as vain little boys could make faces or primp and indulge our juvenile vanities.

In one corner was a rather old but serviceable reed organ on which Father could chord and join in singing. He had a large bass voice. For years he sang with the local German Men's Glee Club. It was truly an impressive singing society which sang mainly for its own amusement, but it did make talent available for community picnics and celebrations. A kerosene lamp with a beautiful shade and with clusters of crystal pendants furnished light for the living room. The lighting of this lamp each evening was virtually a reverent ceremony.

But the prize piece of equipment for this room was the hard-coal stove, resplendent in nickel trim, with a nickel-plated angel perched on top. It had a large door with an isinglass window. When we sat around the base of the stove on cold winter evenings, what a stimulus it was to the imagination to watch sparks dashing like startled deer toward the chimney and wonder whether they ascended to the sky to become so many additional stars in the firmament.

The kitchen was the place where the family spent most of its time. That is where all the meals were served. That is where we lounged in the evening to read. That is where the work was done.

On the floor were carpets made of carpet rags that were woven at a local loom. What an endless job it seemed to save all manner of cloth scraps, cut them into strips, sew them into a seemingly endless string, and roll them into balls the size of large heads of cabbage. Quite often the Ladies' Aid Society was invited to our house to sew carpet rags. When fifty pounds or more had been so prepared, off they went to the loom to come back in resplendent strips to grace the kitchen floor.

A coal-burning range supplied both heat and the fuel for all cooking. Attached to the stove was the water reservoir that was the source of hot water for the traditional Saturday night bath taken in a galvanized tub. Actually a bath on a winter Saturday was an heroic adventure, but Mother always insisted, and she was the boss.

The kitchen was lighted with a hanging kerosene lamp suspended above the dining table. Whether we were at a meal or merely lounging about the kitchen table, if the weather was slightly gusty and the door opened, someone had to jump to his feet quickly and shelter the lamp chimney with a cupped hand before the blaze was extinguished by the wind. There were a few very cheap chromos on the kitchen wall, but to me they seemed so very real. One in particular showed what I thought were the gladiators coming out of their caverns into the Roman Coliseum to confront the lions, tigers, and other wild beasts of the Roman circus days. Actually they were not gladiators but Christian martyrs. Even such a tawdry picture stirred deep emotions in me.

Except for one large bedroom which Mother occupied on the ground floor, all sleeping quarters were on the second level. The walls were calsimined in tinted colors and generously bedecked with rather inferior art, some of which came as premiums for a year's subscription to the daily newspaper and were framed in rude handmade frames. The beds were enormous affairs. A spring, a mattress, and double-decked featherbeds overlaid with sheets and blankets and quilts was really a choice invitation to sleep; but in winter all this was high adventure also. The rooms were almost as porous as a pair of fishnet hose. Snow could and did filter in beside the window casings, so that the first barefooted step out of bed would land on a neat pile of snow and elicit an exclamation both long and horrendous and scarcely polite or complimentary.

There was no inside plumbing. Whatever the demands of nature, they had to be requited with what was referred to in those days as a slopjar, unless one preferred to get semidressed and venture out to that quaint little house with a half-moon carved in the door. It was quite a rugged life.

Attached to this stately menage was an acre of level and fertile soil that was well adapted to my purposes. I had an innate desire to grow things. That acre, therefore, became the most intriguing of all the resources of my childhood and youth. To me it was "one acre and liberty."

There was sufficient land to produce truck crops, not merely for our own table but to be sold about town and ultimately to fill our storage cellar when harvest time really began. It also produced some of the feed with which to fatten three or four pigs and to feed an equal number of milk cows. I found singular pride in weedless rows of radishes, beets, turnips, beans, carrots, and potatoes. Corn ripening in the late autumn sun seemed like one of the mystic wonders of nature. One could lavish almost tender care on such a garden in the spring and watch it come to fruition in the summer. Then came the autumn, when one served as nature's assistant in preparing the garden for winter's sleep. The late harvest provided turnips, parsnips, and carrots to be stored in sand, and potatoes to be stored in a cool dry place. The pigs, which were butchered in the fall, supplied such tasty and delightful things as smoked sausage, hams, and bacon. In addition to all this, there were the hives of bees from which the honey had to be taken and either sold to the local store or peddled from a bicycle. And then came the business of trimming the grapes, berries, and fruit trees against the day when spring would be resurrected.

In those early days, I did very little with flowers and plants. One factor was the cost, the other was that I was quite intrigued with what nature had to offer by way of wild flowers such as violets, jack-in-the-pulpits, may apples, brier roses, lilies of the valley, brown-eyed Susans, trumpet vines, and a good many others. It was something of a challenge to take these wild products of nature and try to domesticate them and make them yield to my rather amateurish touch. Sometimes I succeeded in making them grow in a domestic garden plot, but quite often my efforts did not meet with success. It was, however, an interesting challenge and for that matter still is. These were indeed the carefree halcyon days, when I had nothing more serious to think about.

2

THE GROVES OF ACADEME

I T WAS ARISTOTLE, the Greek philosopher, who strolled through the groves of academe with his disciples, who were known as peripatetics because they walked so much. As they strolled through the groves, he imparted knowledge and wisdom to them. The urge to continue school and stroll through the modern groves of academe at high school was upon me, and I cheerfully enrolled for courses.

One was expected to have at least an inkling of the calling for which he wished to prepare himself, but frankly I did not. I was, however, sure that I did not want to be a senator.

High school was certainly a pleasant adventure. The family income had been improved slightly for my two brothers were working, and it was possible for me to wear clothes that looked a little more presentable. I did a minimum of homework when I was in high school mainly because study was a natural habit and my mind was certainly retentive. Reading was a delightful experience because the supplemental reading that was assigned in the English classes included such works as *Treasure Island, Robinson Crusoe,* and other adventurous tales, the kind of thing a young mind could devour.

I was lucky in my high-school teachers. Miss Anderson, who taught zoology, biology, chemistry, and physics, was a delightful person who made all science courses extremely informal and interesting. Miss Ruhaak, who taught mathematics, always frightened me a little because she was so very prim, severe, and virtually humorless; but she was in truth a great teacher. Either the student did the required work or he did not pass, and the lamentations of parents could not move her.

Miss Baldwin taught history and civics. Only a few years ago I agreed to address the annual Chamber of Commerce banquet in Mattoon, Illinois, and on learning that she was still about and living in Mattoon, I suggested that they make her the guest of honor at the dinner. It proved to be an entrancing evening for there at the speaker's table sat my history teacher of long ago, ornamented with a resplendent orchid and enjoying every minute of the tribute paid to her by the community.

The "acre and liberty" which filled so much of my early life was now about to destroy that "liberty." Milking four cows and peddling the product, the chores of gardening and clerking in a grocery store on Saturdays, along with the regular schoolwork left me little time. Besides, I was interested in some extracurricular activities associated with school.

For a while I thought I could be a great athlete and particularly a track man. I felt that my real strength in this field would be in the one and two-mile events, but the very best I ever seemed to do was to take third place in the annual county track meets.

Football was the most captivating sport, but it was not as important then as it is today, although we worked hard and seriously at it. We could not afford a coach, but a University of Illinois graduate named Nathaniel Green, who lived close to the high school, agreed to coach us in his spare time. I will always be indebted to him for his voluntary service. The uniforms which we inherited from the class before us were anything but serviceable, but where would we find new uniforms? Neither the team nor the athletic department, such as it was, had money, nor was there a school fund or any personal resources from which to buy football gear.

It was at this point that the high-school girls in the Philomathean Literary Society came to the rescue. Candy making was an art even with the young ladies in high school. So they held a meeting of the society, developed a literary program, and sold candy, cookies, fudge, and other goodies. The proceeds were turned over to the football team. This took care of sweaters, pads, and moleskins. But every player had to provide his own shoes. This meant finding a pair of cheap, light shoes and working in the basement at home at night to tack on some makeshift cleats. Somehow it all worked out, and the team was equipped to play a full season of football.

It was an exciting adventure when a game was reasonably far away from home and it became necessary to take a train. In fact, that became one of the major events of the year. When the games were not too far away, public-spirited citizens who could afford automobiles volunteered to take us to the site on Saturdays. This was also a truly adventurous experience, the roads and the cars being what they were then.

On the cultural side there were oratorical contests and amateur theatricals. In this latter field, but unassociated with high school, was a minstrel show which a few interested students put together and took on tour to nearby towns. It was high fun but I had not become accustomed to being away from home overnight. Whether it was fear or timidity or homesickness or the fact that Mother was now quite old and widowed which accounted for it is still something of a mystery. But whatever it was it did account for my walking ten miles at night after the show was over in order to get home. I can still recall that journey rather vividly. Ten miles at night along a rail-road track with a suitcase is not an easy chore. Still, I managed it without ill effects.

At long last came graduation day. My first stroll through the groves of academe had indeed been pleasant. I was the salutatorian of the class. The family circumstances were now such that I bought the first tailored suit I ever enjoyed, with a high collar and a highly starched shirt. I felt trim, stuffy, and stiff and I shall never forget the occasion.

The graduation exercises were held in the opera house. In those days virtually every city and town of any consequence had an opera house to which producers from New York and elsewhere brought stock companies and road shows. They presented such emotional dramas as *East Lynn, David Copperfield,* and *Thorns and Orange Blossoms.* The walls backstage were covered with inscriptions that visiting companies, as well as stagehands, had put there with paint brushes. One of these inscriptions I still remember: "Don't tell us what you did in New York. Do it here."

The only thing that I can remember about the salutatory is the title, since I took the class motto for my theme. It was Latin and read, *Ad Astra per Aspera*—"through difficulties to the heights."

The graduation address was delivered by the local county judge. I particularly remember one word of it, and the reason I do is that I could not pronounce the word. The judge had taken as a title for his address "The Vicissitudes of Life." I simply could not wrap my tongue around the word "vicissitudes" and perhaps that is the reason it stuck in my memory.

With a high-school diploma in my pocket, I began to feel rather important, but I am quite sure that had I been asked I would have said I did not want to be a senator. With a young head filled to overflowing with wisdom and knowledge, it would doubtless be but a few days before some corporate enterprise or bank or a public utility would come and command my services. But strangely enough none came. Mother very quietly suggested that perhaps I should start looking for a job—any kind of a job. Perhaps what frustrated me more was that there was not even a stage offer of any kind, and my pride was hurt. Here was I, the salutatorian of my class, and not a single offer suited to my talent and temperament was ever made.

So I found a job with a corn products refining company in my home town. It consisted of traveling through the plant picking up samples after each processing and taking them to the laboratory for analysis. That was in a day when one did not inquire too deeply into the question of wages, hours, and fringe benefits. The job called for eleven hours each day for one week and thirteen hours each day for the second week. This arrangement required only two shifts in a twenty-four-hour day. The pay was fifty-four dollars a month. Of course, there were no fringe benefits and no retirement pay at that time. After four or five months I was taken into the laboratory to do elementary tests on coal, corn, and processed material. My pride and morale received a real lift with this promotion. They began to refer to me as an assistant chemist. As time went on the prospect of becoming a chemist grew on me, and I began to hope that perhaps I could be a renowned chemical engineer.

Deep down was that constant and irrepressible urge for expression—any kind of expression, spoken or written. The people I knew generally were religious, earthy folks. Anything smacking of art or culture or self-expression had no particular place in their lives. A slightly antisocial complex that had been building up in me for some time drove me into closer companionship with a high-school classmate who had similar tastes. His name was Clarence Hubert Ropp. In high-school days they called him Percy. In later years, when he moved to the Chicago area, he dropped his surname and became known as Hubert. He played the piano quite well and had a real dramatic flair, but above all else he had a pronounced artistic talent whether for art or for the stage. Fortunately he could afford it, and it was my great pleasure to bask in reflected glory. He had plans and dreams that I fully shared, and we became inseparable companions.

Destiny suddenly provided a detour. My half brother lived in Minneapolis, and Mother suggested that since I had been quite a dutiful son and was entitled to a vacation it might be well for me to pay him a visit. I made plans to take a train for what was to be my longest journey away from home. For a week I stayed with him and his family and had an opportunity to look over Minneapolis and St. Paul. It was on this occasion that I paid a visit to the University of Minnesota, which was situated high above the Mississippi River. When I saw this vast aggregation of buildings—the School of Medicine, the School of Engineering, the School of Mines, the School of Law, and others—I decided right then and there that this was for me.

At that point the ever-present subject of money began to intrude. How would I pay the tuition fee and purchase the necessary books? What could I do about renting a room and how would I pay the rent? What could or what would I do to sustain myself while in school? I returned home and discussed the whole matter with my mother and brothers. Out of the pooled resources of the family, they decided that they could afford enough to pay the tuition, buy my books, and provide a small additional supplement for my maintenance until I could find a job. I therefore set in motion the necessary plans for enrolling at the university and also for reducing my workload at home. I reduced the number of milk cows from four to one. I gave up raising pigs. I kept only a few chickens and gradually began to forget all about that acre and liberty. Once more I would be walking in the groves of academe.

Going to a university in a fairly large city was quite an adventure for me. I found a job selling magazines, but evidently I was not born to be a star salesman. It yielded a little but not much. Later I found a job with a rate adjustment bureau checking mistakes of arithmetic in billings of freight shipments. This was rather mechanical and not very inspiring. Somewhat later I became identified with the classified advertising desk of the Minneapolis *Tribune*. I worked twenty-nine nights each month between the hours of six and eleven. The compensation was not particularly impressive, but it was enough for food and room rent provided I was frugal almost to the point of stinginess. It left little time for social or extracurricular activities.

In most ways, college life was for me uneventful mainly because I could not devote any time to the things identified with the campus and with student affairs. All day had to be devoted to study and to class work, and it was far from eventful. Yet there were compensations. Like most students I made a few close friends who somehow continued in and out of my orbit year after year.

One such was Paul Jarocsak. He was of Russian extraction. Paul also had to make sacrifices to remain in school because his parents were quite poor. He was a skilled debater and I was proud of the fact that I was on the debating team with him. He became a lawyer. Long years afterward when I came to know the governor of Minnesota and some of his friends, the opportunity presented itself to make the suggestion that Paul Jarocsak would in my judgment make an excellent judge. I doubt, of course, whether my influence or standing at that time by itself brought it about, but Paul Jarocsak was elevated to the circuit bench in Minnesota, and I am certain that he made an excellent judge.

Still another in that tight circle of friends was William Prosser, who, as I recall, had done some of his undergraduate work at Yale before he came to Minnesota. Probably the reason he came to Minnesota was that his father became the director of Dunwoody Institute in Minneapolis and that became the domicile of the Prosser family. He was brilliant and precocious and ultimately became dean of the law school at Stanford University. He was a skilled debater and served on the team. A third member of our group was Fred Ossanna, of Duluth. He came from a reasonably well-to-do family, was of Italian descent, and was very attractive to the ladies. He too graduated in law. Fred could afford good clothes and wore them extremely well. He became a very successful lawyer later on.

I was the fourth person on the team. We also served together during what was known as University Extension Week. This consisted of an entire week of varied entertainment including debates, lectures, plays, dramatic readings, and similar presentations to audiences in small towns in Minnesota. Sometimes we debated in the afternoon and sometimes in the evening, according to a set schedule. We were glad to have this chance to present ourselves to appreciative audiences in different sections of the state. We developed a degree of poise and learned how to present all sorts of subjects.

At the university I also got my first taste of politics during the 1916 presidential contest between Charles Evans Hughes and Woodrow Wilson. At Minnesota, as elsewhere, the students planned a mock political convention, and a great deal of time, effort, and research went into the preparation of this event. I do not know why the managers of the convention selected me to make the nominating speech for Charles Evans Hughes, but in any event that's what happened. It was quite a spirited affair and the issues of the day were debated in the most lively fashion.

About the same time, I agreed to make a few speeches for a man named Ernest Lundeen who was a candidate for Congress from the university district. He had a brother in the Minnesota Law School whom I came to know quite well. Sponsors of one of the meetings for Mr. Lundeen had handbills printed advertising the meeting that I was to address, and this also turned out to be a lively affair. The handbills were circulated all through the university area and evidently some were dropped on the campus.

Early one morning, as I strode across the campus to get breakfast at the student union, I noticed Professor Thurston, who taught in the School of Law, just ahead of me. He stooped and picked up one of the handbills, glanced at it a moment, and then placed it in his pocket. A few days later he called me to his office and delivered quite a lecture, advising me to make up my mind whether I wanted to be a lawyer or a politician. Not too long thereafter Professor Thurston gave me the lowest possible grade without actually flunking me.

Getting back to Mr. Lundeen, he was elected in that year but was subsequently defeated for opposing the war resolution in 1917. In 1933 when the first New Deal Congress came into being, I was one of the few Republicans elected to Congress. As the newly elected representatives assembled in the House Chamber to be sworn into office, I heard the reading clerk utter the name of Ernest Lundeen. I walked over to where he was seated and asked whether he actually was the same Ernest Lundeen I had campaigned for as a student. He had probably forgotten the incident since it took place seventeen years earlier. This time, he was back to Washington on the New Deal political wave, and despite our political differences we became friends.

Going back again to 1916, I recall that a national oratorical contest was being staged by a national prohibition organization. The event took place in Lexington, Kentucky. I do not now recall if I was picked to enter the contest or how it came about, but in any event I found myself in Lexington as a representative from the University of Minnesota. One rather noteworthy incident that has always remained in my mind was that William Jennings Bryan, the keynote speaker for the event, made a truly great speech. I was quite anxious to meet him and especially so since Bryan was born in Salem, Illinois, and did his undergraduate work at Illinois College in Jacksonville.

The opportunity to meet him came one morning when he was eating breakfast in the hotel dining room. I happened to be there at the right moment. I was quite shy and timid about approaching this man of prominence, but as Lady Macbeth said, "I screwed my courage to the sticking point" and boldly went up to introduce myself. "Mr. Bryan," I said, "could I ask you two questions?"

"Certainly, young man, what are they?"

"Well, Mr. Bryan, I noticed yesterday while you were addressing that huge outdoor crowd that you somehow made them all hear. Is there a secret of some kind?"

"My boy," said Bryan, "all you need to do is to address those in the very last row of the assemblage and all the rest will be able to hear you. Your voice modulation will automatically adjust to the occasion."

"The other question, sir, is this: What do you do about the newspapers who speak so very unkindly about you and your philosophy?"

Mr. Bryan smiled and then replied, "I simply never read them."

So I returned to Minnesota without a prize, but with the satisfaction of having shaken the hand of William Jennings Bryan and of having enjoyed the fellowship of some young men of my own age who gathered from different parts of the country. On returning to the campus I was reasonably sure, however, that I still did not wish to be senator.

The urge to play football remained with me long after my modest service on the high-school football team, but where was I to find time for college football? I finally gave up this activity, but not until I had been asked to tutor two or three men on the team who were great players but rather deficient in mathematics. That proved to be quite a pedagogical experience.

The reason for it was simple enough. One of the law professors who was chairman of the eligibility board was an absolute stickler for schoolwork and simply refused to qualify any player no matter how outstanding or prestigious he was on the gridiron unless he was up to the school's academic standards. So because of Professor Jimmy Paige it was up to me to tutor some members of the football team even though I was not on the team. I could fully appreciate the old adage, "They also serve who only stand and wait."

The president of the university at that time was George Edgar Vincent, who later became head of the Rockefeller Foundation. George Vincent was a dynamic person whenever he addressed student convocations. His speeches were effective, timely, and always concluded on a high and impressive note. On one occasion I asked him about his technique in concluding a speech. "Mr. Dirksen," he said, "I always prepare five or six conclusions every time. I find that if and when I have delivered the message, and if I still have some time to fill, I can draw on first one conclusion and then another and still not do violence to the structure and the purpose of the speech." I never forgot that statement, and in later years I used it quite frequently, particularly when the speech was also going out live to a far larger audience on radio or television. On these media, time and timing are so important.

Money continued to be a problem because I was reluctant to tap the slender resources of our family. As it was, they had been exceedingly generous. The need for funds caused me to sign up with a publishing company for the summer to sell books in the country to farmers. They were the publishers of a home remedy and cookbook which, as I recall, sold for $4.95. Judging from the company reports, there were many other students who had made considerable money with this book, and I felt that with proper diligence I could do equally well. The area assigned to me was Edmunds County, South Dakota, of which the small town of Ipswich was the county seat.

The sales manager was truly an inspired person. He was a born salesman and taught the students how to sell a book and then suggest to the purchaser that one would be glad to trade it out in room and board. That arrangement was designed to make money unnecessary. Generally, but not always, it seemed to work. Yet there were occasions when one had to forsake the book business for a brief while and work in the hay or the harvest field for sufficient cash. I had agreed to remain in Ipswich until just before the convening of classes at the university. I attended church every Sunday so that people who drove in from the farms in the country could see me and anticipate that at some point in time I would be knocking on their doors.

I suppose I would have done fairly well financially except for one factor. Ipswich was in wheat country, and in that year the parasitic fungus called rust got into the wheat and nearly ruined the entire crop. So when a purchaser at the time of delivery said he had no money with which to pay, I had to agree to accept one dollar and return the book to the company. That happened in all too many cases and my profit for the summer was slender indeed.

All sorts of things can befall a person when he ventures out on a book-selling tour in a country where farms are far apart. I spent a lot of time and shoe leather trudging long distances. One of the first things that happened to me was a slight sunstroke. I fell beside the road and a farm family enroute from the county seat to their home hauled me into their buggy and took me home. It was but a slight stroke without serious aftereffects.

On several occasions I was bitten by dogs of a particularly vicious, rangy type, and it became necessary to prepare for this by carrying a very substantial stick with which to ward off their attacks.

About this time, war clouds were already high above the horizon. The farmers in this area had large families, and they were stoutly tied together. They saw looming war as a menace to family life, knowing that the young men in the family of military age might be called into the service. They were, therefore, disposed to argue about war, its causes and effects, and its justification or lack of justification. I found it necessary to be fully alert when such a situation arose. To argue stoutly against their views always jeopardized the sale of a book. On the other hand, to meekly concur might be deemed weakness on my part so I had to pursue a sort of middle course.

World War I had actually been under way since 1914 and had obviously provoked much discussion and conversation in the student union, which was the campus club for the male students. At that time, we were not yet actually in the struggle, and in the landlocked Midwest isolationism ran deep and strong. The general feeling was that it was not our war. Not only was there a substantial body of antiwar opinion, there was a rather unorthodox attitude toward public affairs generally. I believe it can be truthfully said that at some point in time every student is something of a socialist. Norman Thomas and those who were associated with him in the socialist movement were popular in a good many quarters on the campus. By comparison with later years all this seems mild and transitory. I suppose these immaturities are evident in every generation—and always appear to be new and menacing.

But the fact was, as days and weeks went by, that the war seemed to be getting closer to us. Kaiser Wilhelm of Germany began to display an arrogant disregard for our shipping on the high seas. From time to time he uttered warnings that our vessels would not be safe against the torpedoes of the German submarines, or U-boats, as they called them.

To many this was a matter of deep concern. Since the university was a land grant college, military training for one period each week was compulsory for the first two years of enrollment. I entered into this activity with a great deal of enthusiasm. I could have dropped out of the military training course after two years, but I preferred to stay with it and in due time became a battalion major in the cadet corps. Complications then set in.

The torpedoing of the *Lusitania,* which was then one of the largest passenger ships afloat, with its consequent loss of life stirred the feelings of people everywhere, and especially in the United States. The continuing disregard by Germany of our rights on the high seas finally forced the hand of President Woodrow Wilson, and he went before the Congress and asked for a declaration of war. Almost immediately, the national leaders moved to put the nation on a complete war footing. Officer training camps were established for their speedy training. When the first series of these training camp groups completed the program, a second group was established. When these had completed their courses still a third group was established. There was, however, a marked difference between the first two camps and the third. Those who successfully negotiated the first courses were commissioned into the army and assigned to military duty. As I held the rank of major in the university cadet corps, I could doubtless have been qualified and been ready for a commission at the end of the first training camp period. At the time I preferred not to enter.

One day the state adjutant general, who was in charge of military training activities and who had his headquarters in the campus armory, asked me to drop in for a visit. When I did, he administered a sharp lecture on my refusal to enter a training camp and do my duty to the country. That was enough for me. I promptly applied for admittance to the Third Officer Training School but was notified that I had to enlist in the army as a private before I could be admitted. This I did and was given sufficient time to return to Illinois to see my mother and brothers before I departed for military duty.

By that time, my twin brother had married and was, therefore, accorded an exemption on dependency grounds. My older half-brother could not qualify for military service because of an aggravated physical defect. So I became the only soldier in the family.

My mother was quite upset. There were many quiet hours when we sat together mostly in silence thinking of where my military duty would take me and whether or not I would ever return from conflict if I were assigned to overseas service. I tried as best I could to console her. I hoped she would find comfort in the fact that a service star in the front window of our home would be a loud and clear announcement to the neighborhood and to the world that one member of the family was in military service, for we had to remember that we were of German extraction, and there was a certain prejudice about us.

In the course of that visit back home, I noticed the glossy photo of Kaiser Wilhelm and his entire family which was prominently displayed on the wall of our living room. In our town they were still publishing a German language newspaper, and this photograph had come to Mother a few years before as a premium for a year's subscription when paid in advance.

I said to her, "Mother, I believe it would be the wise and discreet thing to remove that photograph from the wall. I would wrap it securely in heavy paper and put it away until this very unpleasant business is over." But she steadfastly refused. She insisted that it was a free country. That was the principal reason why she had come to this country from Germany only a decade or more after the Civil War. She pointed out that there was no law to compel her to remove this picture. She thought the kaiser was a good family man and not to be blamed for what the politicians had done.

"But Mother," I persisted, "there will be not only neighbors but strangers in and out of our house while I am gone. You know that war generates deep feelings and even deeper hates as the war spirit rises. Sentiment against the kaiser may grow to cyclonic proportions; someone will complain about you and that never fails to develop a wretched and embarrassing situation." Despite all my arguments she stood her ground, so as I boarded a train for Camp Custer, Michigan, to be sworn into the army as a private first class, the photograph of the kaiser and his family still hung on our living room wall.

3

"YOU'RE IN THE ARMY NOW"

W AS IT MORE THAN a coincidence that I should land in the army of the United States in time of war and exactly on my twenty-first birthday? I arrived at Camp Custer, Michigan, for induction into the service on January 4, 1917. As I recall, the thermometer indicated a temperature of ten degrees below zero. Could all this have been in my horoscope or was it just plain chance? In any event, there I was among several hundred assorted strangers, all of them potential officers. They would spend the winter in officer training camp and then be diffused into all parts of Europe, the Western Hemisphere, and elsewhere.

The young lieutenant who examined my enlistment papers paused for a moment and said, "I see you were a major in the cadet corps at the University of Minnesota."

"Yes, sir." Secretly I thought this was going to count for something so far as my rapid and steady advancement was concerned, but I was quickly disabused of that idea.

Without smiling he said in a crisp tone, "Just forget what you learned as a college cadet. You'll soon discover this is a different league." So did the mighty fall—even before actually getting into the army.

The training course for this series of officer camps was supposed to include not only a thorough familiarity with the seventy-five millimeter French field piece but also horsemanship, mathematics, firing calculations, and a great many other things both technical and nontechnical.

So far as horsemanship was concerned, it was pretty hard on the horse— we had just one. I suspect the army must have borrowed the animal from some neighboring farmer. The training battery would assemble solemnly around that horse and someone would illustrate how to fold and throw a

blanket onto the horse, then the saddle, and then how to mount and dis-
mount. There was also a textbook course on the care and feeding of horses;
but I wondered some at the time just why this peculiar kind of training was
being offered because we were led to believe generally that war was a grim,
mechanized business. By the time we landed on the Western Front—if we
ever did—that warfare would be completely mechanized and we would have
little interest either in horsemanship or in the care and feeding of horses.

But quite aside from these considerations, I was rather glad that once
upon a time I actually had owned a horse and so knew something about
these critters. In fact, over a period of years I owned first one horse and then
another. But I was not too entranced with a horse as such and preferred to
use the animal's traction power in front of a light-running buggy instead of
riding him. It was infinitely more comfortable.

As for the artillery training with the celebrated seventy-five, they brought
up a single gun carriage stripped of all its equipment and managed to mount
a log about the length of a gun tube on the carriage. That was to be the focal
point of our artillery training. The log, incidentally, did not even have the
virtue of being hollow. But from this quaint arrangement we were expected
to learn all that was to be known about light artillery before we arrived at the
front at some undetermined time in the future. What all this finally meant
was that our training battery had a short textbook course and very little more
before it was shipped to France. All this is what obviously made the whole
exercise so weird.

The battery commander, a captain, was an astonishing personality. He
had been an old army sergeant in the Phillipines and elsewhere. When
World War I broke out and it became necessary to train the young men of an
entire nation, there was a dearth of officers. Thus it was that this grizzled old
army sergeant was elevated to the rank of captain to help whip the new
recruits into condition for action abroad. As far as I could determine, he
knew little or nothing about mathematics and technical matters and con-
tented himself with the administrative chores of operating an artillery battery. Moreover, he was exceedingly careful never to display his lack of learning and knowledge; it was much easier to turn all this over to a half dozen
young lieutenants who, I discovered later, had graduated from officer training camp only a few months before.

They were eager and active and performed their duties quite well. All of
them were college men, but it was painfully evident that they were having a
difficult time keeping ahead of their students in the training course. Despite
what the lieutenant who examined my enlistment papers had said, I was

doubly glad that I had spent three years in the cadet corps at the University of Minnesota, for along with drill formations and the usual exercises which took place on a college campus the cadets spent some weeks in camp where we received highly practical instruction. That information and knowledge proved to be invaluable.

It would be difficult to assess the intellectual level of a training battery of more than three hundred young men, but I can say that generally it was quite high. My bunk buddy was an excellent example of what I mean. He was not only a mathematician but highly knowledgable in the field of astronomy. His name was Ralph. I became deeply interested in him for many reasons. In the first place, he was so very humble and self-effacing that I wondered not only how he had got into the training battery but how he would get along with his associates who were a little more on the rough-and-tumble side. Ralph already had a B.A., an M.A., and a Ph.D. He had a slightly misshapen head which always entranced me. It made me think of Oliver Goldsmith's description of the village schoolmaster in his celebrated poem "The Deserted Village." Goldsmith wrote, "and still they gazed and still the wonder grew that one small head could carry all he knew."

On one occasion I remember that I asked Ralph what the title was of the thesis that he wrote in order to obtain his M.A., and he said it was "The Proper Motion of a Star near Ceres." I did not quiz him any further on this point because I am sure I would have become quite lost in his explanation. But what did occur to me was that they should have been tapping that amazing brain of his for plans which might accelerate the ultimate victory, rather than freezing him into a training battery where his amazing brainpower could not be utilized thoroughly. He seemed out of place. But I was to learn as I pursued an army career that there was nothing unusual about this circumstance.

Still another member of the battery whom I cultivated was a resident of Michigan who was actually president of a corporation that operated three very substantial plants manufacturing goods, equipment, and material which was used for preparatory and war purposes. This would have excused him from military duty if he had pressed the point, but he not only refused to do so but insisted that he be admitted to a training camp and do duty like all others.

Every weekend his wife would come to the Post Tavern Hotel in Battle Creek, Michigan, where Camp Custer was located. She would bring briefcases fairly stuffed with business papers which needed his attention. His weekends were therefore devoted to making decisions, initiating policies to be followed by the various plants over which he presided, and arranging by telephone for the additional financing which was required in order to successfully carry the workload generated by war.

As I think back over the personnel of that training battery, I come to the conclusion that it was an interesting aggregation of potential officers—not excluding the first sergeant, who came from the University of Michigan and who always seemed so prissy, so effeminate, and so affected in his mannerisms. He was the butt of endless jokes and of rough barracks humor.

That training period was beset with extremely cold, rough, snowy weather, and I assume every member of the battery was only too glad when the course ended and we were ready for assignment elsewhere—overseas, we hoped. At the end of the training period came a painful disappointment; we did not receive commissions. Instead we all received certificates as warrant officers, so that we could trade the one stripe of private first class for the three stripes that a line sergeant is privileged to wear. We were kept at Camp Custer, however, until the assignments were completed. The leave gave us an opportunity to suitably observe our graduation day and to arrange for a dinner at the Post Tavern Hotel.

I can recall one incident in connection with that dinner. Obviously there had to be a dinner speaker, and for the occasion one of the local trainees had secured a young Battle Creek lawyer by the name of Hooper. When the speaker was introduced after suitable anecdotes, he arose and told of being introduced at a dinner on another occasion when the chairman had said, "Ladies and gentlemen, let me introduce you to Mr. Lawyer, the rising young Hooper." I thought this was extremely funny at the time, and I have used the story often.

Long after the war had ended and I had been elected to the House of Representatives and was in my second term, on the opening day of that Congress the clerk of the House called the roll to see if all those whose certificates of election had been filed with him were present. When the clerk intoned the name of Hooper from Michigan I became quite intrigued and peered first in one direction and then in another in the hope that I could identify him. Finally I found him and said, "Mr. Hooper, I beg your pardon but your name excites a rather interesting event in my memory. It was in 1917 in Battle Creek, Michigan, that I graduated with the third training battery and we had a graduation dinner at the Post Tavern Hotel." Then I reminded him of the little anecdote.

His face lit up as if he had suddenly discovered a long-lost friend and, in high spirits, he said, "That's me." We later had many occasions to relive some of the interesting earlier days of the war.

While going through the training period in Camp Custer, I learned that the only girl with whom I had ever had a formal date in high school was attending the university in Ann Arbor, Michigan. In those days I had thought she was an angel, and my infatuation blossomed anew. It was like a strange madness. She was dainty, dimpled, and very pretty. Despite my singular innate shyness and timidity where girls were concerned—an affliction which disturbed me not only in high school but through college days as well—I decided to conquer this shyness and made some heroic efforts to get in touch with her. Accordingly, I journeyed to Ann Arbor and found her in one of the very popular sorority houses.

It was a shock to find that she had bobbed her hair. In many quarters, among old-fashioned people, it was then regarded as an altogether sinful business. Next I noticed that she wore rolled hose and, in my book, that was simply unthinkable. That fad had led to a controversy of national proportions. Then came an additional shock; in the presence of other sorority girls she swore—and so did they. You can readily imagine how that cut my old-fashioned rearing. Moreover, it was not exactly polite swearing even to an artilleryman and I was deeply distressed. And to crown it all, out came the cigarettes and all of the girls began to smoke.

She was still as entrancing as when I had had that first date in high school; but I could not reconcile myself to what I thought were unduly modern developments. I returned to my camp that evening still nursing my infatuation after a fashion, but also thoroughly bewildered. For a while we carried on an indifferent correspondence, but that finally languished. It may sound humorous by today's standards, but I felt she had gone to the devil.

It was not long after graduation from the training camp that our assignment came. In short order I was on a train enroute to Camp Jackson, South Carolina, which was the pre-staging area for going overseas. There was no advance training, however, at Camp Jackson. We were assigned routine duties. I became a military policeman with the usual brassard on my sleeve. One of my jobs was to help move the civilian traffic that came to the camp in the morning and left by streetcar in the evening.

At that time I knew exactly nothing about the Jim Crow tradition as it applied to public vehicles. One of the first things I observed in trying to expedite the traffic movement was that there were often a good many seats in the streetcars that were not filled when the cars were ready to leave camp and go to the city. This appeared to be a waste of space and, in short order, I began to urge people, with an occasional shove, to get into the car and occupy all of the vacant seats. It was then that a very irate conductor stepped off the car to ask me if I was aware of the fact that there were Jim Crow laws and ordinances in effect, and that the front seats in the car could not be occupied by colored people. At the time I thought it was just a lot of stuff and gave all of them quite an argument, but the conductor steadfastly refused to move the car until I reentered and asked the colored people in the front seats to leave the car. I received quite a lecture on my general ignorance of customs and habits below the Mason-Dixon Line.

My police experience at Camp Jackson was of very short duration. Being classified as a "casual," without actual attachment to any military organization, I was given a number of assignments including one to teach school. We had inductees in camp who could neither read nor write. To me it seemed surpassing strange and pitiable that they were excellent soldiers in every sense of the word who could do military formations, who could understand plain instructions, and who were excellent marksmen, but who were absolutely illiterate. I was assigned to teach them the alphabet and the rudiments of the English language. It taught me to appreciate, in a very real way, the problems of a country which has a high illiteracy rate. I had never fully appreciated what patience it takes to teach adults the alphabet, the simplest words, and how to write their own names. All through the period I spent in Camp Jackson I stayed with this assignment because I deemed it something of a challenge.

One of the pupils, if he could properly be called a pupil, really intrigued me. He was an Indian. His name was Sam. On one occasion I said to him, "Sam, how do you like the army?"

He puzzled for a moment and then said, "Me no like army."

I asked why, and his answer was simple and quite classic. He said, "Too much salute, not enough shoot."

There were millions of soldiers in those days who undoubtedly shared Sam's views.

Almost fifty years later it became my privilege to revisit Camp Jackson. I went to Columbia, South Carolina, at the invitation of my friend and colleague Senator Strom Thurmond. I went there to address a political dinner. When I accepted the invitation I told him that it would be an anniversary visit and that I would be interested in seeing the transformation of this camp after the lapse of half a century.

To say that it was quite a different place is really an understatement. It had, in fact, been thoroughly modernized and had become a vast training center. The fact that Senator Thurmond was a major general in the reserves and maintained a constant and thoroughgoing interest in all military matters had much to do with the conversion of Camp Jackson into a first-rate training center.

I was accorded full honors, but what intrigued me most was that they had a patient doughboy rigged out in the kind of uniform that we wore in World War I. He wore baggy, ill-fitting outfit with wrap puttees. It was a wonder how military morale could be maintained when one was encased in such an outfit. The contrast between that and the new ones was thoroughly amazing. The members of the military of today are more comfortable and also present a more striking and impressive appearance.

Getting back to my army days, the question uppermost in the minds of all "casual" soldiers, who were not assigned to a definite military organization, was when we were going to be sent to France where the action was. At long last the orders came back. We were not to embark for France but were destined to go to Camp Merritt, somewhere in New Jersey. How long would we be there? Were we to be exposed to more training? Were we to be assigned to routine chores similar to those in Camp Jackson? Nobody had an answer, or, if there was an answer, it was certainly not disclosed to us. Rumors abounded, as they always did in the army, but there was no real information about what our tour of duty in New Jersey would be like. We soon found out, however, after we arrived in Camp Merritt. It was, to say the least, anything but an agreeable assignment.

Virtually in the center of Camp Merritt was a prison stockade to which they committed prisoners—hardened prisoners—who were sent there from army camps in all parts of the United States. Some of them had been found guilty of heinous crimes. They were indeed a rough and tough lot whose characters and whose nature were not improved by prison life. This particular prison was surrounded by barbed wire which was electrified so that a prisoner who sought to escape would receive a severe shock. In addition, the stockade was manned by guards who were stationed about every two hundred feet. On Sundays the camp was filled with visitors from New York, New Jersey, and elsewhere. They liked nothing so much as to watch the men in the stockade and to undertake engaging in the morbid business of conversing with the prisoners. This was strictly prohibited by regulations and the guards were expected to enforce the rule but, frankly, how do you enforce such a rule when the prisoners stand well back from the barbed wire enclosure? And how do you prevail upon visitors to refrain from conversation?

I was one of those guards. What aggravated me most was that the prisoners loved to taunt the guards, using the most profane epithets to show their complete contempt for the army, its officers, its regulations, and for the war itself. As the taunting continued, and quite often evoked bursts of laughter from the visitors, I felt an almost unrestrainable impulse to use a bayonet but I restrained myself. Orders were orders and they must not be ignored or violated by the prison guards.

This went on for several weeks and then one blessed day the orders to report overseas arrived. We were to prepare to leave for France. Reveille was to be sounded at four o'clock in the morning. We were to take our duffel bags and march to the vessel that would take us across the Atlantic. In this case, it happened to be a French ship. Little did I know, at the time, that it was an antiquated vessel that was engaged in cargo service, carrying everything from commodities to live cattle. This gives some hint of how lacking in modern appointments this vessel really was. But who were we to care? We were enroute to France and to the scene of action where we'd soon bring the kaiser to heel.

We were out from port not more than two days before I found my name on the ship's bulletin board. I was designated, along with others, to serve as one of the mess sergeants and was to report to the duty officer for instructions. When I appeared he said, "Sergeant, you will be one of the four who will serve as mess sergeants on this trip."

I puzzled for a moment over this order and then said, "May it please the lieutenant, can you give me some hint of my duties? I have never served as mess sergeant before and, certainly, not on a vessel."

His reply was very short and very sweet. "You will inspect the kitchen, you will supervise the kitchen police and the waiters, you will see that the food is served promptly and that there is ample food for all, and you will see that everything about the ship's mess is kept shipshape."

I had no idea who the other mess sergeants were or where they were to be found, so I entered on my duties as a mess sergeant in a rather independent fashion and started on an investigation of the galley. The kitchen was indeed a mess. The place was infested with roaches and vermin; even Hercules would not have known where to begin. The cooks were messes too, a thoroughly scruffy lot. The uniforms they wore were soiled and untidy and they, themselves, were dirty and did not seem to care whether they kept themselves shaved. Even more than the rolling of the vessel, the mess and everything pertaining to it tended to induce seasickness.

But what was to be done under the circumstances? The cooks were fractious and told me to mind my own business. Sometimes they used far rougher and more abrasive terms. All that could be done, therefore, was to make reasonably certain that there would be enough food to go around and that it would be served on time. Whether the men ate it or not was quite another question. To this very day I contemplate with a feeling of horror the mess aboard that old vessel but, somehow, we all survived the trip and landed at Bordeaux, France, on schedule.

The deck of a troop ship is certainly a wonderful place to reflect on life's course and the vagaries of mankind. I had been in the army for four months and was burning with idealism and a zeal to liquidate the kaiser. I had advanced from private first class to sergeant. That might have been impressive with some but not with me. I had served variously as a military policeman, a teacher, a mess sergeant, and a prison guard. I was convinced that, by temperament and otherwise, I was not meant to be a soldier and live in an environment of discipline. One slight satisfaction did come out of it. I was glad that when, at the end of my high school term, there was an opportunity to secure an appointment to West Point and become a professional soldier, I had declined.

I began to muse about my future. If fate decreed that I was to return alive, I might want to be a senator after all. Senators and congressmen were, in a sense, the direct cause of my being in the military service. To be sure, they had nothing to do with my assignment as a mess sergeant on an antiquated French cattleship, but if they had not voted for a declaration of war in April of 1917, I would still have been on a college campus moving toward the completion of a law degree.

Had I then been in the Senate (unimaginable thought) I would have jousted with such worthies as Senator Claude Swanson, of Virginia; or Wadsworth, of New York; or Key Pittman, of Nevada; or Henry Cabot Lodge, of Massachusetts; or Ollie James, of Kentucky; or Hiram Johnson, of California.

With all the sarcasm at my command, I would have excoriated those who, during the political campaign of 1916, had appealed for votes on the ground that Woodrow Wilson kept us out of war. I would even have turned upon William Jennings Bryan, who lent his eloquence to the plea that Woodrow Wilson kept us out of war but who went even further in his speeches and said, "and will keep us out of war." Yet within five months after that plea, we were in the war and, somewhat later, I was a mess sergeant enroute to the battlefields of France.

4

"LAFAYETTE, WE ARE HERE"

GENERAL JOHN J. PERSHING, commander of the American Expeditionary Forces in France in the first world conflict, is generally credited with saying, when he placed a wreath at the base of the statue of the Marquis de Lafayette in Paris, "Lafayette, we are here." (Actually General Pershing made no such statement, but his name will always be associated with it.)

The statement had some special appeal for me. To be sure, I was quite familiar with the service Lafayette had rendered to George Washington in the course of the American Revolution. But in addition, it is historical fact that Lafayette and his associates penetrated the interior of our country in those early days by way of the Ohio River and actually reached the point at the very southern tip of Illinois where the town of Shawneetown is located. That fact is probably the one and only claim to fame of Shawneetown.

Unlike General Pershing, we were not quite sure where we were when we reached France. We had debarked from the transport in Bordeaux and then marched to a bleak place on the outskirts of the city to a site known as Camp de Souge. It was a miserable night. The rain fell in torrents, and the only shelter we had from rain and mud were the little pup tents issued as regulation equipment to enlisted men. They were only large enough to crawl under and to keep head and shoulders dry. How long we were to remain in Camp de Souge was another question and became a continuing speculation for many days—until orders came to send those who had a smattering of artillery training to the artillery school in Saumur. As I recall, Saumur was an artillery school in the days when Napoleon was emperor of France. Either it had been kept in fair condition all through the years or it had been especially renovated and reconstructed for the training of American artillery officers.

This school was equipped with French instructors, and they were extremely capable. Moreover, it was equipped with something better than the ordinary barracks to which we were accustomed and, above all else, it had the latest artillery equipment, including the French 75-millimeter field piece, which at that time was regarded as the best piece of artillery of this caliber in existence. In addition, the school was equipped with horses and riding equipment for all student personnel, and generally speaking I found it quite comfortable.

The courses were about what one would expect. They followed in a general way the test courses we pursued at Camp Custer, Michigan, except in this case they were implemented with all the necessary equipment plus the firing range where the knowledge we absorbed with respect to artillery could be put into practice.

I never cease to be amazed how theory can go out of the window in the face of reality plus a little common sense. How we struggled over mathematics and textbooks on range finding and the other techniques used by artillery. The French instructors, through long practice and experience, had produced cards on which wind and temperature and pressure corrections were made for any given range. All one needed to do was to take hold of a piece of cord with a weight on it and bring it to the proper place on that card and there was the correct firing data ready to use without the necessity of making mathematical calculations. What a saving of time—and lives. I am sure that artillerymen in the advance zone and under fire had little time or opportunity to sit down with paper and pencil and work out mathematical equations in order to develop the proper range on an enemy target.

The riding horses and the equipment were quite a lure. The equitation courses were excellent and gave us an opportunity to become reasonably proficient in the care of horses. This was, indeed, a pleasant training exercise, and it was only a question of time before it would be put to use in the advanced zone on the Western Front. But on completion of the training course and the receipt of a commission as a second lieutenant, a hitch developed for me.

Somewhere north of the Saumur school was a camp called Coëtquidan, to which I was assigned. When I arrived and reported to the commanding officer of the battery, I was promptly designated as the horse officer. No inquiry was made as to whether I knew anything about horses. He probably assumed that anyone who had finished the course must be an expert in that field. Certainly I had had my fill of horsemeat at the school. It was one of the principal articles of diet. This fact might have shown up in my countenance and in my mannerisms. But for whatever cause, I had in truth and fact become the horse officer of the battery.

When I set out to make my first inspection of the horses which were part of the equipment of this battery, I fairly shuddered. Those horses had been in the advance zone and had been affected by an enemy barrage of mustard and chlorine gas. These terrible gases had burned great patches of hair from the horses and had also produced the ugliest of saddle and collar galls. Certain sergeants accompanied me to the horse lines because the horses were in the open. My first question was to inquire where the stables were, in the hope that some effort could be made to bring these animals under shelter and treat their afflictions.

The answer was a loud and scornful laugh. I remember one of the sergeants saying, "Lieutenant, you must think you are home on the farm." My next inquiry was about feed, such as oats, and that provoked still another laugh. There was a supply of hay but it was so moldy as to be in my judgment unfit for animal feed, but that only provoked another bit of laughter. That was the kind of horse contingent and supply which I inherited when I became the horse officer. Notwithstanding all this, I undertook to improvise as best I could and to procure feed from whatever source it could be obtained. Then I gave full attention to the job of trying to restore the vitality, health, and comfort of these poor wretched creatures which had been through a good part of the war.

Soon another hitch developed. Along with a number of other first and second lieutenants, I was summoned to regimental headquarters for reasons which at the moment were quite unknown to me, but I wasn't long in finding out. A colonel who took charge of the contingent to which I had been assigned told us there was a shortage of balloon observers at the front and that it was necessary to commandeer what talent could be found and trained to meet this deficiency.

To determine our suitability for the balloon service, we were placed one by one in a revolving chair. When the switch was turned, that chair revolved rapidly for several minutes. When the chair stopped, the straps were taken off and the occupant stepped down. Some of these involuntary candidates for the balloon service stumbled about as if intoxicated, and only a few managed to maintain reasonable equilibrium without staggering and losing control. I did my very best to maintain a certain degree of stability, and I evidently succeeded because I suddenly found myself designated for the balloon service without knowing what it was all about.

These balloons, or gas bags, were 150 feet long and 25 feet in diameter and were filled with flammable gas. A basket was anchored to the balloon by means of ropes, or bridles, about 25 feet in length. They were flown about 3,000 feet above the ground. So it was quite apparent that even in a mild breeze the basket would sway. For most persons the airsickness was infinitely worse than the sickness one encounters on turbulent seas. I learned long afterward that some of the men who took this test had been forewarned and knew enough to stagger about until they were quickly tagged as unfit for balloon duty.

Orders to proceed to the front to a balloon company were not long in coming, but once more there was a detour before we reached the advance zone. I well recall that the first stop was a concentration point called La Rochelle, and there we were assigned for some days to what remained of still another old camp that dated back to the days of Napoleon. The structures, however, had been renovated and were at least livable. But while we were there, an epidemic of influenza struck that area and was bad enough to be fatal in many cases. Every day there were a number of funeral services for American soldiers, and I thought the least I could do was to attend these services and pay my respect to the men with whom I had the kinship of the uniform. These services took place in the mornings and sometimes in the afternoons as well. Constant attendance, if it did nothing else, sharpened one's sense of fatalism.

At long last other orders came to proceed from La Rochelle to the city of Toul, and this journey was made in huge trucks, or camions, with stake sides. They bounced over the rough roads and the journey was enough to destroy all vitality for several days. We arrived in Toul in late afternoon. From there my assignment was to find the Nineteenth Balloon Company, wherever it might be. There was no time set for my arrival. My first stop, therefore, was in an area where there was food and shelter and where I could pass the night. I thought it might be just as well to fully enjoy the accommodations of the place because I might not see anything like it for a long time to come.

It was on this night that I had my first taste of a bombing raid. Lights and lamps were always hooded so there would be no glare and no telltale indication to the bomb pilots where to drop their destructive loads. In a single night there were many raids. The sirens would shriek and everyone would rush for the shelters which had been provided. But I could not stay in Toul since the assignment was to go to this specific company on the Western Front. I took time to make a lot of inquiries as to where the Nineteenth Balloon Company might be located, but nobody seemed to know and they cared less. Then I ran into a lieutenant who was making the same inquiry and had the same assignment. We decided therefore to team up and start eastward in the hope that at long last, somehow, somewhere, we might catch up with the unit to which we were assigned.

It was not too difficult to hitch a ride or to get a meal from the military along the way and to continue our inquiries. At long last we encountered some news which gave us a hint as to where our company might be found. We were fortunate while going along the road to hitch a ride on a truck filled with provisions which had been obtained at an army warehouse in Toul. These supplies were being hauled to the Nineteenth Balloon Company. In the late afternoon we came upon a valley where quite a number of cabins and other structures had been built. It was nestling in a heavily wooded area. It proved to be headquarters of the Nineteenth Balloon Company. We had fulfilled the assignment.

The commanding officer of this unit was Captain James Haight, who came from New York. My last information about Jim Haight was that he is still alive and lives in Louisville, Kentucky. We have exchanged letters, but I have not seen him from the day we left the Nineteenth Balloon Company. I have always promised myself that if and when I had occasion to be in the neighborhood of Louisville, I would undertake to find Captain Haight and to relive with him some of those days of long ago. There must have been eight or nine observers from different sections of the country, and everyone was a very agreeable and personable individual. In addition, the personal relations between officers and enlisted men were informal and good.

It might be well to set forth some of the techniques involved in observing and spotting artillery firing from a balloon. These gas bags were large and presented immense targets for German aviators. The balloons were flown aloft at the end of a steel cable which was attached to a winch by means of which it could be raised or lowered. Through the steel cable was a telephone line so that the observer in the balloon basket wearing a telephone headset was in constant contact not only with the machine gun protection on the terrain but also with a communication center and the artillery batteries for which the observers were spotting fire.

When all of this was coordinated and the battery was prepared to open fire, it was the duty of the observers, through a pair of field glasses, to see whether the shell bursts were beyond or short of the target, and also whether they were too far left or right. When these assessments had been made, the battery could then begin firing one salvo after another until the gun tubes became so hot that firing ceased for awhile so they could cool. Ballooning was quite a hazardous business, and perhaps that is the reason it was often referred to as the suicide squad. Enemy planes could spot a whole series of balloons on the Western Front and endeavor to move from one to another and fire tracer bullets into the gas bags, setting the balloons afire. The only gas available in those days was flammable. Sometimes the tracer took effect and sometimes it failed. Usually the only thing that prevented it from igniting the balloon was that the envelope was made of a very tough grade of rubber and even though the bullet actually penetrated the bag, the envelope itself had a sufficiently inhibiting effect to prevent the balloon bag from igniting. If it ignited, the observer was disciplined to quickly remove the headset and bail over the side. He always wore the regulation parachute harness.

The parachute itself was carefully packed in a bell-shaped bag which hung from the side of the balloon basket. These parachutes were made of a fine grade of silk and were sufficiently large to carry the observer to earth at a rate of descent that would prevent broken ankles. Strapped to the parachute ropes within reach of the observer was a very sharp knife and scabbard so when the observer reached the earth, he could unsheath this knife and cut the ropes, for otherwise a ground wind might drag him for a considerable distance.

Once a balloon bag was ignited, it was heavy enough to fall vertically to the earth and particularly so because of the weight of the steel cable. If there was enough wind, the parachute with the dangling observer was carried to one side sufficiently so that the burning balloon did not fall upon him. There were, however, some instances when this was not the case, and the bag fell upon the descending observer and burned him to a crisp.

Some things still stand out rather vividly in my mind in connection with my experiences in the balloon corps. The first was when we were so badly harassed by German planes that we had to entreat the commanding officer to provide plane protection. On one occasion when this request was made, we were advised that the commander was sorry but the pilots were out to tea at the time. You can imagine what this did to troop and observer morale!

The other incident centered around the operations of a big grizzly master sergeant who easily stood six and a half feet tall and weighed at least 250 pounds. We later discovered he had long before been dishonorably discharged from the United States Army. Somehow he managed to reenlist in World War I. He certainly knew his way about, and as a master sergeant he was simply incomparable. He had a sufficient number of cooks whom he kept busy baking the very finest of pies. He always baked a good many more than were necessary for the need of the balloon corps crew. The extra pies would be carefully packed up whenever he started for a commissary warehouse in Toul to procure supplies. There he generously distributed the pies to commissary personnel. They were only too glad to reciprocate. When he returned from his mission with a full truck, he had everything known to man, including jams and jellies, olives and pickles, and many other nonstaple items which were intended for hospital use. Whether or not this sergeant had been dishonorably discharged, he was a good man to have around.

One event which stands out in my mind was the night when we entertained as many as thirty or perhaps forty nurses from the hospital in Toul. They wanted to experience the hazard of the advanced zone, but they wanted to do so in a way that was absolutely safe. The trucks which were available brought them to headquarters, and dinner was served in a vast dugout which had been built by the Germans and must have been at least thirty feet underground, with a concrete roof which seemed absolutely secure against any kind of bomb attack. The dinner which the mess sergeant served that night would have done justice to the old Waldorf Astoria, famed for its food. It proved to be the sole occasion on which we could, for a brief while, forget the annoyances and brutality of war.

To all of this I should add still a fourth item, which is perhaps more important than the others because it happened on the morning of November 11, 1918. There had been rumors of a possible armistice. The rumors added that word would come from the artillery information service at the hour of eleven o'clock in the morning on the eleventh of November 1918. All firing would cease, all hostilities would end, and an armistice would go into effect. Of course, rumors abounded so much of the time that we took these in stride. But this time we were all more than curious as to whether or not the rumor was true. Since I was not on duty as an observer on the morning of November 11, I put on my raincoat and tin derby and hitched a ride on a truck which was going forward to a light artillery battery emplacement not very far from where we were headquartered in the woods. The hour was around ten o'clock. I stood around and talked with the members of the battery, including the battery commander. He felt that there was substance to the armistice rumor and was preparing, after carefully checking all watches, to fire one last barrage at the enemy during the last five minutes before eleven o'clock.

Evidently the German artillery had similar ideas, because at ten minutes to eleven there came a barrage from the German side. I adjusted the tin hat and gas mask, got the raincoat up around my neck, and dropped into a deep trench to wait out the end of the shelling. Sure enough, as my watch moved to eleven o'clock all shelling suddenly ceased and after assuring myself that probably nothing more was going to happen, I stood up, removed the gas mask, and listened to the painful silence—truly, it was a silence heard around the world. At such a moment what should one say? What could one say? Perhaps the first thought was, Where do we go from here? But a more tender thought came into my mind. I looked at the endless trenches which defaced the surface of the earth. I looked at the artillery-scarred trees through a pair of field glasses. I took note of the piles of rubble which were once homes and shelters for people, and then some words from Browning came into my mind. He pictured the Christ on the cross in a dismal world and wrote, "Whose sad face sees only this after the passion of a thousand years."

Intense silence can be noisy. How understandable that is after endless cannonading with howitzers and fieldpieces day in and day out, by night and by day. Suddenly it comes to an end, and the silence is a different kind of noise that crowds upon the senses. It stirs introspection of the deepest sort. Over and over, while continuing the vigil on the front, I kept saying that I would never want to be a professional soldier. I was not sure that I wanted to return to school and complete my law course, but I did know that I wanted to do something to end the madness of conflict and the insane business of arbitrating the differences of men and nations with poison gas and high explosive shells.

It took a few days to adjust to this sudden change in my life, but it was not long before all thought went back to a common denominator: when did we go home? There was little to do except wait. In due course the order came and, strangely enough, it was not to return to a port for the journey home but to report back to Camp de Souge in Bordeaux, of all places. There was no particular hurry to get to Bourdeaux and we had to pass through Paris to reach there. Who cared where I was or what I was doing at any given moment? I felt nothing really mattered except to go home and see my mother.

The journey to Bordeaux via Paris provided an extraordinary opportunity to see the fascinating sights of the great city celebrating the end of a war. We could literally see the lights come on again. There was continuing bedlam in the streets, day after day and night after night, as people observed the announcement of the armistice and the end of the conflict. I had a chance to visit Versailles with those magnificent Gardens, the Louvre with its exquisite works of art, the Tomb of Napoleon, Nôtre Dame, the Opéra, the Champs Elysées, and the hundred other things that make Paris unique. Then we went on to Bordeaux by train.

The commanding officer at Camp de Souge was ready for us. By that I mean he had laid out a whole course of instruction involving the techniques of the balloon service, including textbook work and the making of contour maps. How it all palled after the excitement of the front, but orders were orders so we tried as cheerfully as we might to enter into the spirit of the thing and devote the daytime to something that might prove constructive. The commanding officers were reasonably generous in affording leave to the officers in junior grades who were gathered there, and I lost no time in making application to go to Italy for a few weeks.

The arrival of a good many paychecks, which had not caught up with me because I had been in a travel status, meant I was amply supplied with funds. The day came to leave for Italy and, together with a friend, I left camp to go to Bordeaux reasonably early in the day to catch the very first train for Italy. Then something happened that could have completely marred the trip.

The peace conference at Versailles was beginning, and controversy developed over what the Italian leaders regarded as an affront by President Wilson. As a result, the border between France and Italy was closed. Fortunately several other officers, whom we had encountered in a Bordeaux cafe, had heard this news and suggested that perhaps we should hire a taxicab and go out to the railroad yards and board the train there instead of at the main station, for certainly military police would be patrolling the passenger station and probably barring the way to all passengers to Italy. It was good advice.

We managed to board the train in the yards, but when we got to the Italian border it was a different thing. The military provost marshal and his police were combing all the incoming trains, and we were promptly escorted to headquarters. The provost was a very affable major and we had quite a discussion of our problems. Finally he said, "I'll tell you what I will do. If you will give me your solemn promise that you will come back this same way. I will let you go across the border." Obviously, we were only too glad to give him that assurance; so we were permitted to reboard the train, and we went on for a sightseeing tour to Pisa, Genoa, Florence, Rome, Pompeii, and other points of interest. It turned out to be a fascinating sojourn, and I still think of it as one of the most rewarding periods of my life.

One day a captain attached to our embassy in Rome sat down near me in the Quattro Fontane Hotel, which was quite a gathering place for American personnel both in and out of uniform. After some pleasantries, he asked whether or not I had a working knowledge of the German language and I told him I did—in fact, I could speak the language quite well and also write in German script. The reason for his inquiry was that they needed an interpreter at the United States embassy in Rome, and if I was willing to accept the assignment, they would provide a raise of one grade in rank and, after temporary status as a casual, I would be assigned to the diplomatic service. It was a considerable lure, and I asked to think it over and told him I would give him my answer the following morning. In the night, however, I kept thinking about my mother and my deep desire to go home and see her. In the morning I gave him the answer. It was no.

The following day we were in the same hotel having a drink. The captain was there again and on that occasion advised me that a small supply train was being sent to the Balkans with supplies of food and about forty nurses. Only one officer was available to make the trip, but actually the assignment called for two. Would I accept this assignment with a raise in grade? Once more the thought of advancement began to loom in my mind. It sounded rather romantic, and the Balkan area was completely new ground which I had never visited. That in itself was a strong attraction. Although it sounded so intriguing, there was another night of concern and mental turbulence and once more my mother came so sharply into my thoughts. It was the resolving factor and again I said no. That was the end of offers to keep me in Europe for a longer period of time.

All in all the Italian sojourn was a delightful one, but we became concerned because we actually overstayed our leave period. After visiting Pisa and Livorno we took the next train to return to Bordeaux on the same route which we traversed on the journey to Italy. We stopped for a visit with the provost marshal and thanked him profusely for letting us cross the border.

When we arrived at Camp de Souge there was a message from the commanding colonel. We were notified, since we had overstayed our permissible leave period, that we were under arrest and confined to quarters. This was, indeed, an unhappy state of affairs. But at the musty quarters there was quite a collection of mail, including pay checks which had followed me around Europe and which were just beginning to catch up with me. In that mail was an order to report to Trier, Germany, for duty with the second section of the general's staff. I presume this stemmed from the fact that on the data sheet which I had filled out at time of enlistment I had set down that I had a working knowledge of German and could read and write the language. I summoned an orderly and told him to proceed to headquarters and present the colonel, since I was confined to quarters, with this order. Shortly thereafter the orderly returned. The colonel was ordering me to leave Camp de Souge by seven o'clock on the following morning and carry out the order from Advance Expeditionary Headquarters. That was certainly a break for me.

One could not go to Germany without going through Paris and since no particular time was set out in the order as to when I should report to Trier, I felt that I could afford to do a little more sightseeing. Among other things, I wanted to return to Versailles and make a further inspection of this magnificent palace which had been built by the Bourbons. I remember so well that when I arrived at Versailles, I found the doors closed and then started a systematic search to find some opening through which I might enter and see the magnificent paintings which portrayed the great events in the history of France. At long last there was a response to my continual knocking and rattling of doors, and suddenly a French *poilu,* as they called their soldiers, opened the door. My French was limited, but I greeted him as best I could and told him I would be extremely grateful if he would pilot me about and show me the things of interest.

The first thing I noticed was that he was minus an arm. I pointed to the empty sleeve and simply asked, "La guerre?"

To that he responded very simply, "Oui, monsieur." Since I was in uniform he obviously had no difficulty in identifying me as a member of the American Expeditionary Forces.

His command of English was limited and my command of French was not much better, but somehow we managed. As we trudged from one room to another, he pointed out the significance of the huge paintings and of the historical events which had transpired in the various rooms. It was a fascinating tour and I felt as though I had had a rather thorough lesson in French history.

There were, of course, many other sights of interest in Paris, but now I was becoming curious about my assignment in Germany. I boarded a train to Trier, and when I reached headquarters I found that a billet had been arranged for me. It was in the home of an old lady, then eighty years of age, and her spinster daughter. Since I spoke German, it wasn't overly difficult to become adjusted. I presume the daughter was at least forty-five. In a way she was an astonishing person. She was a superb pianist but played entirely in a mechanical fashion. She seemed to have no ear for harmony and simply pounded out the notes which were on a sheet of music. I remember those occasions when I tried to teach her various melodies in my own limited capacity on the piano and even undertook to sing them in the belief she could chord sufficiently to do a creditable job. I had learned to chord music on an old organ and had some facility in working out various simple songs, however, it did not work at all with her. Neither from my playing nor my singing was it possible for her to play a single melody. To me it was rather strange that a person should be so adept and capable in mechanical application to the piano yet without a sense of harmony.

A few days after my arrival in what was then the occupied zone of Germany, I was assigned to a bureau which controlled the movements of German civilians not only within the country but also across international lines. In due time all of this became something of a routine performance. There were times when this routine work began to pall now that the war was over. My only thought was to hasten the day when I would receive travel orders to return to the United States.

There were, of course, some very interesting occasions in connection with that tour of duty in Germany. The one restriction upon the occupied zone troops was a general order which prohibited fraternization between Germans and American military personnel. After a time such an order can become quite burdensome, and the military personnel found ways to circumvent it.

The American officers, meaning first and second lieutenants for the most part, organized what was called the Harmless Club. The members undertook to have secret sessions, first at one spacious German home and then another. One week the club might meet in the home of a local department store tycoon and the following week it might be the home of a prominent brewer. There were enough people who were only too glad to entertain us, and what added most to the gaiety of these occasions was that there was still a substantial amount of prewar German beer available.

The club never met until after dark and members were cautioned not to arrive in groups. To do so would have excited suspicion and we might have been raided by the members of the provost marshal's force. Meetings continued in a very uneventful way for several months, and then came the news that the commanding colonel in charge of our activities had evidently learned all about the club and its clandestine meetings and was very likely to take disciplinary action. So the ranking leaders of the club convened at a luncheon meeting to discuss the matter and see what might be done to avert such a disaster. After many suggestions had been examined, I suggested that we make the colonel a member of the club. Then the question arose as to who would extend to him an invitation to join. I volunteered for this mission.

I do not know whether the colonel is still alive. I do recall that his name was Rice and that he was a West Point graduate. I presented myself at headquarters to carry out the assigned mission. To Colonel Rice's everlasting credit, he manifested a great sense of good humor about the whole matter and accepted the offer to become a club member. This, of course, meant that along with the rest of us he would have to fraternize with some Germans and, in so doing, violate the general order against fraternization. But the colonel entered into the spirit with great gusto and from then on we had no fear of a raid by the military police. We counted heavily on the cooperation of the colonel to see that this would never happen.

Fraternization often had strange consequences. We had a captain who spoke German very fluently and who was also detailed to do control work among German civilians. Obviously, it afforded an opportunity to become acquainted with all manner of people and very particularly with some entrancing German girls. In this case the captain was carrying on an affair with an attractive girl who had a responsible position in a large store in Trier and, in a sense, also served as the secretary to the owner and proprietor. There came a day when a quarrel developed between the girl and her employer. It was something more than a casual quarrel, because it resulted in her discharge from the store. She was vengeful enough to report the whole matter to her captain friend and, in so doing, advised him also of the store owner's violation of another general order which had been in effect from the very day that occupation troops moved into Germany. It required all civilians to surrender all firearms.

The department store owner was quite a hunter and had retained a dozen very expensive hunting rifles which he used when hunting on a private reservation in Bavaria. The girl even indicated where these rifles were hidden, and the captain promptly notified the provost marshal. He in turn dispatched a detachment of military police and confiscated the entire lot. But that was not quite the end of the story.

The owner of the rifles was charged with a violation of a general order and promptly tried in a military court and sentenced to prison. It was, indeed, a sad blow. The Harmless Club had met at his home on a number of occasions. He was the very soul of courtesy and hospitality, but all that we could do was to bleed silently for him. We were unable under these circumstances to do anything in his behalf.

There was one lieutenant in our club who was an accomplished concert pianist. He, like myself, was always seeking self-expression and there were only limited opportunities for him to keep up with his piano work. When we had some leisure time we talked about music and literature, and we finally decided to compose a comic opera after the manner of Gilbert and Sullivan. It was all in fun. The title we picked was "The Bootlegger's Daughter." I was to write the lyrics and he was to compose the music. Had we had sufficient time, a new work of art might well have seen the light of day on the American stage, but as everyone knows, army life was not particularly conducive to really doing sustained work. When orders to return to the States came, this noble experiment in the comic opera field was ended.

One other item in connection with those days in Germany stood out in my mind: the dice games which took place at the one and only hotel of any real consequence in Trier. It was called the Porta Nigra Hotel and received its name from the remains of an old Roman gate to the city built in the days of the Caesars. This hotel not only served as a billet for the ranking officers, including quite a number of generals, but it had the finest dining room in the city and served as a place where officers could gamble to their heart's content on Saturday nights.

If I remember correctly, no officer below the rank of lieutenant colonel participated in the big dice game. Junior officers could be present and watch if they so desired. On this particular Saturday night on the table there were thirty thousand German marks, still a big sum. Once the game started it went forward at a feverish pitch. The incident that remained indelibly in my memory was the moment when a major general was warming the dice in his hands. He had been losing steadily and this roll meant everything. I shall never forget his prayers and supplications to some harbinger of good fortune. He indulged in such weird antics that the tears rolled down his cheeks. He lost and slunk away, broken in spirit.

Seeing this performance made a deep impression. If I had ever had a desire to gamble, that one incident standing by itself was sufficient to completely destroy any desire in this field.

These were some of the things that occupied leisure moments as we carried on our routine duties of policing that part of the enemy country, which lies east of the Rhine River and was always referred to as the Occupied Area.

Came then the blessed day to go home—a journey which was to be made by rail and ship and rail. The trip in itself was rather uneventful. Like all others, I was subject to but a single emotion, and that was the sheer joy of going home and seeing my mother again after eighteen months of overseas duty.

I shall never forget my arrival in my home city of Pekin. The arrival time and just how I would arrive were publicized well in advance. The least I expected was that the local band would be at the station to greet me, along with a concourse of people. But such was not the case. Only my twin brother was at the station and, without any fanfare whatsoever, we drove straight home where Mother was waiting. It was a tearful blessed moment both for her and for me.

I could now say, "Lafayette, we were there." The first days, and particularly the evenings, after my return were given over to a recital of where I had been and what the war had been like. Among other things, I quickly noticed that the portrait of the kaiser and his family, which I had cautioned Mother to put away for the duration of the war, had disappeared from the dining room wall. "Mother," I asked, "What has happened to the kaiser's picture?" It was then that she unfolded a story which distressed me for a long time.

A group of superpatriots had learned that the portrait was there, and one morning they came to our home and demanded she surrender it. She refused. Obviously without a court order they could not enter the home and snatch that picture from the wall, because it would have been a trespass for one thing and larceny for another. She finally locked the door, but when they had gone she removed the picture and hid it so that these patriots would be unable to find it.

The local newspaper carried a very modest squib which said simply: "Mrs. Dirksen's son, Lieutenant Everett McKinley Dirksen, who served overseas for a period of eighteen months, was separated from the service and arrived home yesterday." Such was the end of this venture which took two years of my life.

In the weeks that followed, I had an opportunity to reflect upon the whole venture of war—this war "to make the world safe for democracy." How many times since then, like Ishmael, I have lifted my eyes to contemplate the results. As I look upon the feverish embattled world today, I wonder again, what has happened to the lesson we were supposed to have learned in that great world struggle more than fifty years ago.

I could and I did do something about it. War is but a form of political action resorted to when all other methods to settle the differences of nations have failed. But how often false pride and a highly nationalistic spirit stand in the way of successful negotiation of settlements of these international differences. If these problems could be approached with proper humility and a realization of the ghastliness of conflict, settlements might be more easily contrived. In any event, the answer now was becoming simpler for me. I must go into politics.

5

FLOUNDERING

I T MAY BE THAT there is some relationship between the fish called a flounder and the adjective "floundering," but I do not know enough about flounders to make such a claim. I do know it's a very flat fish, regarded as a delicacy in some quarters. But to flounder means to struggle as if one were in some kind of mire. If I were permitted to indulge in a pun I might say that kind of a struggle is a flat performance.

In any event, what soldier, what hero, doesn't flounder in mind and spirit when the great struggle is over and he returns to civilian life. It is such a sudden transposition from a life of order and discipline to the exhilaration of freedom. In a way, it was plainly painful. As a second lieutenant, I was a bit above the enlisted grades and just below a lot of superiors. Despite this, I did expect a little more than a dull and undramatic welcome when I returned home.

Of course, it was understandable. Troops in great numbers, both officers and enlisted men, were being sent back home for separation from the service. This had been going on for at least eight months before they got around to me. The delay was occasioned by my assignment to the occupied area of Germany. That left me both unhappy and bewildered because the war itself was over, and now the adjustment had to be made. Many questions popped into my mind. Should I return to school and complete the remaining eighteen months of a law course and then, assuming my successful negotiation of the bar examination, find space in a promising location or team up with some established law firm? I had saved enough money to do so if that should be the next move, but the thought of my being away at school for sustained periods made my mother very unhappy. We discussed it many times, just the two of us. The two-year absence from home had deepened an intense love for my mother. If, therefore, returning to school made her unhappy, I simply would not do so.

I did, however, go back to the University of Minnesota, where I had been in school, to visit with former schoolmates and to get the feel of campus life once more. One of the first people I encountered was John Dahlquist. I liked John. He seemed much more mature than most of the students. Among other things, he had been designated general manager for the university's annual yearbook. That in itself was a very substantial assignment which carried with it many responsibilities. When we met, he was a first lieutenant and still in uniform. That day, we went to lunch at the campus student center. Others who had attended Minnesota when we were there before the war were still about and came to join us. It became a very felicitous occasion. But the basic question with John Dahlquist, and for that matter myself, was whether to remain in the military service or to be separated once and for all, making no effort to maintain a reserve status. For myself, I finally decided not only to achieve complete separation but also to abandon any reserve status as quickly as possible.

First Lieutenant John Dahlquist decided to make the military his career, and certainly what occurred thereafter fully sustained the correctness of his judgment. In due course he became a lieutenant general and commander of the Continental Army. That was indeed a high honor. Many years later we had an opportunity to visit when he was assigned to Washington for a tour of duty, and this enabled us to get together for dinner occasionally. Quite often other Minnesota graduates who were on the campus in our time joined us.

But what now, hero? For the time being at least, school was out of the question. Loafing even for a brief time was quite alien to the whole tradition of the Dirksen family. Life meant work, for only in work could one be happy and really content.

One of my first endeavors, as I began to readjust to civilian life at the hometown level, was to reestablish the relationship which I once enjoyed with a number of other people. Number one on that list was my high-school classmate Clarence Ropp. In both of us there was a common urge for self-expression. He found it at first with a paintbrush and easel; for me it was a case of putting ideas into words and into books. The real difficulty was that all this would pay no grocery bills, and I had to find remunerative work.

Hubert Ropp had an uncle who had invented a special type of vacuum electric washing machine. As a cleansing instrument, the principle of the machine was excellent, but the first model that had been developed clearly indicated that it had some undesirable characteristics. The trend in the washing machine industry at that time was the development of washers that were at once practical and yet so ornamental that they could be set up in the parlor. This particular machine, however, had many castiron parts on the lid of the tub, and it all looked far too heavy for a housewife to lift. In any event, a number of us pooled our resources and made a start at manufacturing these electric washers. It proved to be a very unhappy affair. After the war, the pent-up demand for all kinds of consumer goods resulted in a tight supply situation. Purchasing washing machine tubs and motors and castings and other items necessary was almost impossible. The manufacturers' books were bursting with orders. The result was that the infant company began to languish and its future began to look quite dubious.

As time went by, we had no income coming in, and abundant time to devote to a great many other pursuits. One of these was a request from the deacons of the little frame church which my mother helped to build with her own hands to fill the pulpit on Sunday nights, for the church was without a minister at the time. I was quite willing to accept this uncompensated assignment for a number of reasons.

First of all, it provided the opportunity to go back and pursue the Bible reading course which I had begun at the front many, many months before. In those dreadful hours, I read and reread the khaki-covered Bible that had been given to me in Paris. It became my comfort in those lonely moments and dark hours. Quite often as I read by candlelight in an underground dugout I underscored passages that had some special appeal for me.

Still another reassuring reason was that the selection of a speech or sermon topic, its development, and the research that went into it gave me some mental exercise. For several months, I occupied the pulpit of that little church for Sunday evening services and thereby helped to preserve the morale of the church as the deacons and elders continued their search for a regular minister. All this while I waited for destiny to touch me with so much as a single finger.

Other interests soon developed. In Pekin, there was a very active women's club. They had asked Hubert Ropp to undertake the presentation of a series of one-act plays as part of the club's seasonal program. This, of course, meant selection of the plays and the cast and the supervision of rehearsals, together with other production details. He was quite willing to undertake this and, in due time, he and I discussed the selection of the dramatic vehicles to be used and their presentation. There was this theatrical flair in me, and I was more than glad to participate as an actor and quite generally as the leading character.

I well recall that one of these short plays bore the title *Three Pills in a Bottle*. I must say that this particular play had no great appeal for me, but at least it provided me with a start in the field of drama. Still another was called *The Slave with Two Faces*. It had a cast of only three characters—two female and one male. This particular play we both liked, but for perhaps different reasons. Hubert's artistic instinct made him envision just how a symbolic slave with two faces should look, and I was to discover later that what he had in mind was a character who cavorted around the stage wearing only a very short pair of trunks which were splashed with blue and gold. The female characters wore long flowing white robes and not too much makeup. I shall never forget the presentation of this play. It was performed on the stage of a downtown hall called the Union Mission. The night of the performance was quite cold and the hall was extremely chilly. I can still remember the tatoo that my exposed abdominal muscles played against the rib cage, which made it difficult indeed for me to recite my lines. The reaction of the audience, which in a small town is so quickly conveyed by telephone and otherwise to every citizen, was violent.

The party-line conversation usually began, "Did you attend the performance at the Union Mission last night?" "Did you see that Dirksen boy?" "Did you notice that he cavorted all over the stage with practically no clothes on?" You can imagine what all this did to my image in the community. But there were later plays for other sponsors, and we presented every one of them. I still believe that in so doing we enlivened the community and enriched the sparse local culture.

There were some rather less pleasant things that now come back to me. When I was in the army I had started with a field artillery battery, and we still had horsedrawn artillery. It was difficult for artillerymen on horseback to smoke, particularly if there was much wind. So we naturally fell into the habit of chewing tobacco. I was one of those who contracted the habit, disagreeable as it must have been for others. When I returned home, the habit had become an addiction and difficult to break.

One day, while addressing myself to the very serious business of walking at a brisk rate and chewing tobacco with relish, I found it necessary to go into a stationery store to make a small purchase. There I discovered one of my old school classmates who was one of the clerks. I had not seen her in a long time. She was effervescent and so glad to see me. As she came forward, she reached out to shake hands and said, "Well, Everett, how are you? Tell me about your army days if you have a moment." Obviously, I couldn't talk much about an army career while that quid of tobacco in my mouth was generating a bitter kind of saliva, and soon this turned out to be a very dis-agreeable adventure. There was no place where I could relieve myself of the tobacco, so I hastened to make my purchase and pay for it and then started for the door. The immediate goal was to reach the nearest alley so that I could dispose of the quid, but I failed to make the alley. I swallowed the quid, and when I did I suddenly became as sick as Caesar's horse. It was that adventure that managed to bring to an end the habit of chewing tobacco.

After one has been separated from military service, it takes a long time to divest oneself of the uniform. After all, it does look rather sharp and snappy, set off as it was then by highly polished shoes and leather puttees. The uniform was kept immaculate because one was expected to keep it that way, and this was an added reason for not taking it off too soon. But at long last came the day when this had to be done. Before so doing, there was one social call that I felt I had to make, and that was to a young lady who was a freshman in high school when I was a senior. She and other girls in the community had organized a sewing and knitting club and met one night each week at the county courthouse.

This girl related to me in some detail how many girls had joined the club and how many helmets and scarves and sweaters they had knitted for the men in uniform. I should have been full of deep appreciation, but having been removed from the graces of civilian life for a sustained period, I am afraid my social elegance had forsaken me. At one point in the conversation that evening I had to tell the truth. I said that so many of these helmets were so small and so narrow that we could not get them over our heads; however, they were wonderful to put on the end of a rammerstaff and push it through the tube of a 75-millimeter gun and take out the powder stains. She didn't know whether to be sad or sorry or angry, or to laugh, and I am afraid I did not bother to explain. It was one of those faux pas that obviously I should not have committed.

In this floundering period, the city of Pekin was planning to observe its one hundredth anniversary. When it was first established, it had a very unromantic and unpretentious name. It was called Townsite. The name was changed to Pekin at the suggestion of the wife of an army major who was sent out from Washington to the area near Rock Island, Illinois, where the Indian uprising was taking place. It was, therefore, appropriate that the one hundredth anniversary of the city should be observed properly and that, of course, meant a lot of things. There were many people who would be only too glad to bring forth antiques they had saved or collected and display them in the stores and in the shops of the city. There would be the usual games, athletic events, and other activities to appeal to people young and old, and then there would have to be a pageant to celebrate events in the life of the town.

Perhaps it needed something more than this that might prove to be spectacular. The city officials and others in authority under whose sponsorship all this would take place appealed to my friend Hubert Ropp to undertake some spectacular outdoor presentation, even though it did not confine itself particularly to the events of the last one hundred years.

We were fortunate in that the one park in the city, known as Mineral Springs, had abundant space to accommodate a huge crowd and, in addition, had within it a valley surrounded by hills with gradual sloping sides that could be built up very nicely for seating purposes. It was decided, therefore, that whatever we might present would take place in this bowl.

I recall that in a consultation with a community committee, numbering among its members several ministers, that one of them suggested that the occasion might be observed by presenting the Passion Play. The matter was roundly discussed but then came the question of who would play the part of Christ. This particular minister, who was quite old-fashioned said, "I cannot imagine any human being—I cannot imagine any human embodiment—who could play the character of Christ." I turned to the minister and said, "Doctor, what is your idea of Christ?"

To this he replied, "Well, he is a light, a heavenly light."

I presume out of sheer frustration and from the fact that the conversation was boring everyone, I had the effrontery to say, "Very well, we'll get one of Mr. Edison's lights, hang it up somewhere, put a sign on it, 'This is Christ.'" That came close to breaking up the meeting because my remarks were regarded as sacrilegious to say the least. But what this conversation did was to put all thought of presenting the Passion Play into limbo, and so we began to search for some other suitable vehicle for the occasion.

It was at this point that Hubert Ropp and I began to comb the dramatic works that might be easily staged and used for this anniversary affair. We discovered one such work by an author named Percy Mackaye and its title was *A Thousand Years Ago*. The locale of this pageant, interestingly enough, was in Peking, China. We felt that entrances to and exits from the stage could be properly and efficiently accomplished by amateur performers. Then came the question of casting and also the business of colorful costumes, as it was to be a spectacular.

I must say for my friend Hubert Ropp that he was a perfectionist if I ever knew one. To make sure, for example, that the costumes would be quite authentic and in accord with the time portrayed in the pageant, he journeyed to the public library in Chicago and spent not merely weeks, but literally months, obtaining all the assistance he could to make sure that the costumes and stage properties would be suited to the period. When rehearsals did not go too well, he could scold and he could swear, but all this made for perfection in presenting something quite worthwhile to the community.

Before we could go any further and before rehearsals could begin, we had to select members of the cast. We had to find a leading lady. We had been puzzling over lists of names, but none of them seemed to fit the part because the leading lady was to be the princess. (It was assumed, of course, that I would play the part of the prince.)

Early one evening while Hubert Ropp was sitting in his automobile—a fancy Jordan with wire wheels and by all odds the sleekest-looking car in town—a young lady crossed the main street and was about to walk through the courthouse yard on her way home. Hubert Ropp fairly jumped out of the car and as he did so he said, "There's our leading lady." I did not know her. He ran after her and had quite an animated conversation before returning to the car. He said, "Tonight I will go down and see her mother and talk to her about it." Her name was Louella Carver, and she lived with a widowed mother and grandmother. She was induced to accept the part of the leading lady, and then little by little the cast was assembled and rehearsal was announced.

Play rehearsals in a small town are a considerable social event, and every rehearsal night became a spirited thing. When rehearsals were over, it was the custom for the men to take the girls home. It was only natural, therefore, that the leading man should take the leading lady home. That became one of the regular exercises in connection with the rehearsals.

But before taking a girl home, it was incumbent upon a young man to first take her to the most popular ice cream parlor and treat her to a fancy ice cream dish. That was in the days when people were not so desperately concerned about their weight and their figures. They consumed delicious ice cream sundaes, banana splits, and all those other concoctions that delight the young.

It was at this juncture that my dear mother passed away. She was wonderful. When she died, she left two lost souls. My older brother, Benjamin, and I were desolate. We were now compelled to look after ourselves without the great cohesive force of a mother's personality. We were both unmarried and it became a challenge to us two young bachelors to get along. Somehow, we could not bring ourselves to forsake the ties that went with our old homestead.

A family controversy can be a rather unhappy thing. At some point my mother had suggested to me that I draft a will for her. This I had done. It was very simple. In the main, it took what property there was and bequeathed it to her three sons, Benjamin Harrison Dirksen, Thomas Reed Dirksen, and myself, Everett McKinley Dirksen. We had one half-brother who was still living. He had done exceedingly well in business ventures of one kind or another, and the modest amount in Mother's estate could not have affected him very much one way or another. Perhaps it was the fact that he was left only a small inheritance that brought about the family rift. What added to the family difficulty was that my two brothers worked for my half brother in a wholesale bakery business. He decided it would be a happier situation if they left his employ.

They had had nothing to do with the drafting of the will. It was solely my work and I accepted full responsibility for it. Now my brothers were on their own, and all they really knew was the bakery business, so the question soon arose as to whether some bakery could be purchased for them. Precisely this was done and a new bakery venture began in the city of Pekin. I soon discovered in order to make this venture go, and in order to utilize what acquaintances I had and what knowledge of salesmanship I possessed, I had to get into a delivery truck loaded with bakery goods and go out and sell them to grocers on a wholesale basis within a rather large area. This I undertook to do, and the business was moderately successful for quite some time.

It was in this period that one of the banks came to see me about the prospect of taking over a business enterprise in which the owner and operator had overextended himself and become hopelessly mired in debt. It was a dredging operation. It had four or five different pieces of equipment in operation on land and on the water. Two of these were of the floating variety, and three were of the type that operated on dry land and were engaged mainly in digging ditches. The principal business of the floating equipment was repairing levees along the Illinois River, and sometimes along the Mississippi, and to do ditching jobs in drainage areas in order to keep the water from rising too high and threatening the crops. I took over this business and began to operate it.

The engineer, who gave me professional advice on these projects, lived in Pekin. His name was Leon B. Kinsey. He had graduated in engineering from the University of Illinois. I must say from my long knowledge of the man that he was not only a capable engineer but one who exercised rare judgment.

In this period the real highlight in my life was that the princess whom I had courted in a modest way, in the course of Pekin's centennial anniversary, became my wife. Our wedding was a simple ceremony and resulted in part from the fact that I somehow stumbled into a proposal when I hadn't actually meant to do so at that time. It was in the Christmas season, and I thought it would be most appropriate that I take Louella a Christmas gift. I wanted it to be useful and canvassed a list of possible gifts that I might present to her. One evening when I came back from a long, hard day on the river, I thought it was opportune to ask her about the gift and to find out what she wanted. I suggested that I might present her with a ring or with a radio. A radio was something of a novelty at that time. At this point, perhaps I should amplify a little on my courtship of Louella. It had become something of a habit for me to come to her home at a late hour fairly covered with mud, but she was always such a tolerant and forbearing person. First came the question whether I had had any dinner. After eating, I snuggled close to one of those woodburning stoves. How comfortable it was to one who had been in the cold all day and especially out on the water, where it really does get cold and the cold creeps into the marrow. It did not take long for me to fall into a sound sleep.

I suppose it was a little unusual but my lady love, while I was courting her, would let me sleep and then, at what she thought was an appropriate hour, would tap me on the shoulder and say, "Honey, it is time for you to go home."

But to go back to the Christmas present, I blurted out that I would be happy to give her a ring or a radio set. She did not stutter so much as a moment, "Is it more than a ring?"

Like a country bumpkin I said, "It could be more than just a ring." That's the way it began, and all that remained from then on was to set the time and hold the ceremony.

When I say we had a simple wedding, that's probably the understatement of the time, because the only people present besides the bride and groom were her mother, my brothers, the minister and his wife, and a girlfriend of Louella's from Peoria. It was a home ceremony. It was quickly performed and arranged so that we could still drive to Peoria and catch a midnight train to Chicago for a few days' honeymoon. We walked and walked around the city because our travels seldom took us to Chicago. We attended the theater twice a day and particularly took in several popular plays, which appealed to my theatrical instinct. We also went to a prominent but rather sedate night-club and there enjoyed the show and good food. At the end of two days I said to her, "Darling, it is time for me to go to work and make a living." So our honeymoon ended.

The life of a dredging contractor was not a particularly happy one and there were a good many reasons for it. The dredging rigs operated on the river, and the crewmen remained on duty day after day and sometimes week after week without coming out of the area. They much preferred to put in an entire month and secure a substantial paycheck. During their continuous tours of duty, they operated in an atmosphere of mud and bilge water, prickly horseweeds, and just about every other thing that was offensive to the senses. But at the end of the month, they were paid and they could then go to town and, in fact, be on the town, until the paycheck was exhausted.

Those were the days before the Eighteenth Amendment and the Volstead Law were repealed, so the crewmen had to find surcease from what they must have considered the vexations of life without the benefit of legal liquor. But a great many people had been lured by the fancy returns in the bootleg-ging business, and there was little difficulty in finding some emporium where they could obtain illegal booze. Our crews went at once to speakeasies when they came to town. It did not take too long before the paychecks were squandered and they were prepared to go back to work.

To me it was an unhappy and sometimes a revolting situation because I found it necessary to bail them out of jail on many occasions after their money was gone. In fact, there appeared to be some collusion between certain law-enforcing authorities and the proprietors of the bars where the crewmen were arrested after having imbibed too freely. The bootleggers simply telephoned the police station. Sometimes the proprietor, having taken all of their money for booze or having robbed them in the back room of his place, was generous enough to pay their fines. But when this was not the case, I had to pay the fines before taking them back to the job. That was the nature of the business. For all I know, it still may be, although I fancy and I hope it has undergone a good deal of refinement since those days.

In the course of the almost daily journeys which I made to first one dredging project and then another with Leon Kinsey, we talked about many things and particularly about public affairs and politics. When we were enroute to Beardstown, Illinois, Mr. Kinsey said he was entertaining the idea of becoming a candidate for the office of mayor of the city of Pekin. As the discussion went on, I said, "Lee, I think it is a capital idea. With your engineering background you could, and I am sure you would, make a good mayor, and you would be able to make public improvements in which the city is in great need. Our town needs an engineer's touch." And then by way of a political postscript I said, "Suppose you undertake to run for the office of mayor, and I will run for one of the places on the city commission."

The city of Pekin operated under the commission form of government as authorized by the laws of Illinois. Anyone could become a candidate by filing a petition with a limited number of names of bona fide voters. It was nonpartisan. Out of those who ran, a selection was made in a primary election. The eight highest candidates were selected to appear in a runoff election and four of these were elected. In the case of the mayor, the voters selected two in the primary and the mayor was then chosen at the election.

I recall quite well that when the filing date closed, there were forty-four candidates for the city commission and, I think, five candidates for mayor. I was one of the many nominees for the commission. On one of our journeys to the dredging work down river, I said to Lee Kinsey, "Lee, let me tell you something. I'll bet you the best hat that the John B. Stetson Company ever made that I get more votes than you even though you are running against one opponent and I am actually running against seven others."

Very quickly he said, "It's a deal." So the bet was sealed and then came election day.

As it turned out, I was the high man on the ticket, and Mayor Kinsey promptly paid off with a very handsome Stetson hat, although I must say in my younger days hats did not mean too much. I seldom wore one.

My election campaign for the city commission was carried on in the rear end of a clothing store on the main street. It was known as Goldsmith's Haberdashery, and the chief clerk was a man named Henry Gebhardt. He was very prominent in sports and in any other activity which promoted the well-being of the community. It was in this store that all the decisions were made. This was where we undertook to raise a little money for the campaign, if we could, although in a local election I must say that money is about as scarce as turkey teeth. Whatever we lacked in that field, however, we made up in energy and also in the loyalty and vitality of a great group of friends who were mainly on the younger side and who were willing to get into the campaign and really pitch. That's how I was elected to the city commission of my home city. It was as a result of that election that I developed ideas for conquering larger political fields.

One other thing happened that was quite useful and which became increasingly important before we got through. For a number of years after I returned from the service, I had more or less neglected the military organizations made up of veterans, such as the American Legion, the Veterans of Foreign Wars, the American Veterans, and others. Now I felt I should manifest some interest because the programs that they pursued at national, state, and local levels had great appeal and worked in the interests of the communities the various local posts served. Those identified with the American Legion thought I might do well and serve the legion cause as a district commander. An American Legion district was coextensive with a congressional district, which meant that a commander served the same counties and the same areas as a member of Congress. When I was elected as district commander, it was only a question of how much time I might be able to devote to the duties and responsibilities of that job. It was a big undertaking to say the least, but I did labor at it earnestly and late. I was still doing business as a dredging contractor and also lending an occasional hand in the wholesale bakery that my brothers operated. But I must confess as I look back that I don't know how I did all the physical chores.

In the particular American Legion district in which I served there were thirty-six local posts located for the most part in small towns in the six counties. In addition, each county had an American Legion organization. It was the duty of the district commander to journey as regularly as he could first to one post and then another and also to attend the various county legion meetings. There were also the district conventions. Not the least of the commander's duties was to urge all legion members to recruit other members and make the organization grow. In addition, it was the function of everyone who served in some official capacity to help plan community programs in which the patriotic spirit could be fostered.

In Pekin some imaginative soul thought we should be considering a formal dinner dedicated to the memory and the spirit of George Washington. Before long, the date was set for the First Annual American Legion George Washington Banquet. I was asked to serve as general chairman. I had chores enough as it was, but I was glad to undertake this additional responsibility. Perhaps one of the reasons I was asked was that I had manifested some theatrical talent and was familiar with the theater and entertainment generally. I hoped, therefore, to do quite the right thing, but a rather perverse thought came into my mind. Those members of the American Legion who had served overseas, especially in France, and who had been back from the service only a little while, did not want anything too staid. I felt sure they would not relish a dry and lengthy speech. They would prefer some slightly spicy entertainment to go with the dinner.

Having all this in mind, I journeyed to Chicago and arranged to have some talent come to our city on the twenty-second of February. This talent consisted mainly of dancers and comics. It was my function to serve as toastmaster at the dinner and then present the entertainment. The dinner went very well. After a brief hiatus, I made a very brief speech and then prepared the dinner audience for the talent imported from Chicago. It was the kind of talent that a soldier who had been singing "Hinky Dinky Parlay-voo" could certainly understand. Beyond that it required no further description from me. Before the evening was over, a resolution was passed to hold a Second Annual George Washington Anniversary American Legion Banquet next year. The affair received excellent press coverage. Everybody thought it was a great evening, but we did not fully recognize or appreciate the reaction of the townsfolk. The party lines were buzzing the following morning.

When I came home at lunchtime, I recall my wife said to me, "I understand you had quite a stimulating party last night and that the dancers were superb, if superb is the word for it."

"Well," I said, "Toots, all I can say is that I think they got their money's worth and that everybody liked it. Beyond that, as the lawyers say, 'Deponent saith not.'" And I said nothing more.

The trouble was that all this came just before election day when the voters of the city sallied forth to select members of our commission. I began to wonder whether or not all this might have some adverse effect on the election results. The dinner incident became something of a community scandal, and I thought perhaps that my venture into the political field had been blighted in the bud. But as the ballots were counted and it became apparent that I was high man on the ticket, I felt a sense of elation. Yet I think I learned a lesson.

6

THE COUNCILMAN

C OULD THIS BE A FIRST STEP in the long struggle to go into politics, and did I in fact actually want to do so? This local campaign was, after all, identified with but a single city of moderate size and embraced only a few thousand voters. There were many intervening steps before one finally reached the point of becoming an active candidate for national office—not to mention acquiring the proper organization and the funds to carry on a campaign.

The first and certainly not the least of the advantages of being elected was that it paid the princely sum of seventy-five dollars a month. The compensation was fixed by statute. In times of strained circumstances and slender resources, that was, indeed, an item which could not be ignored. It was also interesting that my fellow citizens began to refer to me jocularly as "Statesman." That in itself was heady stuff. Brokers and bond buyers who came to bid upon the bond issues issued by the city from time to time were deferential, and it was admittedly rather pleasing to be referred to as "Honorable." Thus at the mature age of thirty I thought I was sitting astride the whole wide world.

Perhaps I permitted my ego to persuade me that I had all the answers. I knew, of course, that there were plenty of others who had crawled under the barn for eggs further than I had been away from my home city. How could I possibly know the ins and outs of the great challenging and baffling problems of the time? But I have come to wonder whether the ego that develops in a person in public service is not after all the fault of the public. People think that one does have all the answers no matter how difficult and knotty the problems may be. The kind of glorification and sense of omniscience which a title in public office can give a person is truly amazing. The next step is to be deemed a "know it all" who thinks he has all the answers.

It might be well to go back for a moment to those whom we replaced on the city commission. For the most part they were good, solid citizens who had served long years on the council and had rendered the best service they could. Moreover, they had had the confidence of the people. Consequently, there were great expectations from us who succeeded them.

I suppose it was expected we would do infinitely more for the community, expand cultural and job opportunities, recreational facilities, industries, and make life so much more pleasant for young and old. It reminds me a little of what I think Prime Minister Disraeli said to a friend who queried him concerning what they were doing in London on behalf of the people. The person who addressed himself to Mr. Disraeli said, "Mr. Prime Minister, why don't you let the people of London and England live like gentlemen?"

Disraeli's answer was quite quick. He said, "To do so would simply bankrupt the crown."

It was rather strange, but the newly elected mayor of Pekin was distrusted in certain quarters and, frankly, I never quite knew what the reason could be. He had a charming and gracious wife. He had a young son of whom he was very proud. He was a very competent civil engineer who enjoyed a good reputation in his profession. As serious as he could be on many occasions, there was always a whimsical chuckle which made it appear he was cynical about any suggestion made to him. Yet I and his associates, who all were progressive, knew that his whole hope was to enhance the reputation of our city, to keep it out of difficulty, to bring in new industry, and to make it a better place to live in.

It did not take very long before the novelty of my first public office wore off and real work began. There were so many things that were required in a growing place like Pekin, Illinois. To be sure it was a healthy town, financially speaking. Whenever a bond issue was contemplated, bond buyers were almost like locusts in Egypt. They knew full well that the city's credit was above reproach and that the bonds were gold, not gilt-edged. We had splendid schools and very competent teachers. The treasurer was an appointed official. He was an honest and honorable person who enjoyed the confidence of the community and did his work extremely well. We maintained a close and free relationship with the three local banks. We knew that if we had any difficulty so far as city finances or bond issues, all we would have to do, provided there was legal or statutory authority, would be to go to the bank, sign our names to an appropriate note, and then command within reason whatever funds were necessary for our needs.

As soon as I became oriented as commissioner of finance, I thought perhaps the first job I should undertake was to make an informal examination and a preliminary audit of our municipal streetcar system. With a great deal of fanfare, we had installed that system many years before, and it was symbolic of the success that a municipally owned utility could achieve. On consulting the city clerk, I said, "Now show me your books and how they are kept so I can get a better idea as to what we can look forward to in connection with the streetcar operation."

I am frank to confess that the bookkeeping was as simple as paint on the wall. In one book the clerk carried the names of all the motormen-conductors who were on the various streetcar runs and received fares from passengers. The names of these employees were carried at the heads of columns in a ledger, and it was ruled off to provide a line for every day in the month. By looking at a single page one could see what any motorman-conductor had collected on the first of May, the twenty-third of April, or any other day. It was simple, indeed. In another book, he carried the repairs, itemizing the detailed purchases that were required to keep the cars operating and in good order. This too was a very simple matter; all of it could be boiled down to show a single car in operation for a period of one month.

I then suggested that perhaps we should go to the carbarns so I would have a better idea of how repairs were being handled, the personnel at the barns, and additional overhead expenditures that had to be taken into account. This also was quite simple and offered no problem. We journeyed back to the city hall and I said, "I wish you would show me your depreciation account."

He looked at me a bit startled and then he said, "The depreciation account? We don't keep a depreciation account."

To that I replied, "I took a good look at the underpinnings and the carriages of some of the streetcars in the barn. In the first place, every car is in need of paint. In the second place, all of them are showing signs of wear. I have an idea those axles are getting bad, and it is only a question of time before those cars will have to be replaced. Do you have any idea what they cost new?"

He puzzled for a moment and then said, "I think when we bought them they were second-hand cars and that we paid six thousand dollars for each of them."

I asked, "What do you think a new car would cost today?" He had no idea.

Then I said, "Suppose these cars wear out, what do we do for money in order to replace them?"

His response to that was, "We have not given that any consideration."

All of this, of course, raised quite a few questions, and I felt the necessity of having conferences with the mayor to discuss the future of the transportation system. We could ultimately abandon the system of streetcars and install buses. They would be more manageable, serve wider areas of the city, and render far greater service. But this required a bond issue and such an issue would have to be approved by the electorate. The course was quite clear to me. It would be a case of educating the voters to what the circumstances and conditions really were, what was contemplated to maintain effective transportation, and what would have to be done in order to procure the money for any change. I kept everlastingly at this matter knowing that at the end of the four-year term of the mayor and the commissioners there would have to be an accounting. I did not want to leave the problem without solution any longer than was absolutely necessary. The change to buses was finally made.

Still another challenging problem came to the doorstep of the council. It sprang from the fact that there was a considerable growth in automobile traffic and a scarcity of parking space in the downtown area. What could be done to compel or to persuade shopowners and their clerks to park their vehicles in a parking lot or some rear street, so the customers might find parking room along the curbs of the downtown streets? Pekin was quite a center for farm trade, and it would be such a convenience for the farmers in a wide area if they all would find parking room while they did their shopping.

This matter was discussed in the council meetings, and before long representatives of various manufacturers of parking meters came to the city to demonstrate their products and show how they were superior to those of their competitors. The commissioners became quite familiar with what the probable cost of installation of parking meters in the entire downtown area might be. As figures began to be discussed, some suspicious persons got the idea that in a contract involving so much money there must be graft of some kind. This kind of suspicion and gossip can be the ruination of any community. When those who so glibly talked about it were questioned as to who the grafters might be, they did not say. They insisted, without any foundation whatsoever for their suspicions or their statements, that in a contract of that size somebody would skim the cream from the top. It doesn't take very long for such innuendoes to circulate from one person to another until at long last it becomes a real problem. In this case the council proceeded to enter into a contract. When it was announced, there was considerable hue and cry that surely money must have passed hands in connection with that contract. At such a point, a timid city countil might very well have decided not to go on with the project. I must say for Mayor Kinsey that he had faith in this cause, and that he was prepared to stand by his guns and to defy any of those who said it involved graft and wrongdoing. In due course parking meters were installed, and they proved to be a real boon to the entire community. When enough citizens eventually experienced the inconvenience of having to insert a nickel in the parking meter at the end of an hour, sentiment began to build up for adequate space close to the downtown area. New parking lots were provided, and finally this problem was solved.

In those days it was customary for at least one or more circuses and three or four carnivals to pay a visit to the city each year and remain for an entire week. There were a number of areas not too far from the downtown section that were adequate for their tents and sideshows and the paraphernalia they brought with them. It wasn't too long before somebody thought surely a circus or carnival, in obtaining a license from the city, must receive other concessions for which there was some cost. The question then arose as to whether these costs were legitimately taxed to them or whether there was something skimmed off the top and put in somebody's pocket? To me it was always amazing how these unjustified and unwarranted allegations could be manufactured out of whole cloth and made to reflect upon the integrity of the commissioners.

Something of the same problem manifested itself when at least three members of the city council thought that the city should buy one or more motorized streetsweepers for use in the paved downtown streets. This matter was discussed several times in open sessions with a good many of the citizens present, and it was finally determined that on a given Saturday all members of the council would journey to a distant city to see a demonstration of various streetsweepers and to determine whether or not the performance was such as to justify a purchase.

At that time, as I recall, there were only two companies in the United States manufacturing motorized sweepers. In one of them the broom was in front; in the other the broom was at the rear of the sweeper. There was no other substantial difference in their performances and, as I remember, the prices of the two were identical, six thousand dollars. That was a great deal of money then for a piece of rolling equipment of this size. But we wanted to be sure and so we embarked on still another journey for a further demonstration of the streetsweepers. In the course of the day, we called on the city councilmen of the city we visited and had lunch with them. We invited the salesmen representing the two companies to join us. Then early in the afternoon we returned to Pekin.

It seemed to me a bit strange that an alderman from the neighboring city had been following me around most of the day and was determined to make the journey back in the car that transported me. He called attention to the fact that the salesman for one of the sweepers was a very fine person, and he began to give that particular sweeper a considerable buildup. I wondered why he was so deeply interested. I quickly found out when we reached home. He pushed me off to a corner and said, "You know there is a consideration in this if you will recommend this particular sweeper."

My reply was, "I am the commissioner of finance and not the commissioner of streets and public improvements." He said he knew this full well but that he had been talking to one or two of the other commissioners, and they had agreed they would doubtless follow whatever recommendation I made. To all of this I said, "Thanks for the suggestion." We left it there.

This happened over the weekend, but early in the following week the salesman for the other company dropped in at our business establishment for a visit. He was an extremely pleasant, agreeable person and the first thing I noticed was that he wore an American Legion button in his lapel. "I understand," he said, "that you are the district commander of the American Legion here. I am a member of the legion in the northern part of the state. As one soldier to another, I guess we can talk to each other with all the cards on the table. You know there are just two sweepers; both of them are pretty good performers. Obviously, the one I sell I believe is the best. I can take you and the members of the city council anywhere, anytime for further demonstrations, but that is it. We have nothing to offer. There are no commissions or concessions nor come ons—there is no rake-off in this business. We sell them at a given price. We believe we have a good article and we do get our share of the business." He was, indeed, frank and disarming and I was quite taken with him.

Before the day was over I had occasion to journey to the city hall and there I found the mayor. I discussed the matter with him at length and, among other things, I said, "I am just afraid that one sweeper salesman may have made an offer somewhere to someone at the wrong time and the wrong place, and we might be very justly scolded if we purchase his sweeper. I do not say that this is correct, but I do say that I could read it in the conversation of the legionnaire who came to see me. The strict fact of the matter is that an offer *was* made to one member of the council. It should not take very long for the council to buy the sweeper sold by the legionnaire."

The same problem arose when at long last it was indicated that the city was in need of at least one additional firetruck of large dimensions. They cost a considerable amount, and it was again a case in which there were some who believed that when the price tag is high, there must be a discount which goes into somebody's pocket. Actually, the purchase of a firetruck became a real community issue. Salesmen for firefighting apparatus were in and out of the community for a good many months. I became familiar with all manner of firefighting equipment. It was decided in open sessions of the city council, which were fairly packed by the citizens, and as I look back I can only observe that the city got its money's worth.

Despite such problems from time to time, which to some people seemed almost world shaking, life generally moved at an even and peaceful pace. My operations in the city council were reported in the local press from time to time and I was in some demand to participate in programs of different kinds. I remember one time in particular when a press account of a program made it difficult for me for quite a long time after the report appeared. I had appeared in a church in the very small town of Tremont. The parishioners had managed to collect enough money to pay off the mortgage on the church and the parsonage, and they thought it would be a fine thing to have a mortgage-burning ceremony. The minister phoned me and asked if he could persuade me to come and participate in this ceremony and make a brief speech. I told him that I would be glad to come and added, with some enthusiasm, that I was always ready and willing to see a church mortgage burned so that it could plan for greater things.

It turned out to be quite an impressive ceremony and when it was over the local newspaper referred to me as "Reverend Everett Dirksen." So I became known in a very considerable area as the "Reverend Dirksen." It took quite some time to dissuade people from the belief that I was an ordained minister. To my friends it was a never-ending source of delight. They enjoyed making all manner of quips about the Reverend Dirksen.

It was at this point in my life that I received my first honorarium for a speech. To me it seems a little strange even now. I recall very well being at the backdoor of our bakery in white baker's clothes when a friend of mine, who was one of the prominent embalmers and undertakers in our city, came through the bakery and found me. He had with him a very impressive looking person who was immaculately dressed. He began by saying, "Everett, this is my friend from Chicago, the president of the Illinois Embalmers. He is here to see whether or not you are willing to accept an engagement to address the state convention of embalmers and undertakers which will be held in Peoria."

Then the president of the embalmers took over the conversation and said,

"I should tell you that there is a rather substantial honorarium attached, and what we want is a stimulating speech that has lots of humor in it, something unlike what we have had before. Certainly, we want nothing like the speech we had last year. We invited one of those inspirational speakers who, when he was introduced from the head table, came marching down the center aisle of the dining hall shaking a quart fruit jar filled with navy beans and one walnut. What he was trying to prove was that if you shake the jar long enough the walnut invariably comes to the top. That is just plain nonsense in our book, and what we want is some entertainment in a speech."

I puzzled for a moment and then said, "Well, sir, I am not particularly an entertainer but if you want to take me at face value, we will see what can be done." So, the agreement was made and sometime later I addressed the embalmer's convention. I spent quite some time on that speech and, I must say, it turned out to be rather humorous, judging by the laughter and applause. One thing I did remember to include was the parting salute that Digger O'Dell always gave when he appeared on the Fred Allen radio program in those earlier days. It would do as the embalmer's salute, "Drop over sometime." That was the theme of the speech I gave.

That first professional engagement for an honorarium still comes back to me and leaves me with a bit of a chuckle. But one thing also comes back; the dinner was held in a large auditorium and all of the paraphernalia and apparatus of the embalmer's and undertaker's art was on display. Surrounding that dinner crowd on every side was an endless array of caskets, hearses, and other fixtures used in the profession. And there I was in those surroundings undertaking to make a humorous speech. In any event it was, to say the least, a funereal atmosphere and yet I thoroughly enjoyed it.

I remember one other anecdote which I still use when I try to emphasize the advisability of brevity. It was the story of a cub reporter on a New York newspaper who was turning in such long stories that he was roundly criticized by the managing editor. On a certain day the editor called him in and told him to, "Get yourself out to Park Row where they found a man dead as the result of an explosion, and make it short."

The young reporter grabbed a cab and journeyed out to Park Row and, after locating the place of the accident, made all possible inquiry and then turned in this story: "John Jackson lighted a match to see whether there was gas in the tank. There was. Funeral Tuesday."

In those days, as a part of my chores in the wholesale bakery, I drove a truck around town to sell and deliver bread and rolls and other baked products to grocers, delicatessen stores, hotels, and other establishments. It is really a great experience for one who is also a member of a city council. After a time the citizens know fairly well about where I would be on my delivery route at a given hour, and they congregated there and ventilated their complaints and grievances. This was one way of becoming accessible to the citizens of all parts of the community.

The grievances were legion. They would recite that their alleys could not be negotiated in wet weather and asked what was the matter with a city council that it did not keep these important accessible thoroughfares passable so that coal and food and other things might be delivered. Cellars would fill with water, and when that happened the people's imprecations were unending. When a storm felled a tree and it dropped across a roadway and no city employee was available to proceed quickly to the spot and remove the impediment, there was raucous scolding about the inefficiency of the city council. These were but some of the constant complaints. I, as the member of the council most accessible to them, had to hear these endless complaints.

The stores and shops where I delivered bakery products really became political centers, and I like to think back on the expediency with which we settled national and international problems. No matter what the size of the store or meat market might be, we settled all these problems to our deep satisfaction in a way that would have made a deliberative body like the United States Senate turn green with envy. Alas, they were not durably settled nor were their voices heard beyond the confines of the store.

I had one experience with the police department in my city which gave me an insight into crime and the growth of criminal activity among all age groups and in all quarters of the city. There was a man of my acquaintance with a family of five children who often said that he would like to be considered whenever a vacancy occurred in the police department. He had no special training for this type of work, but I thought because of his courage and character that he probably would make a good police officer.

I prevailed upon the commissioner in charge of police assignments to hire him and he did. Before entering on his duties as a policeman, he came to see me and I said, "Johnnie, I have no special instructions for you. You are generally familiar with the conditions that exist in this community, and if it should be your lot to encounter hardened criminals and desperadoes engaged in crime, take no chance. Shoot first and argue afterward."

It could have been as much as six or seven months after he joined the police department that my doorbell rang about two o'clock in the morning and there he was. Even in the semidarkness I could see he was pale and trembling. I said, "What brings you here at this unearthly hour?"

He stuttered a bit and then said, "I just killed two burglars."

"Tell me about it," I said. So he recited the circumstances as briefly as he could. When it was over I said, "Suppose you try to forget it for the moment and go back to your duty. If perchance you may need a lawyer, I'll see you get a good one, and I will be glad to be on hand to see that you are fully taken care of."

What had happened was that the professional bootleggers in Chicago who had their stills and cookers along the Illinois River some distance south of our city had to send their trucks transporting illicit alcohol to Chicago through Pekin. This meant, of course, that desperadoes and ruffians were on hand to make certain that the trucks were not molested. If they could bribe their way, they would. If the effort at bribery was not effective, then it was often necessary to shoot it out with law officials. I had given one other instruction to the new policeman, and he had followed it. It was simply this, "Keep your feet on the ground, keep your head, don't be unduly hasty, but if you have to shoot, be sure your aim is good." This is exactly what he had done. When the case came up he was exonerated, but soon after he retired from the police force.

Perhaps the incident of the installation of ornamental lighting should be mentioned. I must reaffirm what I said before, that the mayor was indeed progressive and did much to improve the town and give it a slightly spectacular appearance. That meant ornamental lighting on the main street and on some of the residential streets. It was, however, not negotiated without difficulty. I remember our first effort in this field when the residents could not agree on the type of lighting they desired. There were quite a number of mass meetings before the matter was finally settled, and I recall that the preference was for a fixture referred to as a Georgian lantern. The last time I had a chance to observe, and that is not too long ago, those same lanterns were still in place and have been producing light, comfort, and security for nearly forty years.

There was one comic incident involving our fire department. It was an excellent and efficient department even though quite small, and despite the fact that the fire chief was regarded as entirely too old and too gabby. He may have been old, but he was wiry and energetic and a good man in his field. He had actually devoted a lifetime to the business of fighting fires. Along with all else, he had a great sense of humor. But the incident that intrigued me was one occasion when the firebells sounded and the fire equipment started across town in the direction of the blaze. The chief always wore a celluloid collar. On this occasion he got a little too close to the blaze, and a spark managed to drop on his collar and it flared up in a blaze as celluloid will do, fortunately doing no real damage. An account of this was carried in virtually every trade paper, magazine, and newspaper in the United States: "The Fire Chief Catches on Fire."

As our community grew and the population increased, the question of city planning and city zoning became quite a problem. There were, of course, those who did not want any regulation. Fortunately, the mayor was one of those who fully understood these developments, since he had served as a consultant to other communities. He and I discussed at length the desirability of a building code, a planning ordinance, and a zoning ordinance. In due course we laid the matter in preliminary form before the council. The question of bringing in expert talent was also explored, but since this required the appropriation of funds, it was finally decided that perhaps I should devote weekends and spare time to making a general outline of such ordinances, after which they could be discussed and perfected. I agreed to do so and actually spent some eighteen months assembling building codes, planning ordinances, and other material, as well as holding meetings with contractors who would be affected by whatever requirements might be imposed.

I soon discovered that it was not an easy undertaking, but it was fascinating and I labored with it early and late. At long last, when I thought I had this whole matter fairly well in hand, I submitted the building code to the members of the council so that we could discuss it before calling in affected persons. When we held the first open meeting, the council chamber was packed to overflowing with contractors, bricklayers, carpenters, and others. We went through those ordinances line by line so that we might ascertain points of agreement and disagreement.

This same procedure was employed in the consideration of a zoning ordinance because it meant that certain property in certain areas could not be used for commercial purposes, and this of course had an impact on property owners who used to be entirely free as to how their property was to be used. The planning ordinance proved to be even more difficult than the building code. It became necessary, in order to appease the wrath of the citizens, to hold a mass meeting of the people living in particularly affected areas so that their grievances might be heard. One such meeting I shall never forget.

It was indeed a grievance meeting attended by virtually every adult property owner in the area. The high school auditorium where the meeting was held was filled to overflowing. The property owners had collected a substantial sum of money with which they engaged two excellent attorneys. In the mass meeting they considered various aspects of the planning ordinance and concluded that if the council undertook to enact it, they would authorize the attorneys to appeal the ordinance to the Supreme Court of the state as a violation of the intent of state law which covered the ability of municipalities to engage in such activities.

When the night for the mass meeting came, I decided for myself that, not as a member of the city council but rather as a property owner in this area, I was entitled to attend. When I arrived, I found about eight hundred highly hostile people. I took a seat in the front row of the auditorium and watched the proceeding unfold. I listened intently as various citizens ventilated their feelings. I listened to the attorneys as they undertook to explain what, in their judgment, was illegal about this proceeding and how they intended to proceed in any appeal to the courts.

At about this point I arose and addressed myself to the chairman of the meeting. Someone in the audience shouted that I was out of order. Still another shouted that I had no business at the meeting. Still another stated in a loud voice that I had not been invited. I insisted that I was a property owner and that I was fully entitled to be there whether I was invited or not. That seemed to make little difference. An emotional wave developed, and then several persons shouted, "Throw him out." A substantial phalanx came up the center aisle and gave me a moment to consider whether I would walk out under my own power or whether I would be physically evicted from the meeting. There was a moment of banter and discussion, and then it happened. These were rugged, hard-working people, and enough of them took hold of me, carried me to the door of the school, and bounced me out on the sidewalk. That certainly did not improve my feelings one bit.

The net result of all this was that the council adopted a planning ordinance, which was appealed to the Illinois Supreme Court. The court found that the city council had not acted in conformity with the requirements of the state statute, and so the planning ordinance was nullified. Later a revised ordinance was approved.

All this had at least one interesting compensatory incident. It related to one who had been a longtime friend. He was in the grocery business on the north side of town and he was in fact one of the customers for our bakery products, and I called at his store every day. When the mass meeting was over, I had lost a customer, but that's not the interesting aspect of the matter. He had built himself a very spacious two-story frame house located about three lots from a street intersection. Sometime after I had been given the bum's rush, I found him sitting on my front porch one evening when I came home from work. There was no good reason why I should be very friendly in view of his activities against the planning ordinance and at the mass meeting which had resulted in my eviction.

As I stepped inside the porch I simply said, "How are you?"

He said, "Quite all right."

To this I added, "I am a little surprised to see you here because when I last saw you you were quite angry with me over my efforts to bring about the adoption of a planning ordinance, and I had some doubts that you would ever speak to me again."

He was a bit abashed at all this and then said rather meekly, "I have a problem." I asked him to tell me about it in detail. And then he cited the fact that there were vacant lots lying between his newly built residence and the corner, and that somebody had already taken an option on the corner and was preparing to erect a gasoline service station there for all and sundry who might patronize it. He then went into a real tirade against the idea of erecting a commercial business so close to his residence, because all it could do would be to impair the value of his property.

When he subsided I simply said, "Didn't I tell you that the only thing we were endeavoring to do in the adoption of a zoning and planning ordinance was to give protection to existing property and to aid the orderly growth of the community? You have become a victim of the very thing we were trying to prevent. You were the ringleader in seeking to undo all this, and now you are one of the first victims of the failure to adopt just such an effective ordinance. I am very sorry. I do not believe I care to make this effort again because those planning and zoning ordinances represent an investment of time and effort on my part which runs over a period of nearly two years. I am afraid the damage is done, and you will have to find someone besides me to undertake that task."

He became pathetically appealing. "But there is no one on our city council who can, or who would, undertake this job except you, and I hope you will reconsider that decision."

"Nelson," I said, "I am truly sorry, but I prefer not to undertake this, knowing what it has cost me in sweat and effort."

One other incident comes to mind, because there was also something pathetic about it to engrave it on my memory. It was a situation which developed as a result of an extended improvement project embracing the paving of virtually a quarter of all the streets in the city. There was a widow who owned a residential property and also several lots which were located on

a corner. Notwithstanding the amounts that were levied against public benefits, I knew that it would be a hardship on her. I knew her very well and
always referred to her as Aunt Lou. She and my mother had come from the
old country about the same time. I drove out to see her. Almost immediately
she began quite a tirade about what the paving would cost, and that she
might lose her home, and then she fairly exploded. She said, "You young
crook, how much do you get out of this? What would your mother say if she
were still alive? She would be ashamed of you." She continued in that
fashion for quite a little while.

Finally I said as humbly and apologetically as I could, "Aunt Lou, one
family, ten families, twenty families cannot stand in the way of progress in a
community. I know that some people will be hurt. It has always been so and
it will always be so." The tirade began all over again and I realized that it was
a fruitless and abortive effort on my part, so I gave up.

Despite the headaches and heartaches which one may suffer in public
service at the local level, there is still a great lure about it. There is some
glorification, meager as it may be. It is exhilarating when something is
accomplished. There is the pride of accomplishment, and finally there is
some recognition, no matter how humble the office. As one moves up the
ladder, that recognition becomes even greater and the glorification a little
more widespread, all of which is by way of saying that even serving on a city
council in a community of less than twenty thousand population, one is
flattered by being referred to as "Honorable Commissioner." There is usually enough written in the local press to satisfy whatever egotism one may
possess. I was no exception to all this. I regarded myself as a normal human being with normal tastes and weaknesses, and with that feeling of delight that goes with hearing yourself referred to as "The Honorable Everett McKinley Dirksen, Commissioner of Finance of the city of Pekin." It
sounded pretty good to me, I admit.

Almost immediately there comes a feeling that there is higher ground and
larger authority to be enjoyed over a wider area. As I looked down the vista of
the future, I thought that this could take many forms. I might become a
candidate for the state legislature or the state senate and represent not one
community, but many communities in Springfield, Illinois. I might also
become a candidate for Congress. Actually I had little interest in being a
candidate for state office. I assume this could have sprung from the fact that
in college days in Minnesota when we sat around in the student union, the
budding politicians discussed the various things they hoped to accomplish
in life, and their horizons were usually far beyond that of the state legislature.

Certainly I was a veritable tyro so far as political organizations were concerned. Our community elections were conducted on an entirely non-partisan basis, so party organization did not figure in local affairs. I did not have anyone I could turn to for sound and candid advice. Whatever decisions were to be made I had to make on my own and as best I could. At long last I did make a decision. In fact I made several. The first was that I would not again be a candidate for the city council. Once was enough. I had experienced all the frustrations, the heartaches, the headaches, the delights, the joys of accomplishment, and every other thing that local office had to offer. The second decision—and it was a firm decision—was that I would not be a candidate for the state legislature. But by far the most important decision, and one made with firmness and determination, was that I was certain that my future had to be found in the domain of public service. The final decision, and at the moment it was necessarily slightly tentative, was that at some point in time I would become a candidate for the Congress of the United States. It was at the national level that I wanted to serve. I wanted to be a part of the nation's hub. I felt it was, and would continue to be, the political hub of the whole wide world.

The congressional district in which I lived consisted of six counties. If I expected to succeed, it would be necessary to become a candidate in the primary election against an incumbent Republican. At that time, the occupant of the congressional seat had been in Congress for ten years. His name was William Edgar Hull. He was a very successful businessman and a substantial figure in the community. He had made lots of money and could afford to spend it very freely in perpetuating himself in office. He would be my opposition if I decided to make the race. Then came the all-important question of how to go about getting the nomination. I puzzled over it and thought perhaps the best way to approach it was to let the news of my decision seep into the district from the outside.

I was still active as a district commander of the American Legion, and the legion districts were coextensive with the Congressional districts. I could continue service in the legion as an officer, since our form of government in Pekin was nonpartisan and that did not disqualify me.

About that time it so happened on a Saturday and Sunday in the late fall that the Illinois department of the American Legion was having its annual conference of adjutants and commanders at state headquarters in Bloomington, Illinois. I knew most of the staff members. When we arrived on Saturday at noon, I went to headquarters and selected one man whom I felt I could fully entrust with a strictly confidential matter. I told him very frankly what I had in mind. I told him also that I had prepared a short statement that could be released in the Sunday paper in Bloomington, which was located in a congressional district adjoining my own. My friend at headquarters, who had been in the newspaper business, summoned a reporter from the Bloomington *Pantagraph*. We made him a part of this very polite conspiracy. Incidentally, this newspaper was owned in part by the family of Adlai Stevenson, who was one day to become governor of Illinois and, at a later date, a candidate for the presidency of the United States. I gave the reporter whatever background material he required along with the statement that I had rather carefully developed, and I told him that my candidacy was now in his hands.

The story appeared exactly as it was planned and things began to happen quickly. The report was placed on the wire and was quickly picked up by every daily and weekly newspaper in the Sixteenth Congressional District. In fact, it appeared all over the state of Illinois. Very shortly after it appeared, various editors undertook to editorialize on the brashness of a young man who was trying to unseat a seasoned legislator who had been in Congress for nearly ten years.

At this point, it might be fitting to observe that sometimes history and destiny hang by a hair. Had the editors completely ignored my candidacy and devoted no space to it, it might have died aborning. This, however, they did not do. Considerable editorial space was devoted to me and this quickly began to intrigue the curiosity of people, and they began to inquire who this young guy Dirksen, a baker from Pekin, really was, and why he thought he could be elected to Congress in the place of a very seasoned legislator.

The more they wrote, the better I liked it. Not the least of the political art is exposing one's name and image and personality. As the saying goes, the fat was now in the fire. It was necessary to secure petitions to be signed by qualified voters of my party as required by the state law. It was not too difficult to secure the requisite signatures, and when the petition was filed and acknowledged by the secretary of the state, I was a candidate for nomination to Congress. I prepared to start campaigning wherever there were people who were willing to listen to what I had to say.

I shall never forget the first meeting in that campaign. The county chairman of Peoria County, the largest of the six counties in that congressional district, was an excellent organizer and liked to start the campaign with a spectacular meeting. It was held in the Majestic Theatre in Peoria. All of the ambitious party candidates were on hand. They were seeking every position on the ballot. These included state senator, state representative, clerk of the supreme court, clerk of the appellate court, sheriff, county judge, probate judge, county assessor, county treasurer, and perhaps other offices. The stage of the theater was filled with candidates. The county chairman came to where I was sitting on the stage and said that he would introduce the candidates for all other offices and since I was the only candidate other than the incumbent congressman who was running for Congress, he would save me until last.

This proved to be a real advantage. Most of the candidates took only a few minutes to announce to a packed theater the office which they were seeking and that they deemed themselves qualified to discharge the duties and functions of that office. Nearly all of them stated that at the request or even the insistent demand of many friends and associates, they had decided to become candidates. Finally, the list was exhausted and they were ready for me.

It had been a rather lengthy meeting, and I know how restive people can be in a political assembly if it runs too late. But strangely enough no one appeared to leave the theater. I had given the county chairman just a few biographical essentials about myself so that he could present me in an authentic way.

I began my speech by saying that I had become a candidate for the Congress without a request or a demand from any friends and well-wishers. In fact, I could not be sure that even my wife approved of my being a candidate, and that on occasions I had noticed her look at me from the corner of her eye as much as to question whether I knew what I was really doing. I confessed, therefore, to the audience that I was a candidate for Congress because I wanted to go there, that I felt there was a place for me in national life, and that I would continue my effort to find that place no matter how long it took to do it. This gained a great burst of applause. I spoke very frankly to that audience. I said I respected the congressman who now occupied the seat, but that in all life change was eternal. I advised them that it would take some money to carry on the campaign and that I had no money unless I could borrow from the bank on an unsecured note. I emphasized those points by stating that my conviction about it was such that I was willing to pit young energy against organization and money in the hope that this would have appeal for the electorate. I did not try to discuss more than one or two issues in that opening speech because there would be plenty of time for that at a later date.

Somehow, my candor and frankness seemed to catch on with this big crowd. When the speech was concluded there was a burst of applause such as I had never hoped for. They all left the theater chattering to one another. I knew I had tapped a live body that would advertise my name and that it would go out into far reaches of the congressional district. That is how the campaign for Congress in the year 1930 got underway. It was implemented the next morning in the press. The reporters treated me generously, but the editors undertook to make light of it all. In quiet moments I somehow felt deep in my heart that if I could be elected to Congress it would be just another step in the direction of becoming a senator, and so from time to time I said to myself, "So you want to be a senator?" But that was still a long way off.

7

MR. SMITH DOES NOT GO
TO WASHINGTON

A GOOD MANY CLOSE FRIENDS wondered whether I should undertake a primary election contest in view of the fact that the incumbent congressman from the Sixteenth Illinois Congressional District was a Republican, a multimillionaire, a ten-year veteran of Congress. In fact some of these friends had serious doubts about my mental equilibrium. They pointed out rather candidly that I would have only meager funds with which to conduct the campaign and that these would necessarily have to come from close friends who could contribute only modest amounts. They also pointed out that I could expect no support from the daily newspapers nor from the influential weeklies. Finally, they made a special point of the fact that the incumbent congressman was in a position to make very substantial sums available to the Republican organizations in the six counties, and that that would have real effect so far as organizational Republicans were concerned, including the entire precinct structure.

I listened attentively to all of these representations. The best I could say without giving offense was what Abraham Lincoln said to his friends who sought to dissuade him from seeking the presidency. It was a rough road for him, and one of the phrases he used was, "The taste is a little in my mouth."

I got the first test of all this when I began to campaign actively. It meant that all the candidates, local and state, would be on hand at whatever meetings were set in the various counties. I experienced a sense of distress when I noted that they were not too anxious to be seen in my company or to have very much to do with me. I should have expected this. All these candidates wanted the support of the party organization in the primary election. Only qualified Republican voters could vote in the primary, and that included the precinct committeemen and their wives and their associates throughout the six counties. But at long last my determination hardened, although I must confess that many a turbulent thought crossed my mind when I was on the highways alone late at night after political meetings. I knew also that regardless of how late I managed to find the comfort of my own bed at home, that it would be necessary for me to be on hand early in the morning to do my share of the chores connected with the dredging and bakery enterprises.

It was astonishing how many things crowded through the mind not only with respect to the sacrifice which was to be made but also whether or not I was on the right road. Did I actually want to be a senator? For that matter, did I really want to be a congressman? Why should I make the many sacrifices that would be imperative and why expend every ounce of vitality for a mere political goal? There were, after all, so many other things which might be done, and not the least of these was the prospect of returning to school and completing the remaining three semesters of my unfinished law course so that I might be admitted to the bar and become a practicing lawyer. But always and always I was confronted with the Lincoln experience; the taste was still a little in my mouth.

Finally these somewhat troublesome thoughts were dispelled, and I set myself to the arduous and serious business of winning the primary election. It occurred to me that to arouse the interest of the voters, an expression must be coined, directing attention to me and diminishing the interest of the average voter in my opponent. In the light of hindsight, I suppose I regret what happened and, frankly, it only happened one other time in my political career. I was rather idealistic about the whole domain of politics, and I did not want to be charged with saying something that might be regarded as particularly unkind about an opponent. Generally speaking, I pursued the theory that an opponent in a political contest was free to sell his merchandise and his image as best he could and that I would undertake to sell my merchandise and my image. Yet there was the hard realistic fact that interest had to be created in the primary election, because so often less than 30 percent of the party voters went to the polls in a primary contest. In that mood an expression began to take form in my mind. It was "Hull, Hooey, and Horsefeathers."

I blush, because as an expression it actually did not make too much sense. It was true that he emphasized what were then some far-out ideas. Those associated with him in conducting the campaign left a clear impression that his proposal for the improvement of the Illinois River would make it a deep waterway, and that the citizens could envision the time when ocean-going vessels would be traveling up and down that river.

As a contractor I had had experience with that river. I knew as an irrefutable fact that the measure which he had introduced in the Congress called for a waterway two hundred feet wide and nine feet deep. Anyone having any experience with navigable waters knew that the best any such waterway could handle would be barges loaded with bulk commodities, for the most part pushed by a tugboat. Ocean-going vessels and, for that matter, even vessels that could ply the Great Lakes area would not dare to travel a channel only nine feet deep. Since the Illinois River was close to most of the counties in the congressional district, it was readily apparent what kind of appeal this plea would have. It inspired visions of world markets, improved farm prices, expanded markets for industrial products, and a great many other benefits.

It seemed to me fair to expose this matter in terms that the voters could understand. (Frankly, there are no better weapons in the political field than sarcasm and ridicule.) This I could make quite persuasive out of my experiences as a dredge contractor. Thus it was that I could make abundantly clear how far afield my opponent was on the subject of a deep waterway.

Inasmuch as the primary election in the state of Illinois in 1930 came in the month of April, it was quite obvious that much of the campaign had to be pursued at the end of the winter season when heavy snow still lay upon the highways, and it wasn't always easy, particularly at night, to move from one meeting to another. Under the circumstances I should have had someone travel with me at all times, but that offered real difficulty. I could not very well prevail upon a friend, no matter how deep his devotion, to spend so much time in my behalf. At the same time, out of my slender resources, I could not afford to engage the services of someone who might serve as both driver and companion. And I suffered setbacks.

I recall on one occasion in Lacon, in Marshall County, where I called upon one of the leading citizens, who was the president of a woolen mill, which at that time had contracts with the army. I was sure my opponent had, quite rightly, assisted him in getting the contracts. His name was Paul Grieves. It was natural that at some point in the campaign I should call upon him in the hope of enlisting his support. When I did, I was very gentlemanly about it, and when the discussion was over he said, "Young fellow, I can only say to you, Ed Hull is my friend. He has been good to me. He has been good to this industry and we intend to support him. But if you should win the Republican nomination in the primary election, we will support you with equal vigor." Marshall County was small, and I knew what the influence of Paul Grieves in that county could do, and I began to think in terms of defeat—at least there.

But another factor entered into the campaign. The Illinois River had become in a sense a part of the drainage canal for the city of Chicago. That metropolis had made little effort to build plants for the treatment of raw sewage. Instead, they built a drainage canal from Lake Michigan into the Illinois River, so the effluents of this large city polluted the river water. Indeed it was a ghastly situation, and nothing had been done to remedy it. To a considerable extent the basic reason was that the Chicago sanitary district, which was charged with the responsibility of disposing of Chicago sewerage, was a powerful organization and could easily put an end to the political ambitions of anyone who took sharp exception to what it was doing. It was finally disclosed that members of both branches of the Illinois legislature were on the sanitary district payroll, so no mandatory legislation could be enacted to compel action on a sewage treatment program.

The net result was that the Illinois River, which in 1900 had probably ranked next to the Columbia River as a fish-producing stream, became so polluted that for all practical purposes fishing came to an end. I made a very considerable point of all this, largely so because Mr. Hull continued to talk about his deep waterway and said very little about clean water. The more I discussed this issue, the more interest developed among the outdoor and recreational organizations. As a result of this, interested people organized the Illinois Hunters' and Fishers' Association. They suggested that I serve as president and I accepted, because I saw not merely its immediate implications but its potential in future years. All this served to bring sportsmen to my cause and enlarged my hopes very considerably.

One real handicap from which I suffered was that I could get very few people to undertake platform assignments in my behalf. There were a few, who were definitely on the younger side. I have some satisfaction in noting that those who helped me have come reasonably far in the political field. But to meet and confront the voters was a big task for me, and that meant a greater expenditure of energy day by day.

I recall that on one occasion when I was invited to a meeting in Woodruff High School, in the northern part of the city of Peoria, I arrived a little late to find a prominent attorney on the platform speaking on my opponent's behalf. I stood in the doorway and listened to his concluding remarks. When he left the platform I shook his hand and suggested that he stay and hear what I had to say. He preferred not to remain.

I moved to the platform and received quite a generous ovation from the crowd. After a brief introduction I said, "Ladies and gentlemen, I came in the door just in time to hear Mr. Heyl conclude his remarks on behalf of my opponent. I was a little intrigued by his statement that you would not want to send a storyteller to Congress." This was an allusion to the fact that I tried always to drive home a point with the audience by means of a suitable anecdote. I felt, over a period of time, that quite often people in the audience would forget the point I made, but when they recalled the story it would come back. Now I made this comment, "In 1848 this general area sent a man to Congress who was regarded as one of the most capable storytellers of his time. So many of those stories have been saved for posterity and on occasion I have used some of them myself to illustrate a point. That man's name was Abraham Lincoln."

That observation brought forth a great salvo of applause, and I knew by that time that my audience was not hostile, even though Peoria was the native city of Mr. Hull. I was, however, bothered that prominent attorneys like Mr. Heyl were taking up the cause of my opponent. Mr. Hull was apparently paying $250 for each speech made on his behalf. He could well afford it, and I, on the other hand, could not engage the services of any speaker who might present my cause in a persuasive and satisfactory way.

One other thing is quickly learned in a political campaign of this kind, and that is that the combative instinct in many people is quite close to the surface. They like to fight. This is indicated by the fact that men and women attend boxing contests, wrestling and football games, and shout at the very tops of their voices for one party or one team or the other. A political campaign stirs that same barbarian spirit in people. They become quite combative, because it gives them a sense of personal involvement in a fight. Think of the people who used to attend meetings addressed by former President Truman, and at some appropriate moment would in a loud voice yell, "Give 'em hell, Harry." All of this served to inject spirit and heat into the campaign, and that spirit was conveyed to the audiences as the campaign unfolded.

I began to feel a little more certain that I could win, but as my chances improved there also developed new difficulties, some of which I did not exactly anticipate. A candidate begins with a certain circle of friends, and then other groups of friends emerge and attempt to take over the management of the campaign. Quite some time before the date of the primary election, some of these friends began to think in terms of political patronage. The reasoning was that if I emerged as the winner in the primary, it was quite certain that I could and would win in the November election, because it was essentially and predominantly a Republican district. In that case, jobs and patronage might become available, particularly the appointment of postmasters, United States marshals, federal judges, rural mail carriers, and others. Some of the groups became rather demanding and insisted on firm promises, or else they would drop their support of my campaign.

I pointed out as carefully and inoffensively as I could that every candidate for Congress was bound by the provision in a federal statute, which was referred to as the Federal Corrupt Practices Act. Among other things in that statute was the requirement, under oath, that no promises had been made to anyone in return for their support.

The other aspect of the campaign which these groups forgot was that once a primary election was over, the regular Republican county organizations would take over the management of the campaign in each county. So far as past experience indicated, the county organizations were very jealous of their patronage prerogatives. If successful in the election, they would not countenance the dictation of jobs by any other group.

One other thing continues to come back to me, and that is the situation that prevailed in the northernmost county of the congressional district, which was, incidentally, the third largest county. The state senator from the district, Dr. Thomas Gunning, was a practicing dentist when he wasn't legislating. He was a very religious and extremely straitlaced person. He had his office on the second floor of an office building in Princeton, Illinois. It seemed to me as if the stairway by which one reached the second floor was almost as long as the steps in the Washington Monument, and the climb completely deprived me of all breath before I reached the top landing. I opened the door and fortunately the doctor had no patient in the chair at the moment. I greeted him, shook hands, told him my name, and said that I was a candidate for Congress on the Republican ticket.

He looked at me with a steely eye and asked, "Do you drink?"

"Well," I said, "Doctor, if you will just give me a minute to catch my breath I will discuss the matter with you."

That incident pointed up an interesting aspect of the situation in Bureau County, because all this came in prohibition days. One part of the county was heavily populated by people of Italian extraction and was given over in considerable measure to the business of making and selling bootleg whiskey and home brew. The other side of the county, where Dr. Gunning lived, included the city of Princeton, the county seat, where the people were mainly abstainers and teetotalers. Strangely enough, these two different areas of Bureau County got along quite well, and those who were devoted to the bootlegging art always supported Dr. Gunning for the state senate in spite of his violent aversion to liquor. That may be one of those things that is difficult to understand, but it is an indication of what must be taken into account when one enters any campaign covering a very diverse area.

When I reminded Senator Gunning that my opponent, Mr. Hull, had made his millions out of whiskey, he said, "That does not make the slightest difference. The point is that he does not drink."

I did not challenge Senator Gunning's logic, because it would have done no good. I must say that he really was a very able and honorable public official, even though I did not understand him and found myself on the other side of a good many issues.

Still another incident occurred in that campaign which added to my difficulties. One day the Honorable William Hale Thompson, better known as "Big Bill Thompson," mayor of the city of Chicago, chartered a river vessel, loaded it with people and public officials, and started down the Illinois River on a cruise. They made stops at a number of places in the congressional district, including Peoria. The mayor was a rather close friend of my opponent, Mr. Hull. It was quite natural, therefore, that far and wide the managers of my opponent's campaign freely availed themselves of every bit of publicity in connection with Mayor Thompson's excursion. It was something I had not expected, but I anticipated that it would serve my opponent well and add some votes to his total.

Mayor Thompson was a colorful character. He was the one who came to international fame, or shall one say notoriety, when he told the whole world that he proposed to go to Great Britain and punch King George V on the snoot. Of course, such a thing never took place, but it made good headlines everywhere. When he arrived in the Sixteenth Congressional District, he immediately endorsed my opponent. I did not know Bill Thompson at that time and so I couldn't complain about it. If it had been done for me, I would have welcomed the gesture no less.

One thing I could say about my many appearances in every part of the district during the campaign was that they served as lifters for the Republican party and put spirit into both the party and the campaign. As we approached primary day, I knew from the subtle communications that were directed toward me by Mr. Hull's managers that they were getting quite alarmed about the progress I was making. It is at that point in any campaign that the lures usually begin.

First one friend and then another would come and discuss my campaign and my hopes, in a rather general way, and then subtly observe, "Ev, you know that you cannot win. Why don't you think about getting out of the race now while you still have time? I've got some connections. I feel quite certain that if you agree to run for the state senate or the general assembly that those who are backing your opponent will pay all of your expenses and then some, and you will be sure to win." My only comment was that I had thought it through very carefully, that I thought there was a chance to win, that I had expended too much energy in the campaign already, and that I could not afford to withdraw.

The lures were then followed by threats. These also came from friends. Usually they began by discussing the campaign and the alarm which my progress had created in some quarters, and that they were afraid that something would happen to me. There were occasions when little notes in the form of threats were tied to the doorhandle of my automobile. I revealed this to a few friends who were active in the American Legion and, from that time on through the rest of the campaign, they set up a security guard and accompanied me wherever I went until I was safely on the road back home for the night.

Important as the fulfillment of the political ambition might be, one matter of far greater significance was in the process of being consummated in nature's own good time. Simply stated, Mrs. Dirksen was pregnant, and we fervently hoped and prayed that we might be blessed with a perfect baby—whether a boy or a girl. I was a bit apprehensive about not being present, as so many meetings were fifty or sixty miles from home, but the fates were kind.

It happened to be a terrible winter night with a freezing rain that converted the highways into glass. It was the night that the American Legion's society "40 and 8" had set for the initiation of new members, and it was quite certain that a substantial crowd would be on hand. The society was really a sort of fun organization or auxiliary of the legion. The name derived from the French railroad boxcars with which all soldiers who served in France were familiar. These cars were labeled "40 hommes" or "8 chevaux," meaning that they would accommodate 40 men or 8 horses.

The initiation ceremonies of the society were fun affairs, but sometimes they became slightly rough, yet it was all done in high spirits. When the meeting was about half over, a telephone call came. Mrs. Dirksen had been taken to the hospital—of course, I knew what the implications were.

One of my most devoted friends, a frequent guest in our home, was Louis Stacy, the building manager for the Peoria Life Insurance Company. I sought him out in the crowd and said, "Lou, they have just taken Louella to the hospital. It looks as if the baby could arrive anytime and certainly before morning."

"Wonderful," he said. "I'll drive you."

The twelve miles over incredibly slippery highways provided a journey I will always remember. The car skidded from side to side. I wasn't sure that the expected child would have a father. But once more the fates were kind, and Louis deposited me at the hospital door before midnight.

I quickly made known to the nurses and the attending physician that I was there and the vigil began. What a cavalcade of diverse thoughts creeps through the mind as one sits outside a hospital door waiting to hear the first birth cry and know that another soul has come into the world. Would it be a boy or a girl? Would it be a perfect baby or would it have some deformity? Would it be strong enough to sustain life or would it be weak and have only a minimal chance to survive? Would it have blue eyes and brown hair like the father or brown eyes and dark hair like the mother?

Then came the question of a name. Mrs. Dirksen and I had reached an agreement. If it was a boy, she was to name him. If it was a girl, it would be my privilege. Having a feeling for alliteration, I thought it should be something to go with "D" for Dirksen. Many names came to mind, but at long last I hit upon the name "Danice." Danice Dirksen! And then she must have a middle name. I tried out a good many. Finally, the name "Joy" came to mind. Danice Joy Dirksen! That name became settled in my mind.

While the vigil continued, the hospital attendants supplied me with coffee. As the minutes ticked off, I noticed that it was after one o'clock in the morning on the tenth of February. Ten minutes later I was sure I heard the birth cry. Surely this was it. And in a few minutes the nurse opened the door, ever so slightly, and said, "A perfect little girl with so much dark hair that it would do justice to an adult." It was the first child, and somehow it brought an overwhelming feeling of gratitude that the tradition of the family would be sustained.

Then came the innuendos which seem to have been so long accepted, particularly in political campaigns. One night I returned home very late and found Mrs. Dirksen was waiting for me. She had not gone to bed. I noticed the tears when I walked in the door. I gave her a pat and said, "Now what?"

For a little while she was reluctant to say anything, but at long last she did say, "There is a vile and vicious story going around not only about you but about me."

"Well, my dear," I said, "what is it?"

She blubbered a bit and said, "It's that our daughter, Joy, was born out of wedlock, that we were never married, and she is an illegitimate child." At that point she really did weep.

My response was, "Those things happen in every campaign. I should tell you about the Scotsman who became a candidate for office in Scotland and returned home one evening and said to his wife, 'Mither, they are charging me with stealing sheep.' At the time he didn't make too much of it, but a few nights later when he returned home, he said, 'Mither, they're not only charging me with stealing sheep—they proved it on me.'"

In any event, such rumors, such gossip, such vile talk is always a bit hard to take. Certainly it was hard for people who lived in a small town and sought to live a sedate Christian life, but it was part of the business and I was compelled to put up with it.

At long last primary day came. That night all ears were glued to the radio. The returns began to come in. Scores of people moved in and out of our home. About two o'clock in the morning we felt that it was time to retire, and the last guest finally went home. The latest news on the radio indicated that I was leading Mr. Hull by a majority of forty-four hundred votes. As Mrs. Dirksen and I went up the stairway to go to bed, she began to cry a little. The fact that I was leading made her quite happy, but I said to her, "Mother, don't set your cap too high. The feel is not right. Somehow victory is not in the air." There is a peculiar psyche of some kind which makes one sense whether victory or defeat is in the air. In any event, it did not feel right to me, and my fears were justified.

Normally the vote in a district of that kind was rather quickly tallied and phoned to headquarters, and one had a fair idea of what the outcome was going to be, notwithstanding an uncanny feeling about it. But it was late on the following day before the final return was published. I had been defeated by eleven hundred votes in my first congressional contest.

Frankly, the defeat by so narrow a margin was disappointing, and I found it difficult indeed to conceal that disappointment. Things had gone so well toward the latter part of the campaign and there was so much encouragement from so many sources that my confidence in a victory had been built up to the point where I fully expected to win. I had not been in this particular field of activity long enough to develop that kind of tough skin that must come to all politicians, because of the uncertainty of political life. The defeat did not improve my morale.

Not the least troublesome of all the aspects of the matter was that at two o'clock in the morning, on retiring, I could be ahead by forty-four hundred votes and yet in the afternoon of the following day be counted out by eleven hundred. Somehow it didn't seem right.

Analyzing the vote, I could only wonder what had happened in Bureau

County. There must be an explanation. It takes a little time, but sooner or later the truth will out. There were too many very close friends who had been watching and taking count of every move in the campaign. It was reported to me that on the night before the election someone had journeyed to Bureau County with a large quantity of handbills which had been circulated in the heavily Catholic part of the county. The handbills were printed in large letters and simply said, "Dirksen is a member of the Ku Klux Klan." It did not require any more than that, because it was like a red flag to voters to find the handbills in their mailboxes and on their doorsteps on election day. Obviously, there was nothing to be done about it. It was, of course, an unmitigated falsehood. But this was enough of a clue to continue the exploration, and finally it was disclosed who had lent himself to this nefarious undertaking.

The first thing that shocked me about it all was that it came from a legionnaire. The second thing was that he was a state highway officer, and the third thing was that he must have been compensated well for such a mission. It was quite clear, as we continued the investigation, where he had got the handbills. He was fairly well known in Bureau County and he knew who in that county would undertake to distribute them. With this evidence, we set up a meeting and confronted him with the facts. He readily confessed that he had done it. The obvious effect was to impair one's faith in human nature, and I became quite cynical about any kind of political venture.

The slender defeat also set in motion a wave of indignation. Groups of friends came promptly to insist that I run as an independent candidate. They gave me every assurance that they would raise the money. They promised to subscribe to my candidacy. I permitted them to build up the idea to a point and then finally said, "Now look here, I am sorry, but I cannot undertake an independent campaign. I am a Republican. I am not so old and there will be another time. I will watch the future and try to build my case a little better and then determine what may happen two years hence. The listing of an independent candidate must be at the extreme right on the ballot and it will be difficult, indeed, to persuade people to forsake the party lists and cross over to mark ballots for an independent. I must prefer to wait." That ended all efforts in this direction, but it did not assuage the feeling that developed as the result of this incident.

A few days after election day I was on the main street of Peoria and there I encountered Howard Fuller, the political editor of the *Peoria Star*. He was a genial person and not unfriendly. The things he had written in connection with the campaign, however, obviously had to conform to the political views of the newspaper. To me he said, "What are you doing up here on the street in Peoria so early in the morning?"

To that I said, "Howard, I am campaigning."

"You have just been defeated," he said.

"Oh," I said, "that was just a trial heat. I think I have discovered two things as a result of the campaign. The first is that I learned a lot, and the second is that I believe I discovered what I must do in life, and I am prepared to go at it hammer and tongs, because I must find my place in the political field."

There was ample time to meditate, and certainly one of the things that continued to occur to me was why political life had to be such a dirty business. Did I really, under those circumstances, want to be a congressman after all? Would I really want to be a senator? At times the game did not seem to be worth the gamble, if it had to be played in that fashion and if dirt had to be matched with dirt.

But surely there must be a public conscience that would at some time rebel against this business if it could be stirred to the quick. I gradually made up my mind that it was one of the things to which I would set myself. I decided that when I became a candidate for public office again—and certainly the mood was still upon me—I would do what I could to arouse the electorate to the need for clean campaigns. This was the idealist in me speaking. I expected as much from others who ventured into the political field. I had to make myself believe that political life and public service must be placed on a pedestal if it was to beget the faith, the confidence, and the trust of the people. On that line I was prepared to fight.

8

MR. DIRKSEN GOES TO

WASHINGTON

THEY SAY TIME MARCHES ON. Well, really, time does not march on. The fact is that sage people march through time, and as we go we make history. Time itself is stationary.

As we moved along toward 1932 I thought that I perceived quite well what the general political pattern would be. The groundwork had been well laid in the campaign in 1930, but there would be a different situation in 1932. There were advanced indications at an early date that the magic of Franklin Delano Roosevelt would be sweeping the country. I, however, could not be too concerned about that, for somehow destiny had already laid out the pattern for me and I had no choice but to follow it.

In the period between the election of 1930 and the time for the primary election in 1932, I continued to campaign as much and as best I could. By that time I had a distinct advantage because people in large towns and small, in every one of the six counties, knew who I was. My unmanageable hair had become something of a trademark, and even children could identify me on the street. Moreover, audiences of all kinds had become quite familiar with my speaking style, and the invitations to come for lodge meetings, luncheon clubs, churches, men's groups, public dinners, and every other variety of meetings were far beyond my capacity to accept. This then was a real advantage.

Nor were the county chairmen and the precinct committeemen strangers to me any longer. I began to cultivate them and to make a special point of remembering their names. By primary time in 1932, I believe I had persuaded most of them that that would be the year for me despite the popularity of Democrat Franklin Delano Roosevelt. Members of the American Legion in some thirty or more posts, or in county organizations, were now very definitely in my corner, and this could be a deciding factor. In addition there were many who had had military service, but who were not particularly active in the Veterans of Foreign Wars or the American Legion or any other similar organization, who looked rather kindly upon my ambitions and were enthusiastically willing to help the cause.

That was also true of many institutions. I made a special practice whenever and wherever it could be contrived to appear before high-school student bodies, because I knew how active they could be, particularly in carrying messages to fathers and mothers. I carefully watched as the holidays came and made certain that I would have a number of meetings to address. Memorial Day is a good example. In some small towns it was the custom to hold a public ceremony in the morning and stage a parade. In other areas this was done in the afternoon. I found, therefore, that I could meet with two or even three groups on the same day and thereby enlarge my image. This was equally true of Armistice Day, which was so revered by the veterans of World War I. Wherever they had a fairly substantial group, they did their very best to bring out a crowd on that day.

Then, of course, there were the many fall festivals, harvest home picnics, and homecoming ceremonies. Usually these were the last of the meetings before chilled autumn air cut down the size of crowds. It is at meetings of this kind that one becomes quite intimate with almost everybody in the community, and it was possible to develop points of interest and to deliver a message that proved quite suitable.

Generally the ladies of the town, whether they were identified with the church or a lodge, would undertake to feed all who might wish to come. This had the added incentive of providing a little extra money for the organization staging these affairs. It was also very informal. One could spend an entire day just standing in one spot in the center of the area, shaking hands with people who came up to introduce themselves.

One other factor at issue intruded itself into the campaign, and that was the so-called Jones Act, which had been introduced by Congressman Jones and approved by both branches of Congress. I learned, on examining the *Congressional Record,* that Congressman Hull had voted for the Jones Act. It was quite an extreme measure and provided that a person could be sentenced to the penitentiary if found in possession of a pint of liquor. This act became known all over the country as "The Living for a Pint Act." Quite obviously it placed a man who had amassed most of his fortune from the sale of whiskey in a rather difficult position. Since Hull had voted for it, I made quite an issue of that fact.

This was a particularly potent factor because the Sixteenth Congressional District contained my home city and also the city of Peoria, where quite a number of distilleries had operated. They gave employment to many people, both men and women. I endeavored, sometimes in a sarcastic or cynical way and at other times in a whimsical way, to paint the picture of a great whiskey salesman voting for the Jones Act. One result of the act, of course, was that the distilleries could continue to make and distribute alcoholic beverages only to the extent permitted by federal law, and it became necessary in some cases for them to convert into distilleries for the production of industrial alcohol. Even where they were converted, the impact on jobs was very heavy.

Then, of course, the old issue of the deep water route was still there. My opponent continued to refer to it when, in fact, as I had indicated in the primary of 1930, it was nothing more than a channel in the middle of the river, two hundred feet wide and nine feet deep and navigable for the most part only by barges carrying bulk material. There was disillusionment among the people, since the ocean-going vessels which had been so glibly promised had not materialized and the river remained a dirty barge canal.

Since the primary election came in the month of April under Illinois law, the period in the month of February just before the observance of Lincoln's birthday was a tremendously popular time for holding meetings of all kinds. Among other things, these meetings provided an excellent opportunity to galvanize the spirit of local Republican workers in every one of the counties and helped in raising funds for the party to carry on the campaign. Though there was but one actual birthday for Abraham Lincoln, the various Republican organizations usually started their meetings three or four days prior to the twelfth of February and continued three or four days after. I visited most of them but devoted time only to those dinners that were held in communities within the confines of the Sixteenth Congressional District. These helped the party and I am quite sure they also helped me.

One interesting incident occurred at that time and became a rather powerful political incentive. I continued my chores at the wholesale bakery. We operated a small retail shop in connection with the bakery, and anyone who was available at a given time would wait upon the customers who came in to purchase bakery goods. On one occasion I heard the door open, and as I looked around from the desk where I was sitting, a young man came in. He was a bit furtive and seemed to be extremely fearful about something. I said, "My friend, what can I do for you?"

He looked around at the door and then said, "I escaped from the law."

"What do you mean that you escaped from the law?" I asked.

He replied, "I escaped from the jail in Peoria and I need help."

"Who sent you here?" I asked.

The young man replied, "Father O'Brien of St. Joseph's Catholic Church."

Then I asked, "How did you come to Pekin to find Father O'Brien?"

He said, "I went to a priest in Peoria who knows Father O'Brien and he suggested that I go and see him."

"Why not sit down and tell me your whole story."

He explained that he had been working on a dredge rig operating on the river about fifteen miles north of Peoria. He had a pistol in his belongings on which the stock was broken, and some weeks before, he had gone to Peoria to have it repaired in one of the small shops on South Adams Street. A few weeks later, as soon as he could get away from the dredge, he went to pick it up. A police officer was standing just outside the door of the little shop as he walked out with the pistol in a paper sack.

The young man told me what had happened. "The cop tapped me on the shoulder and said, 'What have you got in that package?' I told him it was a gun I brought down to have repaired."

" 'Well, you'll have to come along with me. You are carrying a concealed weapon and I am compelled to get a warrant for your arrest,' the cop said. So he took me along. I appeared before a magistrate and then they put me in jail. I was a stranger in town and did not know to whom I might turn. But I suppose because I was so young my jailer didn't think I could be a very desperate character, and they did not place me under the strictest kind of security. After some days, the sheriff made me a trusty, and the opportunity came to break from the jail and finally get here, as I told you. First I went to see the boss of the dredge rig and told him what had happened and why I hadn't been working. To that he said, 'I am sorry but I cannot take you back because you are a fugitive from the law. First you will have to call the authorities and get this straightened out before I dare put you back to work.' "

Such was the story this young fellow unfolded. I puzzled over it a little and decided to call the sheriff, whom I knew quite well because I had campaigned with him in 1930. I recited the essentials of the case as they had been told me, and the sheriff advised that it was substantially true. Then I asked if it would be possible to drop the charges so that this boy might go back to work. He agreed to do this.

But to make certain that trouble would not develop from some other source, I called the chief of police in Peoria. He was remotely related to Mrs. Dirksen. I repeated the story to him, and finally he said, "Tell the boy it will be all right and he will not be molested again." Then I called up the boss of the dredge rig, who had a downtown office in Peoria. He thanked me and told me to tell the youngster to come back to work.

I then turned to the young fellow and told him the result of my calls. He fell on his knees, threw his arms around my legs, and began to weep. It was simply unspoken gratitude. I said, "Better get to your feet and get ready to show up for work in the morning. Do you have car fare to get back to Peoria and to the dredge rig? Have you any money at all?"

He said he had no money, and I gave him several dollars for transportation. Then he said, "How can I ever repay you for all this and especially since I am a perfect stranger to you?"

I said, "Young man, you can repay me for all this. Before you leave Pekin, go back to Father O'Brien's, because it is only six or seven blocks from here, and tell him that the man who helped you out and got you back to work is the one who two years ago was charged on election handbills distributed in Bureau County with being a member of the Ku Klux Klan."

I must say that he and Father O'Brien repaid me with compound interest because it was only a few days later, while I was moving in and out of stores in a small town named Chillicothe, that I ran into a very bright young priest by the name of Father Spaulding. We knew each other quite well. As we shook hands, Father Spaulding said to me, "We have already heard what you did for that young deckhand on the dredge, and we fully intend to see that our church is not going to be made a political football any longer. The word will go out that you should be helped." I was, and it proved to be a big reward indeed for a small kindness.

In the political season, audiences are indeed very strange at times. I recall that the weather was threatening one night when I went to the little town of Brimfield in Peoria County for their annual homecoming. A fabulous crowd had assembled, and when I was introduced I said, "Let me make a bargain with you. If I read the signs correctly, it is pretty certain we will have a heavy shower. But you are all home and I am not. It will be very easy for you to get dry clothes, but I am thirty miles from home and must continue to wear wet clothes until I get back there later tonight. I offer you this bargain. If it does begin to rain, I will stay right up on this platform and get wet if you will stay and get wet with me." There were some chuckles and some murmurs. But in a very few minutes the rain began. There was a mad dash in the direction of the city hall just across the way, and I quickly learned that a crowd simply melts in the face of a rain.

Still another incident comes back to me. Only a few miles from my home city was a large area underlaid with a very fine quality of bituminous coal. It was the custom to operate a miners' train from Peoria to the mine and to take the miners back home in the late afternoon. I familiarized myself with the timetable so that I could drive to the mine and get on the train which they called Number 6. It was well filled, and I quickly embraced the opportunity to go from one coach to another shaking hands with the grimy miners, telling them who I was and discussing anything on which they might have questions. What was important about this was that these people seldom ventured out to political meetings, and obviously this was about the only way to contact them and tell my story. I rode that miners' train several times before election day.

I had an opportunity to tell them about the Bible covered with khaki cloth that I picked up in Paris before I went to the front in World War I. I told the miners that that also was a rather hazardous line of endeavor, since one never knew when the balloon might be burned by enemy planes and char the observer into a cinder. I also told them that, in the dark hours when one was in a deep dugout and fairly safe from bombs and heavy howitzer shells, I would light a candle and read the Bible and underscore many passages that had particular appeal for me. So here were the miners just out of a coal mine finding that same kind of comfort from that same book.

Quite often people wonder why I interlard speeches with quotations from the Scriptures. The reason is twofold. There is the fact that in the quiet examination of the Bible under the conditions on the front, there were so many passages which seemed to fit every circumstance of life; and, second, I discovered so many meanings which had previously seemed rather obscure. It was only natural, therefore, that these should creep into my ordinary speech as well as into speeches which had been prepared for certain occasions.

Again I had to deal with that interesting area in the Sixteenth Congressional District which was populated in considerable part by people of Italian extraction. When the Eighteenth Amendment was enforced, many of the people in this area became engaged in the business of manufacturing and distributing bootleg liquor. No use moralizing on the subject—it was a condition that existed. In some of the communities in this area, the bars were quite open, despite the danger of being raided by prohibition agents. The general public could enter and be served.

The one establishment that intrigued me most, however, was a funeral parlor. In the front section there was a display of caskets and other paraphernalia of the undertaker's business, but a door led from this room to a room in the rear which seemed to have about the longest bar I had seen. The place was quite filled when I entered, and it seemed to be a jolly, carefree crowd. They were drinking quite freely, quite oblivious of the fact that all this was in violation of existing law.

Regardless of this, I realized that they were all voters, and I circulated among them, shook hands with everyone, and indicated my great desire to go to Congress. I expressed the fervent hope that they might vote for me. These were really very decent people. They worked hard. They went to church. They were frugal. They raised families. They paid their taxes. In the main, they were law abiding; their one weakness was that they did not believe that a government should undertake to control the tastes and habits of the people, and they were determined not to comply with the Eighteenth Amendment. What is more, despite my experience in the 1930 campaign when at the last minute they had charged me with being a member of the Ku Klux Klan, they were now in an entirely different mood and completely trusted me. They became my friends and I felt certain that this time I would receive my share of that vote.

The economic slump began in October 1929 and had settled like some evil pall upon the economic structure of the country. It began to spell itself out in terms of lower prices, a slowdown in business, and resulting jobless-ness. As time went by, it became evident that this creeping dislocation was going to have a deep impact upon the elections. One very expressive and unrestrained state senator who was a candidate for reelection limited his speeches to three items. He would go before an audience and, in a most vigorous way, begin by saying, "Ladies and Gentlmen, the issues in this campaign are very simple. They are bread, booze, and business." In a sense he was quite right, because those were the issues to which the public re-sponded, and they were issues moving to the fore as the primary election came closer.

In the final stages of the campaign, my opponent resorted to virtually every device that was honorable to secure the nomination for his twelfth term in Congress. He made unlimited use of radio, newspapers, handbills, sound trucks, and every other publicity device. He had an unlimited amount of money to spend for this purpose. Even in the second primary campaign, I had limited funds and had to offset all of this advertising by my own energy and invention. There were no other forces I could bring to bear.

From time to time I have mentioned the American Legion and how much it meant to me. Perhaps in justice to the American Legion I should make it plain that it was not a political organization. As a matter of fact, no one can occupy an office in the American Legion if he occupies a political-party office for which he receives compensation. But because of the kinship of the uniform and the common purposes to which we were all dedicated, the veterans of World War I became an exceedingly powerful influence at the polls—serving as workers, providing the poll watchers, electioneering day after day, and doing all those things that assure a fair and honest election.

My visits to the men's clubs of the various churches in the six counties proved to be one of the most effective activities in which I engaged. Even in the smaller communities, these clubs were exceedingly well attended by men who were active in the affairs of the community, and that meant, among other things, political affairs. They could have a decisive effect upon the outcome of any election.

My visits to the high schools and colleges in the district continued as before. One particular high-school incident still comes back to me when I think of this rugged struggle. I was invited to address the students on Armistice Day. It was the largest school in the congressional district and had the largest student body. When I arrived the principal looked at me and said, "Young man, have you ever had any experience in addressing a large audience of lusty, vocal and uninhibited high-school students?" I said that I had had some. Then he observed, "I should warn you that if they do not like you and what you say, they can be a rather boisterous lot and they manifest their feelings in a resounding way. In view of all this, do you feel that we should go through with this program?"

"Oh, I think so," I said.

And so at the appropriate time the students filed into the auditorium. I must say that it was a large and vigorous-looking crowd. The principal presented me in a short statement and remarked that I was seeking the congressional nomination. From that point I was on my own. There was a tremendous cheer, after which I tried to tell my story. When I had finished they stood up and gave me a standing ovation. Although for the most part they were not old enough to be voters, I knew that they would certainly report to their fathers and mothers at dinner and probably to others before election day.

In that second campaign, we had a candidate for the office of sheriff who had a very impressive war record. As I recall, he had been decorated with the Distinguished Service Cross. Having been a soldier myself and having had some experience, I knew what a soldier had to do to earn such a coveted medal. It required service which was regarded as over and above and beyond the call of duty.

At some point rather late in the campaign, when most of the candidates had finished their late meetings, he said, "Well, fellows, it looks as if the campaign is about over. Why not come out to my place. I may be able to find a little drink for you."

"I believe I would enjoy a drink, because I am tired and weary," I said. "This daily grind is really taking its toll."

There were at least a half dozen other candidates for different offices, and we all went to our friend's house and there had a drink. It was quite customary each evening to recount the highlights of the day and the week and to recall the different experiences each of us had had. We had all become good friends and wished each other success on the great day which lay immediately ahead.

While the banter and conversation continued, there was a knock on the door and our host went to respond. He opened the door rather cautiously and stepped out on the porch. He was gone for quite some time. Meanwhile, I had pushed a curtain aside to see what was going on at such a late hour. I could not make out who the man was on the porch, but I noticed that they were carrying on a very animated conversation. I also noticed one other thing; there were at least four large automobiles along the curb in front of our host's house, and my immediate appraisal was that they were Cadillacs. After a time he returned to us.

As he rejoined the group of candidates, I said, "Who were your late callers? It is nearly midnight."

"Well," he said, "you may believe it or not, but they are all from Chicago."

Then I asked, "What in the world are they doing down here at this hour?"

He looked a little sideways and said, "You fellows have all been in the army and you know how it is. During your army career you make a lot of buddies and friends from all over, and you never know what happens to them or what activities they may get into once the war is over. These fellows, frankly, have gotten into the rackets in Chicago. I knew them back in army days. They just heard that I am a candidate for sheriff, so they decided to drive down and reconnoiter and see whether or not they could be helpful. Believe it or not, they brought all their equipment and their hardware, and when I say hardware, I am certain you know exactly what I mean."

My comment was, "I hope you sent them on their way and told them not to come back."

To that he responded by saying, "I told them that we did not run elections down here like they do in some areas in Chicago." That seemed to be the end of the incident, but I could not avoid noting the irony of this offer on the part of Chicago's leading racketeers to help elect a sheriff.

I have said over and over again that as election day activities move along and one notes carloads of men and women going to the polls to vote, either in charge of election workers or on their own, one gets a feeling of elation. It is in the air. I do not know what the experience of other candidates has been in this respect, but I know full well what has happened in my case. I had felt two years earlier that somehow there was something wrong; this time it was quite different. Victory was in the air, and I was quite certain that I would win.

In a small city like Pekin, election night brought out the people to listen to the returns wherever they could. Early in the evening, candidates and their friends usually met at the *Pekin Daily Times* office where the staff sought to monitor every area in the county and district to get results as quickly as possible. Sometimes they gathered a little later at the office of the county clerk, because precinct committeemen and county chairmen usually had instructions to phone the county clerk as soon as the vote had been counted and a report was available. Later in the evening, they repaired to a candidate's home knowing there would be radio facilities to get returns from the entire district. And so it was. Little by little as the returns came in, they were reassuring, especially from the counties furthest away from my home town. And when it appeared that the votes had finally been counted every-where, it was indicated that I had actually won the Republican nomination for Congress by twenty-three hundred votes.

In that year of 1932, the Democratic party in Illinois's Sixteenth District had nominated a very kindly old gentleman by the name of Dr. Carr. He was a retired minister. I liked Dr. Carr. I had occasion to visit with him a good many times in the course of the campaign. I assured him that I would be a gentleman in every respect and conduct a campaign based upon the issues involved. No personalities would be involved. He gave me a similar as-surance. I went on the theory that it was up to him to sell his own candidacy and it was up to me to sell mine. I undertook it in a very simple, direct way during the summer and autumn. It was a very active campaign, but not especially eventful. By election day my candidate for Congress had had a lib-eral education. Certainly I knew a great deal more than I had in 1930, and many fine people had helped me to learn some hard facts about politics.

The first of these was my wife. She had an unerring instinct for determin-ing whether a certain appeal to the electorate would or would not be effective, and in this respect I came to value her judgment highly. She had also been an auditor in a large retail store and had a very well defined sense of accounting. We determined that we would not go through the heartbreaking experience of concluding a campaign with a deficit. If the bills have not been paid when a campaign is over, it is difficult to obtain contributions to pay them. I know of nothing which can so handicap a candidate as to have a deficit when he cannot afford it.

Often candidates, even for the office of Representative in Congress, have discovered that they were commited by friends and associates for thousands upon thousands of dollars which they could not pay, and we were determined to avoid that kind of postelection grief.

There was one dedicated friend to whom I owe so much and I would be remiss indeed if I failed to mention him. His name was George Chiames. He was of Greek ancestry. In his earlier years he drove a Checker taxicab in Chicago, a tough assignment which can develop character or destroy it. George Chiames could be rough and tough, or he could speak eloquently of the classical authors, leaders, and dramatists in the Golden Age of ancient Greece.

George Chiames realized, reasonably early in his career, that driving a taxicab had no future for a person with ambition and a fine, perceptive mind. So there came a day when he shook the dust of Chicago from his shoes, and with only modest resources boarded a train for Peoria. There were quite a number of people of Greek ancestry there, and it did not take long for him to identify himself with this group. He began to explore various opportunities and possibilities. As a result, he developed a very successful billiard parlor which was patronized by all groups in the city. He ventured into other enterprises and all those were quite successful; he had a bit of the Midas touch. He became active in a number of organizations, including the American Legion and the American Hellenic Educational and Progress Association. He dabbled a bit in politics, and it was through this medium that we became firm friends.

Whenever the campaign required additional funds, he addressed himself to raising them with vigor and also with success. I became the godfather of his first child and maintained a close personal relationship with the entire family. Now we count his widow and his children among our best friends.

One other devoted friend whom I would like to salute was then an assistant cashier at the Central National Bank in Peoria. His name was N. Curtis Cation. I recall that before I went to the Congress I journeyed to Peoria to bid him goodbye. We shook hands as I sat down with him at his desk in the bank, and I said, "Well, Curt, the great day of my life is at hand. Perhaps you may have a word of advice before I depart?"

He puzzled for a moment and finally said, "Ev, I don't believe you need any advice from me, although I might make this observation as you go to assume some great responsibilities in Washington. As a general proposition it will not be too important how you vote but rather *why* you vote for or against some measure. If you have a good reason for voting as you do, certainly you will be able to defend that vote." I needed nothing more. As events unfolded, I had reason to think about Curt Cation many times. How many measures there were where politics dictated a vote on one side, but reason and logic indicated an opposite vote.

In a political campaign of congressional dimensions, if a candidate is a conformist and follows the usual political pattern, he purchases small cards with his name and picture and a few details concerning election day. He uses these when he shakes hands with voters to be sure that the name and the image register. He also purchases handbills and usually writes his own text for these. He buys cards about eight inches by twelve inches, which are generally tacked on telephone and highway poles. These must be printed in a union shop; they must be stamped by an authorized union billposter and in some cases actually tacked up by a member of an authorized union. He must have a great supply of circulars to be used at political meetings. These give some biographical details and quote some complimentary comments by newspaper writers and others.

I went through all this like every other candidate because it appeared to be the accepted thing to do, but I learned quickly that the accepted thing was not always the effective thing. First of all, the placards were usually so small and the print so fine that people had to resort to bifocals to read even the larger print. Accordingly, I insisted on much larger cards with a minimum of print and with my name in heavy letters so they would not forget it. I learned also that motorists on the highways, looking at cards tacked on poles, could scarcely make out the name or the photographs at a speed of forty miles an hour or more. Inasmuch as larger cards would not solve the problem, I rapidly abandoned the idea of using this type of advertising. Instead we used billboards, but the only thing of value was the name and the office in large print, preferably in color together with a very good likeness. For people on the highways this was, by all odds, the very best kind of advertising. I also learned that instead of having a variety of campaign folders, I could have just one with a modest amount of reading matter. These one could have printed in large quantities at a minimum cost.

I also noticed in the various political meetings that age was dominant. By this I mean that older people were deeply interested in campaign meetings. They would not forget to vote on election day, and hence these people became an area of special appeal.

As the campaign moved closer and closer to election day in November 1932, it was quite evident that the market crash was really taking its political toll. Farm prices continued to drop and farmers generally became quite sour on the Republican administration. The number of jobless began to multiply and, in the shadow of the election, the number had run to many millions in all parts of the country. The aggravation which had developed over the Eighteenth Amendment to the Constitution was enhanced by enforcement of that amendment and the implementing statutes. Business was generally in the doldrums. The state senator who summed up the issues of 1932 as "Bread, Booze, and Business" was not far wrong. These were creature issues which could be simply stated and were very effective. It was quite evident by election time that they would determine the outcome.

To this, of course, one must add the appeal and the personality of Franklin Delano Roosevelt. The Democratic high command had excellent speech writers. They coined phrases that people liked to hear. They kept those speeches on very simple lines, and the methods of communication with the voter were excellent. It was a new approach, politically.

The Republicans in our district had hoped somehow to offset all this by negotiating with the national committee to have the train that took President Hoover across the country to come into our area. At long last we succeeded. The date and the time were set for the president to come through and make brief appearances at a number of stops and a short platform speech at Peoria.

On the appointed day, as I recall, the train was to arrive in Peoria about one o'clock in the afternoon. Harry Scranton, the Republican county chairman, had undertaken to advertise in every publicity medium at his command in the hope of developing a real crowd, not merely to honor the president of the United States, but to reap the benefit of all this in the coming elections. He estimated seventy-five thousand people had gathered in the area near the Rock Island Railroad Station in Peoria.

The occasion afforded an opportunity to present to this huge crowd all the local, county, and state candidates. It also gave me an opportunity to address the crowd until the train arrived. It was an intriguing experience. It was a good deal like building a house one room at a time, not knowing how many rooms there would be. All the while the crowd was alert to any train whistle that might indicate that the Hoover train was approaching.

I am quite certain, as I try to remember, that I must have addressed that crowd for nearly ninety minutes and used virtually every political story and anecdote I knew in order to retain their attention and to keep them from becoming weary, because they were standing, of course.

I watched that huge crowd and noted that they shifted weight from one leg to another. I could detect a certain weariness the longer they stood, and I tried to stir their attention at regular intervals by stories told slowly and in simple language so that all could understand. If it was a good story it begot a vigorous laugh, and that laugh had the biological effect of accelerating the blood flow of those in the crowd, and then their attention quickly came back to the business at hand. It was a curious experience and from it I learned something of the storytelling art.

At long last came the train whistle. I uttered a fervent prayer of thanks. I was beginning to run out of time, energy, stories, and ideas suited to the occasion, since there was no way of properly organizing a speech of that kind. The train finally moved into the station with the last car closest to the special platform that had been set up. President Hoover made a very short speech. He expressed his gratitude for the opportunity to be in Peoria. He sought to pinpoint and emphasize two or three issues without much amplification. In a short time there came a loud toot of the locomotive whistle, and everybody knew that that was the end of the speech and that the train would be moving off toward other cities.

As it moved away and finally out of sight, Chairman Scranton was still with me on the platform. The first thing he said was, "Did you notice that not a single hat went into the air?"

"Yes, Harry, I noticed it, and I also noticed that there was virtually no applause when President Hoover finished. There was some but not much."

He turned to me and said, "Ev, I'm afraid we're sunk."

I thought that over for a moment and finally said, "Harry, that may be true for a good deal of the Republican ticket, but I do not believe that it will include one person."

"Who's that?" he asked.

I said, "That's me!"

He looked at me with some astonishment and said, "You don't believe you are going to win do you?" My rejoinder to that was, "Why do you think I have been working like a madman, trying to put the personal touch on every aspect of this campaign from the day it started? I do not know how the other candidates will fare, but I do know that I am going to win."

Election day came. The spirit and hopes of all those associated with me in the campaign were high. We had endeavored to touch every base. We had our poll watchers, suitably armed with the necessary certificates signed by the candidate, so that every polling place could be monitored to insure a fair and honest crowd.

It turned out as I expected. When the votes of the Sixteenth Congressional District were counted, the score sheet showed that the voters had chosen Franklin Delano Roosevelt, the Democratic candidate for president, by twenty-three thousand votes, and had also elected Everett McKinley Dirksen, the Republican candidate for Congress, by twenty-three thousand. What could be fairer than that?

Did I still want to be a senator? That question certainly took on fresh significance.

9

"YOU ONE-TERMER"

WHAT A GREAT ADVENTURE this was to be in my life—to be one of 435 representatives in Congress. I was then thirty-six years of age. It was not the custom in Illinois to elect younger men to Congress, for reasons quite unknown to me. It seemed to be a traditional concept that anyone seeking to represent a constituency consisting of six counties with about 350,000 people should have already had a successful business career and have developed the judgment that comes with the years before undertaking to help make the nation's laws. Evidently I had broken that tradition, and obviously it would be public life in a goldfish bowl. I noticed, however, that there were many young men from different states who had been elected to Congress on what seemed like a new wave in public life, and I was certain that, whether they were Democrats or Republicans, they would be good company.

First came the many housekeeping chores. I called them housekeeping chores for want of a better term. It appeared to me that every real-estate agency and broker in the District of Columbia had something to sell or rent; they fortified me with telegrams, letters, and brochures long before I left Illinois. There was a mountain of requests for positions on whatever staff I must set up. The huge displacement of incumbent members in 1932 meant that their personnel would be unemployed at the end of the session. They were about to be uprooted and that, of course, was a thoroughly serious matter for them.

Election to a high public office quickly generates all manner of demands on the pocketbook for the newly elected official no matter how slender his resources may be. Organized charities from every section of the country were quick to present their causes to me and to ask for assistance. There were churches that had been beset with one form of catastrophe or another, whether it was fire or tornado damage or something else that required a rebuilding of the church edifice. Any number of churches felt it was necessary to install a pipe organ and would be delighted with a contribution for that purpose. Lodges and fraternal organizations were sponsoring girls' basketball teams or boys' football teams or some other athletic organization, and since it would cost money to send them afield to play in competitive contests, they welcomed donations. There came requests for autographed books, and for discarded hats and neckties—preferably autographed—which could be raffled at public functions to develop funds.

And then, of course, there were the individual demands. A candidate never knows how many ardent admirers and faithful workers he has in a campaign until it is over and he has been successful. Individuals who were hard pressed for funds were quick to describe how diligently they had worked in the campaign and ask whether I could spare a hundred dollars for three or four months? Previous experience had taught me that these were not loans but gifts. But there were other requests also, and some were most intriguing. There was, for example, a neighbor in my home city who was building a rock garden and who thought that rocks from different parts of the country would give it tone and prestige. Accordingly, she asked if I would be so kind as to go down to the Chesapeake Bay and gather some rocks that might look good in her rock garden. They were not to be so large that the parcel post cost would be too great. Frivolous as this sounds, there were many requests of this nature. I suppose it is all a part of our democracy.

One item that never ceased to interest me was that the federal government had discontinued the practice of sending out free garden and flower seeds. At one time these could be had for the asking, and even if a constituent made no request, he was likely to receive a large assortment of such seeds in a manila envelope anyway. It was quite evident that there were many who thought the practice continued, even though it had been abandoned for nearly a decade. And then came those back home who were interested in federal positions. It was their conviction that, as a new congressman, I would shake the federal plum tree and have all manner of federal jobs fall in my lap. They had forgotten, first of all, that a Democratic president was being inaugurated and, second, that since the complexion of the new Congress was decidedly Democratic, there would be few jobs for the Republican party. Answering these requests and making the answers sound plausible and persuasive was not an easy task. But it had to be done and, in due course, I set myself to it as firmly as I could.

What sheer exhilaration it was for a country boy to see the illuminated dome of the Capitol of the United States of America for the first time in his life! I picked up my bags and walked out of Union Station in Washington, and there within a stone's throw was the Capitol. It is a difficult thing to describe now precisely how I felt on that occasion, knowing that I was to become a part of the national scene.

But I was equally jubilant of spirit as I saw other institutions in the nation's capital. There was the Lincoln Memorial built from subscriptions of youngsters in the forty-eight states, with the huge bronze statue of Lincoln suffused with soft light, giving him an almost eerie appearance. There were the wide avenues and the many government structures. There was the Smithsonian Institution, which, strangely enough, had been built with a legacy left to this country by an Englishman named James Smithson. There was that immensely impressive obelisk that had been erected in memory of George Washington. It was more than five hundred feet high and was bathed in soft light. These were but a few of the things that deeply impressed me, and I felt a little like a bewildered schoolboy.

One of the most intriguing things in Washington to me was the statue erected to the memory of William Jennings Bryan. It was of more than casual interest to me since Bryan was born in Illinois and did his college work at Illinois State College at Jacksonville. I remembered him, in part, as the great temperance crusader and dry reformer. And how ironic it was that his statue was erected quite close to the only brewery in Washington that might operate again whenever the Congress repealed the statutes implementing the Eighteenth Amendment to the Constitution. Here, then, history had been made and here more history was to be made, and I would be a part of it.

The first official matters that had to be disposed of were essentially routine. I had settled the secretarial problem by engaging the services of a man who had been the secretary to a Republican congressman twelve or fourteen years before. I learned of him quite by accident and took the initiative in having him come to see me to determine whether he was interested in returning to Washington, and also to find out whether he had an agreeable personality and would, in my judgment, make a good secretary.

He was quite familiar with the usual routine of filing for office space, which was allotted on the basis of seniority; doing whatever was required to obtain stationery and establish a stationery account; preparing biographical data for the *Congressional Directory;* putting committee preferences in proper hands; and letting it be generally known that, as one of the few surviving

Republican candidates in the last election, I esteemed myself to be a big frog in the legislative puddle—a fact which I felt should be suitably recognized. I discovered, to my discomfiture, that all this was not too important after all.

The first Republican party conference was held on the morning of the day that the Seventy-third Congress was to convene. At that conference the party leaders would be selected and presented to the House for approval. This included a candidate for the speakership, for parliamentarian, for sergeant at arms, for clerk of the House, and certain other party offices. Of course, all this was not taken too seriously. In the House of Representatives, the New Deal landslide accounted for 313 Democrats. There were only 117 Republicans. Since House officials were elected on a strict party basis, the Republicans knew at the very outset that the conference was merely going through the motions. At the other end of the Capitol this situation was not quite so bad, and yet it was decidedly in a state of imbalance, because the new Congress would be graced with 59 Democratic senators and 36 Republican senators.

It may be interesting to note, after the lapse of many years, that of the 531 men and women who served in the House and Senate in the Seventy-third Congress, only six still remained when the Ninety-first Congress convened. Such is attrition in public life. The six out of that great body who were still there in 1969 included Senator Richard Russell, of Georgia; Senator Stephen Young, of Ohio; Senator Jennings Randolph, of West Virginia; Congressman Wright Patman, of Texas; Speaker John McCormack, of Massachusetts; and myself.

I watched intently as the party conference selected Congressman Bertrand Snell, of Potsdam, New York, to be the Republican floor leader and Congressman Joseph Martin of Massachusetts to be the whip or deputy leader. At a subsequent meeting of the conference, the chairman and members of the Republican National Congressional Campaign Committee would be selected. I was fascinated to see the chairman and members of the committee, whose function it was to consider the composition of the various House committees, note the number of committee vacancies occasioned by election defeats, strike an agreement with the Democratic committee as to the ratio of the two parties on the various committees, and then proceed to make assignments to all those yet unassigned.

When this seemingly routine business was concluded, there came from members who had served in the Congress over a period of years the post-mortems over the election of 1932. At that moment, I recall that a sense of disillusionment struck me. The longer the discussion continued, the more these questions haunted my mind. Where are the Daniel Websters and the Henry Clays? Where are the Calhouns and the Bentons? Where are the Garfields and McKinleys? Where are the James Manns and the Joseph Cannons? Where are all the great, thundering leaders I had expected to see? These were all people not unlike the people I encountered in the six counties that comprised the Illinois's Sixteenth Congressional District. I presume many others before my time have experienced a similar disillusionment and, perhaps, I was expecting entirely too much.

On that same day—March 4, 1933—the House of Representatives was called to order by the clerk of the House. This is the usual procedure. There was a call of the roll and one had a chance, for the first time, to follow the names of those who were swept into office in the 1932 landslide. There was the usual routine business and it was quickly dispatched. The party slates for the various House posts were presented and quickly disposed of. When I say "disposed," I mean that the Republican slate was quickly and decisively voted down, because these matters are dispatched by a strictly party line vote. There was much chuckling as the various routine matters were handled because our Democratic brethren were already conscious of our vows. They were, of course, quite courteous but also a bit arrogant about it all, and why not? They had the presidency along with comfortable majorities in both branches. Comfortable is an understatement—their majority was roughly three to one. What was equally obvious was that this great Democratic host could be expected to hew to the party line, and it would not be unduly difficult for the Roosevelt regime to push its program through Congress.

I wondered, from the day I set foot in the nation's capital, what I should or could do so far as social obligations were concerned. Certainly in my state of nonaffluence it would be impossible to cut a wide social swath. A little of it, of course, by way of extracurricular life would spring from committee assignments. When I was named to the Committee on the District of Columbia, I explored the matter and discovered that Washington had no local government. It operated under a three-man board of commissioners. They were appointed by the president, and one had to be an officer in the Corps of Engineers. While these were the titular heads of the local government, the real force in all affairs relating to the District lay with the Board of Trade. It had an endless number of committees to deal with taxes, improvements, bridges, relations with Congress, and many others. Those who were assigned to these tasks were very diligent indeed. This meant that I was invited to the Board of Trade dinners, and there I quickly encountered some of the leading lights in Washington society.

But I pursued this social matter because I wanted to be so very correct in what I did. After I had been in the Congress some weeks, I took account of a congressman from Pennsylvania by the name of Louis McFadden. He either had been or was at that time chairman of the House Committee on Banking and Currency, and I struck up an attachment with him in the belief that he could be useful and helpful when the occasion presented itself. I said to him one day, "Mr. McFadden, I am a new member of Congress and you've been here for some time."

To that he said, "Well, Dirksen, I have been and I am still in the banking business in Pennsylvania. Long years ago I began to wonder about Congress and what it would be like to be a member and to inflict my views on that body. I decided to run for the office and promised myself that I would not stay longer than one term. I was elected but I didn't keep that promise to myself, and now I have been here for sixteen years."

"Well, Mr. McFadden," I went on, "what I wanted to ask was how much social activity must one engage in in order to get along? I've been told that you can make little or no progress unless you join a country club to which other members of the House belong, as this gives you an opportunity to speak with them about all the matters you would like to see accomplished."

Almost immediately he pooh-poohed the idea. He said, "Do not let anybody sell you that bill of goods. I have participated in virtually no social activities, but I got along and moved to the top in the committee structure because I did my homework and paid attention to my legislative chores." His advice gave me a modest amount of comfort, and it proved sound.

One other thing happened in the early weeks that gave me a little concern. Washington, as everybody knows, has its little poker parties and is very clubby. Members of the House and Senate and their friends attended weekly poker parties in a room above the Occidental Restaurant or at the University Club. All these were well attended, and the stakes, according to reports, were quite high. Those who were active with the cards kept a constant lookout for new recruits and new prey (if that is the appropriate word). As a result, a member who had been in Congress for some years engaged my ear while we were standing beside the House rail enjoying a smoke. "Dirksen," he said, "I've an idea that perhaps you'd like to sit in on a little poker party one night this week at the University Club. It is a nice friendly game, and most of us who attend are members of the House."

I puzzled for a moment over this and then said, much to his chagrin and disappointment, "Dan, of all the things I do not have first on the list is what you would call card sense. I am simply not card minded or gambling minded. I know full well that I have no competence in that field and, more than that, I've never actually had the urge to gamble. If I ever did, it would have been cured by an incident which happened in Germany when I was on patrol duty in the town of Trier." I told him about what I had seen at the celebrated Porta Nigra Hotel.

My sheer jubilation over being a congressman was rather short lived. The very first bill to be presented to the House was, at the moment, not even in printed form. It had been rushed through a committee by securing unanimous consent to depart from the standing rules of the House, and it was first considered while still in typewritten form. The history books refer to it as the Economy Act, but its actual legislative title was A Bill to Maintain the Credit of the United States Government. Since there were no copies to go around, we had to be content with an explanation of this measure by the persons in charge. The debate was rather sharply limited.

I listened carefully. It became quite clear that the first target of the Economy Act was to be the veterans of World War I who were disabled but whose disabilities were not connected with military service. This was a substantial group and the measure proposed to chop them off the rolls.

The second group to feel the blow were those on the civilian rolls of the federal government. As I contemplated the idea of the administration's building an economy-and-frugality image on a foundation consisting of disabled veterans and civilian workers, I concluded that it was unfair, unjust, and indefensible. I could not bring myself to support it. So, the very first vote that I cast on the record in the Seventy-third Congress was in opposition to the program of President Franklin D. Roosevelt.

In a few days the deluge came. There were letters and telegrams by the thousands. They came from political friends and enemies alike. I watched them pile up on my desk and, after examining perhaps a hundred or more, I began to feel that my budding political career was to come to an end almost before it was born. I wept. My mind went back to the advice of my old friend Curtis Cation, the banker in Peoria, when he assured me that it was not how I voted but the reason for voting in a particular way that would count because it could be defended.

Perhaps the greatest blow of all was a telegram from a very special friend for whom I had high respect and great affection. In his wire he did not even bother to salute me by saying "Dear Everett" or "Dear Congressman" or "Dear Ev." He merely said, "You one-termer, time cannot move fast enough to vote you out of office." As I looked at that telegram I thought of the wounded Caesar who, looking up, saw Brutus in the band of assassins stabbing him and said, "Et tu, Brute."

That first session of Seventy-third Congress was often referred to as the hundred-day session, but actually it was only ninety-nine days. It was indeed a romping legislative lark. The New Deal theme for the session was built around the three Rs—relief, reform, and recovery.

One of the first orders of business was the repeal of the Eighteenth Amendment, which prohibited the manufacture and sale of intoxicating beverages in interstate commerce. This was the so-called Prohibition Amendment. I had often thought of this amendment not simply in terms of its restriction upon the tastes and habits of the people, but rather as the only amendment to the Constitution that raised a stop sign upon the people rather than on government. If one takes time to examine amendments like those contained in the Bill of Rights, he will quickly note that they all begin by saying, "Congress shall make no law . . . " The Eighteenth Amendment, however, approached this problem from an entirely opposite standpoint. The marvel is that it was ever passed by Congress and ratified by the necessary number of states. The resolution for a new amendment, to repeal the Eighteenth Amendment, went through the New Deal Congress in February by an overwhelming vote and was sent to the forty-eight states for ratification. It was ratified by the requisite number of states in December. That was the only time in our constitutional history that an amendment was proposed, approved, sent to the states, and ratified in a period of nine months. This was quite understandable, because it was alien to the preamble, which begins with the words, "We the people . . . "

As I recall, it was in that first session of the Seventy-third Congress that the Tennessee Valley Authority was created and launched. Prior to that time it had been generally referred to as Muscle Shoals. But from 1933 until this hour it has been known as the Tennessee Valley Authority. Since then it has been expanded and reexpanded until today it is a giant enterprise. All this was done to the great dismay of those involved in utilities.

It was also in that first session of the Seventy-third Congress that a bank holiday for a period of four days was declared and the banks were closed. There were thousands of visitors in Washington who had come with their checkbooks but with only a modest amount of currency. They found themselves stranded, and I recall how many people from home came to tax my slender resources. Actually, it offered no real difficulty because the House of Representatives maintained a kind of private bank of its own in the disbursing office, which was under the direction of the sergeant at arms. On this bank I could write private checks in a checkbook specially printed for the members of Congress, and, in fact, I could write postdated checks and obtain cash with which I could help friends and constituents until the bank holiday came to an end. This was also the session in which the National Industrial Recovery Act was placed on the statute books.

This Emergency Banking Act also called in all gold and all gold certificates. A great many people were outraged and thought President Roosevelt was about to set himself up as a dictator. Some citizens threatened to move to Canada or Peru or other places. They were quite outraged and wondered what would come next. To be exact, the next proposal on which the Congress took action was a relief measure. It was the creation of the Civilian Conservation Corps. The purpose was to enroll 250,000 jobless young men between the ages of eighteen and twenty-five and put them to work on reforestation, soil conservation, and related activities. I recall that at one point they were rather derisively referred to as the "Sapling Army." They were under military direction and there were those who began to speculate as to whether this might be the beginning of an effort to militarize the country.

As I recall, the camps were desegregated, but racial feeling was not so high in those days and not too many complaints were entered or arguments offered on this score. It was necessary to build wooden barracks to house this young army, and that meant that the location of a camp had some impact upon trade and commerce in a given area. The locations of these camps became a matter of some concern to congressmen and senators and was regarded as a type of patronage. It was later that other difficulties came to the fore. Local patriots who had occasion to examine the camp libraries, which were used in the instruction of the young men, pointed out that they included volumes that were then regarded as pro-communist, and this evoked many fulminations in different parts of the country.

But it was in May of the celebrated ninety-nine-day session that the alphabet soup really began to boil. Its ingredients included FERA, AAA, TVA, USES, HOLC, FCA and NIRA. At a later time there were to be a good many others.

The FERA meant the Federal Emergency Relief Administration. This was the day and age of Harry Hopkins, who had been appointed as the relief administrator. Mr. Hopkins had been identified with relief work for a number of years and finally found himself in New York, where he became a friend to Governor Roosevelt. It was through this connection that he was made administrator. It was he who coined the slogan "We shall spend and spend, tax and tax, elect and elect." He became the symbol of the New Deal to those who violently disagreed with it. Actually, Harry Hopkins was a shy and retiring type. Whenever I saw him he did not seem to be very well and, as the history books indicate, he died at the age of fifty-six.

Then came the Agricultural Adjustment Administration to deal with the depressed conditions of farmers everywhere. Farm prices had dropped into the cellar. This was true of virtually every basic farm commodity, including corn and wheat, cotton and rice, hogs and dairy products. It was proposed to use the so-called parity formula, which sought to balance farm prices with farm expenditures for a base period from 1909 to 1914.

The approach of this new concept in agriculture was simple enough. We were confronted with a huge surplus of most farm commodities, and the hope was to equate supply and demand so that prices would rise. This was expected to develop a market economy. There was, therefore, a call upon farmers to reduce their acres and in return receive a benefit or rental payment from the federal government. I shall never forget the day when I encountered the Honorable Cordell Hull, secretary of state, and asked him rather casually what he thought of the farm program. His reply was a classic. He said, "At first they will demur at the idea of subsidies, later they will expect them, and still later they will demand them."

With Secretary Henry Agard Wallace presiding over the destinies of the Department of Agriculture, this program had full official blessing, and he really worked at it with conviction and some emotion. First came the plow-under-crops campaign, and later the liquidation of an estimated fifteen million little pigs that were committed to the rendering vats.

The program contained, however, another item. This was the famous Thomas Amendment, named for Senator John Thomas of Oklahoma. It permitted the president to inflate the currency in a number of ways: he could change the gold content of the dollar; he could decree the free coinage of silver at a ratio to gold which he was to determine; and he could also, by presidential order, decree the issuance of paper currency to the amount of three billion dollars. What upset conservatives and critics of the New Deal was, however, the devaluation of the gold content of the dollar, which had been fixed by law many years before and which had remained stable for a long period of time. I can still hear the imprecations on the floor of Congress which were hurled at the administration. I can still hear the prophecies of doom and disaster for the country. How interesting it is to look back over the years and to note that we are still wrestling with the farm problem and with the same basic concept of seeking to equate supply and demand in one way or another.

Then came the TVA Act, for which Senator George Norris of Nebraska carried on a vigorous crusade. He proposed to build dams, power plants, fertilizer plants, explosive plants, and transmission lines. He wanted to provide electric power to the municipalities in that general area and to engage in related activities. One look at the area that would be served in seven states quickly indicated that, in due course, this would become an empire in itself.

When this act went on the books there came a great cry of anguish from those identified with private utilities and from the holders of utilities stock. They saw in all this a huge all-powerful competitor, and it brought fear and misgiving, but it has grown steadily from the day that the TVA Act was placed on the statute books. It always interested me that one of the three appointed directors was David E. Lilienthal, born in my home county in Illinois in a modest town called Morton.

The next New Deal venture was the creation of USES, the United States Employment Service. It was to be a cooperative venture between the states and the federal government. There was to be a nationwide system of employment offices, but both states and the federal government were to contribute to its operation and maintenance. It has continued from that day to this.

Then came the HOLC, the Homeowners Loan Corporation. It took account of the fact that, as a result of depressed conditions, many mortgages on homes were in a state of default and the owners were in danger of losing their properties. The corporation was, therefore, authorized to issue two billion dollars in bonds to refinance such home mortgages and make money available at lower rates for longer periods.

The administrator was John Fahy, a very kindly gentleman with a Van-dyke beard. He came from Boston and had been the head of a well-known department store, Filene's. The matter of refinancing home mortgages was a field in which I had had some experience. I had served as a director of a savings and loan association in my home city and, among other things, had been assigned to go around the city to examine properties, estimate values, determine the amount of money the association could and should reasonably loan on such properties, and keep an eye upon the performance of the mortgagee in making payments and in keeping the property in good condition.

On the basis of this background, I undertook seeing Administrator Fahy on a number of occasions and, in fact, harassed him a little about statistics. At a time well beyond the ninety-nine days, I continued to probe the operations of HOLC because I apprehended that whereas in the most depressed days banks, insurance companies, savings and loan associations, and other lenders had the burden of foreclosing on properties of the citizens, in due course it would become the disagreeable function of the federal government to undertake similar foreclosures. As a postscript to all this, I believe, if memory serves me correctly, that the federal government finally did foreclose on 250,000 properties, and that, of course, made great campaign material.

In mid-June Congress approved, and the president signed, the act creating the National Industrial Recovery Administration, which had a variety of purposes. By far its principal purpose was to bring about industrial recovery through fair pricing. It was to be administered under what were known as fair practice codes. There finally came into existence more than five hundred orders relating to all forms of business covering more than twenty-two million workers. In referring to those agreements, which had presidential approval as fair practice codes, it was not specifically stated that the antitrust laws were thereby suspended, but that, in fact, was what happened.

A very vigorous brigadier general named Hugh Johnson was designated as administrator of NIRA, and his publicity staff quickly created the blue eagle as a symbol of compliance with the codes. There were huge billboards displaying the blue eagle, designed to develop a compliance psychology on every hand. There were blue eagle buttons to be worn by everybody and anybody. There were blue eagle stickers which housewives were expected to paste in their windows. It was, in a sense, a truly majestic assault on the forces of depression, but the weaknesses of this measure soon became evident.

There were those who thought that the antitrust laws were something out of the gospel and should not be impaired or destroyed under any circumstances. There was also a growing group of consumers who saw in all this a business and industry effort to push prices higher and higher. There were those who saw in section 7(a) of the act an effort at unionization, because it assured the right to organize and bargain collectively through representatives of their own choosing.

And then there was the second title of the act, which created the Public Works Administration and authorized about three and one-third billion dollars for this effort. Harold L. Ickes, the secretary of the interior, was made the administrator of the Public Works Administration. It was expected that many public projects of all kinds which had lain dormant for years on the shelves in the city halls, courthouses, and statehouses of the country would be taken down, dusted off, and processed with the aid of federal money.

This also was a grand assault upon the depression but, once again, the New Deal did not fully recognize the obstacles. A rather obscure poultry dealer in New York City named the Schechter Poultry Corporation refused to comply with the provisions of the fair practice code relating to the poultry industry, and when cited for violation, it promptly took the case to the courts. It was only two years later, in May of 1935, that the Supreme Court declared that NIRA was encouraging monopoly and cartelization at the expense of the little businessman and, thus, held the act to be unconstitutional.

There were still other exciting things that took place in that first session of the Seventy-third Congress. These included the abrogation of the gold clause in public and private contracts. This also provoked a resounding outcry from many sources. The Railroad Coordination Act had set up a federal coordinator for transportation who soon found himself at loggerheads with the rail carriers of the country.

But when one reflects upon the fruit of the first ninety-nine days, it could well be agreed that Congress had never in the history of the country been subjected to such a barrage of ideas and programs. When it adjourned, Congress was quite exhausted.

One did not have to be in the nation's capital very long before beginning to wonder about its social life and precisely where one might fit in. In earlier days under the Republicans, there was a good deal of pomp and glitter. But when the New Deal took over, life became chummier; the people who replaced the outgoing Republicans set up a new type of society which was more intimate and clubby in nature.

When it was all put together I was a rather unhappy freshman congressman. The gloating of the New Dealers did not ease my pain or anguish. The radical design of the legislation which had been pummeled through Congress by overwhelming votes seemed alien to my conservative nature and so, on June 15, 1933, I felt relief when adjournment of this first historic session came. But there was that telegram I had received after we voted on the proposal for economic recovery. It was the one from a friend who said "You one-termer!"

I must now go home and give an account of my stewardship. What would I say? How would I confront them? And then I fell into a state of self-pity. Why be a congressman after all? Why be a senator? Hadn't they capitulated in both bodies to the emotional surge which had washed the New Deal in on the wings of the depression? My spirits were low, and the ambition to reach out for the Senate at some future date was even lower.

IO

THE NEW DEAL AND I

Y OU HAVE READ ENOUGH of this book, I hope, to know that during my boyhood and high-school days I was not particularly a social butterfly. As a youngster I was extremely shy, but when I mentioned that fact in later years, after appearing before so many audiences, few would believe it. That shyness, however, remained with me not only in grade-school days but in high-school years as well. Perhaps it was only natural in beginning my life in Washington as a member of Congress that I was not too deeply interested in my attire, or that I should be regarded as one of the best dressed men in the capital.

Before making the journey to the capital I conferred with a few friends at home, particularly with one devout friend who was known as the "Talkative Tailor." His real name was Richard Bradley. He was a great jokester on the platform and had an unending fund of stories and witticisms. His circuit was lunch clubs, church brotherhoods, and the like in central Illinois. Along with it he ran a high-class tailoring shop.

We decided that, among other things, I should have two new suits that I could wear everyday, a semimorning suit, which was really a dark suit coat with striped pants and a buff-colored vest, and a tuxedo. I did not bother with formal evening attire, meaning the long-tailed coat and white trimmings, because we believed that a tuxedo would be ample for all purposes.

The first formal gathering to which I was invited was President Roosevelt's reception for Congress, which came early in the year. I wondered whether a tuxedo was quite the appropriate dress for the occasion and, hence, I made inquiry among my colleagues in the House on this point. They were about equally divided as to whether I should wear a long-tailed coat or a tuxedo. There were many, of course, who had been members of

Congress for some years, and they did not bother to attend the White House reception at all. For me, in my first term, it was on the "must" list. I had to be in attendance and suitably attired. I decided to wear tails.

Since I did not own such formal wear, it was necessary for me to shop among the many Washington rental emporiums for a tailcoat that I hoped would fit. I spent one entire morning on this matter, going from place to place. Generally the answer to my inquiry was that other senators and congressmen had been there before me and that all of the good ones had already been taken. In any event, I finally found what seemed to be necessary with the required trimmings, and I felt proud of the fact that I had accomplished all this in the space of a single morning. When I arrived at my office in the Old House Office Building about noon, a regional reporter of the Associated Press was on hand. Jerry Miller, who happened to be from Illinois, was a friendly chap with a great sense of humor.

As I entered the office he asked me quite brashly, "Where have you been all morning? What will your constituents say about a new congressman who does not show up in his office for work until noon? Suppose I write a front page story and tell the folks back home that already, so early in your first term, you are neglecting your duties?"

To this observation I said, "Jerry, I hope you won't do that, because I have been out of the office on very serious business. I've been trying to find out from the House membership the appropriate thing to wear to my first White House reception, and I got a mixture of answers. So I decided I should do it up proud and appear in a formal tailcoat and, since I do not own one, I started on a shopping venture which took me all morning in order to get one that would fit. I had to call at a dozen places before I found what I wanted. Now that is the whole story." He snickered a bit and said very little, and I was certainly not prepared for what was going to happen before that day came to an end.

About five o'clock in the afternoon, the late edition of the *Washington Star* appeared on the newsstands with the front page printed on pink paper. There on the front page was a photo of me together with the story as written by Jerry Miller. He did full justice by the story and even let his imagination roam rather freely as he recounted my efforts to find this elusive long-tailed coat. Seeing myself on the front page was truly a shock, and the shock gave way to an overwhelming embarrassment. By this time, however, there was no backing out.

I decided to wait in the office until the very last moment before I went to the hotel to wriggle into this stuffy evening attire. During that wait in the office every Washington paper called to verify the story. There were calls from the press in New York and, above all things, there was a call from Will Rogers, the very celebrated raconteur from Oklahoma who was appearing in the floor show at the Shoreham Hotel. He asked whether I would object if he clowned a little at my expense by tearing the lining out of his own tuxedo and letting it hang down to the back of his knees in imitation of what I was to wear that night at the White House. I said, "Mr. Rogers, at this point I do not suppose that it really matters; the newspapers have done their worst, so it's all yours."

With fear and trepidation I hailed a taxicab and finally repaired to my downtown hotel room to get myself into these clothes and let come what would.

While I was engaged in this effort, the hotel clerk called to say that a young photographer wanted to come up to my room and to ask whether I would see him. My first impulse was to tell him to go fly a kite, but on second thought, it occurred to me that I should not be offensive to the press. When he entered the room I said with some petulance, "Go ahead and shoot your picture and let's get this over with." He managed to assume a pained expression and said, "Gee, Congressman, this is going to be my first scoop. Won't you please let me take your picture struggling into that iron shirt?" My sense of humor got the better of me, and I proceeded to oblige him by getting into that highly starched shirt and then made valiant efforts to tie a white bow tie that might be reasonably presentable.

I carefully noted the time before I went downstairs and engaged a taxicab to take me to the proper entrance at the White House. As I walked into the East Room where everybody was gathering, I suddenly found myself the center of all eyes. It seemed as if everybody in Washington had read that front page story. My face fairly burned with a fever of embarrassment as the crowd receded to the walls and left me standing all alone in the middle of the East Room of the White House.

Someday I am going to remember a certain lady in my will if she outlives me. She is Genevieve Forbes Herrick, who was a Washington reporter. She came out of the crowd, covered me with genuine sympathy, and defended me and my action against my tormentors. I never felt such a sense of relief in my life, and that is why I shall always remember and love her.

Year after year, for at least a dozen years, this matter of renting a tailcoat for White House receptions came up, and the press never failed to come and inquire whether or not there would be a repeat performance and did I mind if they alluded to it in whimsical and other ways. As inadvertent publicity it paid big dividends.

But there was another reaction that I certainly did not anticipate. The people back home in Illinois's Sixteenth Congressional District had considerable pride in me, and certainly they wanted their representative in Congress to look fit for every occasion. As a result, some of my close friends held a meeting to determine what might be done. They finally decided to collect money to be used for proper attire for me. The effort was an instant success and about twenty-five hundred dollars was raised without difficulty. The next move was up to me. It embarrassed me no end because I could not determine what to do with the money. It had to go for clothes for the congressman or for some far worthier purpose. I finally concluded that whatever they raised should be divided into three parts and made available to three organizations that made provision for poor and needy families in my district at Christmas. When I submitted that suggestion, it was very promptly publicized on the front page of the newspaper at home so my embarrassment, in part, paid off there too.

As a general observation about social activities in the early days of the New Deal, I soon discovered that those who came to Washington for the first time then were far more interested in small chummy parties in their homes or in the office than in the lavish displays of the earlier days. It was interesting to hear some of the old-time waiters at the top hotels and restaurants, particularly those who came from the old country and who had been trained in the art of waiting and serving at big and fashionable functions, lamenting the passing of the good old days. To be sure there were a great many outstanding dinners, but I am speaking now about the general social going and coming of many people who were invited to Washington to man the New Deal battlements and who thus ingratiated themselves little by little into the structure of government.

On the political side there were, of course, outstanding personalities like James A. Farley, the postmaster general, and Marvin McIntyre and Louis McHenry Howe, who were the close and intimate secretary and assistant to the president. Then, of course, came the other cabinet members and heads of the many bureaus and agencies in government.

The cabinet member who was probably closest to me, in the sense that he presided over a department of government whose dominant interest was closest to my own, was Henry Wallace of Iowa, the secretary of agriculture. He was, in fact, the first cabinet member upon whom I called, and I did so because the farmers in the Sixteenth Congressional District were tremendously interested in the New Deal plans to meet the problem of depressed prices and huge surpluses.

The reason for this interest was quite obvious. When the depression was triggered by the slide of the market in October of 1929, farm prices went to the very bottom. Farms were steadily going under the foreclosing hammer simply because farm prices did not enable farmers to pay their bills and interest on the mortgages on their property and machinery. To be sure, all this was equally true in business and industry. The prime reason for the first overall attempt to develop a relief agency, under the direction of Harry Hopkins, was to create jobs regardless of how constructive they were and get money into the hands of the unemployed.

After these programs got underway, they were quite cynically referred to as "leaf raking" programs. There were many other names not nearly so mild and unabrasive which were applied to these projects. Certain it is that little caution was employed in the administration of the program, but it did put funds into the hands of many people and helped them to keep body and soul together.

Benevolent as many of these programs were in purpose and design, they did not set too well with the average taxpaying citizen who still had a job and who saw the waste in this government effort day after day. It was not merely the fact that it was wasteful but also that it seemed an alien idea, at least to those in my party.

My mother had been left a widow with a brood of youngsters when I was but five years old, and there were no relief agencies worthy of the name to lend a helping hand. We knew, however, that there was one way to get relief and that was to work. To people brought up in that fashion, the payment of money out of the public purse to reduce farm acreage and bring about a scarcity situation seemed to be wholly unjustified. The idea of suspending operation of the antitrust acts in order to let trade associations dictate prices brought an equally sharp reaction from many people. I knew, of course, that those amazing programs were effected simply because of the tremendous majorities which the New Deal had in both the Senate and the House of Representatives. With the celebrated ninety-nine-day session behind it, the Seventy-third Congress then devoted itself to many other programs which had broad social connotations. One of the biggest was the so-called Social Security Act, which was enacted in 1934. I believe I applied myself to this amazingly complicated legislation about as diligently as any member. I found it difficult indeed to support this legislation because there were such sharp departures from some very basic and fundamental principles.

A good deal of the inspiration for the Social Security system was derived from what was being done in Great Britain. Over there a royal commission had been appointed to work out a pattern that they thought would be justifiable and suitable and, above all else, sound. As I recall, Lord Beveridge was the chairman of the commission. It runs in my mind that the hearings they held and the testimony they took were never published, but they made a report and recommended an essentially sound program. Had it been adhered to, Britain would never have been beleaguered by the excessive costs and the abuses that crept into the plan. This, I presume, was a result of the modifications which were introduced in the House of Commons. We could have profited from the British experience but we did not do so.

The adoption of a Social Security system should not be dismissed without pointing an accusing finger at people high in the insurance industry who might have been extremely helpful when this program was being prepared. Their dislike for Franklin Roosevelt was so intense that they had no interest in appearing before congressional committees to assist in the preparatory work, and the net result was that all social planning and direction was left in the hands of the extremely liberal professionals in this field. Had the best talent in the insurance industry made any real effort to assist conservative members of the Congress in eliminating weaknesses in the program, it would not have been necessary, over a long course of years, to add first one amendatory plaster and then another in order to make the system work. As a matter of fact, there has been no session of Congress that I recall where this act has not been amended in one part or another.

One other matter in which the House had only a general public interest at the time when it was submitted, but which in due course would have to come to our attention in the Congress, was the proposal of the president to enlarge the Supreme Court because that body seemed out of sympathy with his New Deal program and had struck down some of his pet concepts. In enlarging the Supreme Court, the president was expected to appoint additional justices of known views so that he might be sure of a majority of that court when constitutional questions involving New Deal measures were submitted.

The matter was initiated through the United States Senate and almost immediately stirred that body and the country. A veritable avalanche of mail and telegrams came from men and women and even youngsters in high school and college who looked askance at this idea of prostituting the highest court in the country. They ventilated their views in no uncertain fashion.

I recall so very well the thousands of letters I received on the subject. They were impressive, to say the least. It was not because they were on fine paper and dictated to a secretary, but rather because they were handwritten letters on whatever stationery might be available at the moment. I know from a personal search through that mail that there were men and women and particularly housewives who, when they returned home after a shopping venture at the store, would take a piece of wrapping paper and with a short and somewhat unsharpened pencil put down the words as best they could: "Dear Mr. Dirksen, don't let them pak the cort." The fact that they could not spell the words "pack" or "court" made little difference. They knew what they wanted to say; that was the important thing.

In puzzling over this court episode it occurred to me that the great outpouring of views on court-packing by the citizens was, in a sense, a great tribute to the schoolteachers of this country in an earlier day. Wherever they went, their influence was felt. They emphasized a reverence for our free constitutional system and for the institutions which were created under that constitution. Over the years they came from the seaboard through the Allegheny and Appalachian passes into the prairies of Ohio, Indiana, and Illinois. The tide moved ever westward into the Great Plains. Finally they moved to the Pacific and so foreclosed the frontier. And so the court-packing proposal failed in its tracks and has not been attempted by any president since that time.

I suppose I could describe my congressional existence over the years as a diligent effort to remain abreast of every legislative proposal which was submitted to Congress, to answer the mail as expeditiously as possible, to process the complaints, and to do the errands requested by constituents at home.

One thing which left me quite cold so far as New Deal projects were concerned was the bread-and-butter attempt to move into the cultural picture. I did not realize how my own interest in the arts, and my desire to place the emphasis on excellence in the cultural field, would move toward a collision course with the New Deal administration in this field.

I was not unaware of the fact that the market crash in 1929 and the ensuing economic dislocation would place its heavy hand upon artists, actresses, and musicians, as well as upon people who worked on the farms or in the stores, shops, and factories. In fact, I felt that even though it might be unpopular, these groups merited some assistance from the government, but I was not prepared for what finally resulted.

Among other things, traveling groups of actors, actresses, and musicians were organized and provided with tents and other facilities so that they might go through the country and present whatever they thought would be entertaining and of cultural interest to the people. I deemed it quite appropriate to insist that I be supplied with a list of the dramatic vehicles which they proposed to dish up for the delight of the people. It was then that I discovered that, among other things, they were presenting some of Avery Hopwood's choicest pen children such as *Up in Mabel's Room* or *Getting Gertie's Garter*. I regarded these as baneful potboilers that were about as close to culture as the equator is to the North Pole. To be sure, they brought in money at the box office and had a certain appeal, but I knew of no one who would contend that they were very high on the cultural list. Perhaps I should take some of the curse from this statement by saying that certainly Avery Hopwood showed a flair for the theater even when I was a student at the University of Minnesota. His work paid off big at the box office and that was important. These were depression days. There was so much gloom and melancholy, and having a traveling company go into a town of modest size, set up a huge tent, get out its publicity, start rehearsals, and then subject the town to *Up in Mabel's Room* or *Getting Gertie's Garter* seemed incredible. I felt there must be something better to give than such farces.

All of this cost money, and those who were sponsoring projects of this type had to come before the appropriate committee of Congress and estimate how much money they needed for this purpose. It was then necessary to go before the respective appropriation committees and plead for funds. It was when such measures were reported to the House of Representatives that we had an opportunity, by means of sarcasm and ridicule, to keep such projects within reasonable bounds.

Still another project comes to mind every time I look at a certain oil painting on the wall of my home. It is kept only as a reminder of another day and age when art was about to become an assembly-line technique. Since artists, like all other people, had to be sustained and to eat, an art project was organized, and artists from all over the country were encouraged to work their will on cloth or canvas or hardboard or whatever medium they chose in which to express the artistic searching of their souls. The question was what to do with all this art—good, bad, indifferent, and horrible—after it had been completed.

The use of one of the temporary buildings which stood on the Mall somewhere between the Capitol and the Lincoln Memorial was finally obtained. It was a wartime structure and here the fruits of the paintbrush, the crayon, and the pencil were finally warehoused. The word went out that any member of Congress who was interested could come and make a selection with which to adorn his office. I went for a look, and for an afternoon of real enjoyment to wander around in this maze of artistry. The largest canvas was nine feet by twelve feet, but huge as some of them were and huge as the overall project was, the faults and the failures and the weaknesses were even greater. Most of those renditions could not even approach professional art.

We were invited to select as many things as we desired, and many members of Congress availed themselves of the chance to haul a host of art forms to the Capitol to grace their office walls. Some were hideous indeed and it was interesting, as a commentary on art appreciation by senators and congressmen, to see what was selected to adorn the offices.

It would take volumes to describe all the experiences that took place in those hectic New Deal days but, perhaps, it can all be disposed of by simply saying that it was an intrusion of the federal government into every activity of the American people, and it seemed quite alien to me. I supported some of the New Deal adventures and proposals, but there were some that simply taxed my credibility, and those I refused to accept.

It was later in this period that the Republican National Convention of 1936 was held in Cleveland, Ohio. By this time I was in my second term, and it was generally believed that I should seek to be a delegate to the convention. There appeared to be little or no excitement about it and little conjecture that the Republicans could win the presidency in that year. My party nominated Governor Alf Landon, of Kansas, for the presidency and Colonel Frank Knox, publisher of the *Chicago Daily News,* for the vice-presidency. It turned out to be a dispirited campaign, and the results called for that whimsical expression of Jim Farley to the effect that, "As Maine goes, so goes New Hampshire and Vermont."

Thinking of the diverse personalities I encountered in Congress in these years, I will start with Congressman Finley H. Gray, of Indiana. What a quaint character he really was. To me, he symbolized Ichabod Crane. I used to refer to him as the "Gray Ghost of the Wabash." He had long straggly hair and wore a long Prince Albert coat. He was terribly nearsighted and was forever taking off and putting on his pince-nez glasses. He was, indeed, an uninhibited person.

Whenever I was aware that Congressman Gray was to make a speech to the House, I was present to listen. His discourses almost always related to the fascinating subject of money. Invariably he would start a speech by saying, "I am advised that there are only thirteen people in the United States who really know anything about the subject of money. Gentlemen and Ladies of the Congress, I am not one of the thirteen and, therefore, I propose to lecture you for the next hour on the subject of money." This always evoked great guffaws on the part of the members and they tolerated Finley Gray in a big and enthusiastic way.

There was one occasion when I am afraid I must have offended Mr. Gray. We were walking together from the Capitol to the Old House Office Building and, to this day, I don't know what peculiar urge ever possessed me to say it but I did. I said, "Finley, I believe I could make a lot of money with you!"

"How's that, my boy?" he asked.

Then I said, "I could use you to haunt houses and what a project that would be." He lapsed into a dismal silence and I knew then that my suggestion was not taken very kindly.

We had another interesting member of the House from upper Michigan by the name of Frank Hook. As I recall, he represented a constituency where people of Finnish extraction dominated. Frank was the pugnacious type. He had a genius for making some slurring remark about some person present and would then follow up by saying that if there was anybody in the room who did not like it he was prepared to put on the gloves. What intrigued me most about Frank, though, was that he once appeared on the floor with a pair of blackened eyes which were almost classic in their artistry. There was a great deal of curiosity about what might have happened. I sat down beside him, uttered a few sympathetic sentiments, and asked, "Frank, what in the world happened to you?" He then unfurled quite a recital about journeying to the ranch of Congressman Frank Boykin of Alabama along with a number of other members of the House. He related that while there for the weekend he ran into a tree in broad daylight and, hence, the discolored optics.

To this account I simply said, "Why, Frank, it takes sheer genius to run into a tree in broad daylight and come up with such a result."

His explanation did not satisfy me, and out of pure mischief I pursued the incident and discovered what had really happened. A very intense poker game was taking place, and Frank Hook took it upon himself to wander around the table and do a bit of kibitzing to the dismay of the participants in the game. One of the players was a peppery young chap who had been in the prize ring for a number of years and did not like Mr. Hook's gratuitous observations. He said as much, and it was then that Mr. Hook undertook to threaten him and invite him to come out and settle it, man-to-man. The young fellow did exactly that, and before Frank Hook could so much as read one paragraph in the *Congressional Record,* he was the recipient of the old one-two punch. That was the real reason for his black eyes.

There was another extremely interesting character in Congress, Lawrence Lewis from Colorado. He was diminutive in size and had a built-in twinkle in his eyes. He was diligent and extraordinarily attentive to the desires and interests of his constituents. On one occasion when the business before the House was an authorization bill for the Works Progress Administration, which was a kind of "make-work" operation, I had done my homework rather carefully and prepared an extended speech on the pending bill. In the course of that speech I included a comment which I found in *Reader's Digest.* It purported to be the slogan of the senior graduating class of the high school of the town of Golden, Colorado. They were permitted to edit the final edition of the school paper for that year, and at the top of the full page they placed this headline, "WPA, Here We Come," implying that they had only to graduate to go into the Works Progress Administration. I thought it was a delicious and riotous piece of humor and chuckled audibly when I read it. Congressman Lewis was up out of his seat in an instant and challenged the authenticity of this little anecdote. I gave him all of the documentation and read it again for the edification of the members of the House. Up to that time Mr. Lewis and I had visited every morning at considerable length, and our fellowship was heightened somewhat by the fact that a free-lance reporter whom we both knew quite well was serving as the Washington correspondent for a Denver newspaper and also for one in Peoria, Illinois. This little incident about the graduating class of Golden, Colorado, breached that friendship and it was months before the congressman spoke to me again.

During my tenure in the House of Representatives there was a highly respected member from Auburn, New York, named John Taber, who was the ranking Republican member of the Appropriations Committee. Since the Democrats were in the majority, Congressman Clarence Cannon of Missouri was the chairman. They were both staunch and rugged people. Mr. Cannon was a little more on the liberal side, except when it came to legislation and appropriations in the field of agriculture. (Among other things he was an orchardist and a livestock grower.) John Taber, on the other hand, was a rugged archconservative.

The Appropriations Committee office was just off of the House chamber, and it was quite common for members of the committee to enter the committee room either on business or to chat with the clerks and the staff of the various subcommittees. One day there was occasion for me to go to the committee room to see the chairman. When I inquired in the outer office, they did not know where the chairman might be. Without hindrance, therefore, I walked into the chairman's office and discovered something for which I was not prepared. There was John Taber—sober, serious, and well behaved—lying on his back on a divan in Chairman Cannon's office, and there was the chairman with his hands on Congressman Taber's throat trying to choke him. I had to separate them.

I promised never to mention it and I never have until this good hour, but I have thought of it a great many times. To me it was a spectacle to see two men who were both in their sixties, and who had gone far in public life, become so upset about a public question that they undertook to settle it by main force. Had I not accidentally walked into the chairman's office, I am not sure what would have happened. Certain it is that had it been fatal, it would have convulsed the House of Representatives for years to come.

Congressmen, or shall I say most of them, develop senses of humor. Sometimes it can be quaint and quite weird. Nor does it always add up to the benefit of the member. From Connecticut came a member named Herman Kopplemann. It seems that every other term in that particular constituency, Connecticut was in the habit of changing from a Republican to a Democrat and then back to a Republican. Mr. Kopplemann was a Democrat. His main business was newspaper circulation work and he had done extremely well. We also had a congressman from Missouri by the name of Joseph Shannon. He was thoroughly Irish with an Irish sense of humor. He was somewhat beyond the average age of members of Congress and loved to indulge in practical jokes.

It was the custom after dinner for the congressmen and senators who lived at the Mayflower Hotel, where we then lived, to meet in the lobby to exchange anecdotes and whimsy and then repair to our rooms and apartments for the evening.

On this particular occasion when we gathered—and there were two dozen or more—I noticed that Mr. Kopplemann and Mr. Shannon were both on hand. Congressman Shannon walked over to where Congressman Kopplemann stood and said, "Herman, I saw your wife a little while ago. She went upstairs."

"Oh! is that so?" said Mr. Kopplemann.

Then Congressman Shannon said, "I told her I saw you on the corner of Connecticut and K Street and she wanted to know what you were doing. Quite obviously I had to tell her that you were standing on the corner talking to two very lovely blondes, the loveliest that I have seen in all my days in Washington. She didn't say anything more and went upstairs to her apartment. Now, Herman, what I said was certainly not out of the way was it?"

To this Mr. Kopplemann replied, "It certainly was going out of your way. I wasn't talking to anybody, I didn't see any blondes, I didn't stand on the corner of Connecticut and K Street or any other place. Joe, you just made up this story out of a hole in your head but it will cost me a lot." We did not find out until later what it did cost Mr. Kopplemann.

His recital went something like this: "You fellows will never quite know what happened to me after I got upstairs. Mrs. Kopplemann had already gone to bed and I was preparing to follow her. Suddenly she sat upright and asked, 'Who were those blondes you were talking to down on Connecticut and K Street?'

"I said, 'Mother, I wasn't talking to any blondes. I don't know what you are talking about.'

" 'Well, Mr. Shannon told me he saw you talking to two blondes.'

" 'Mr. Shannon stretches the truth now and then.' I thought at that point she would subside and go to sleep but it only lasted about thirty minutes. Then she started the argument all over again, and this kept up the whole night through. It was one of the weirdest nights I have spent since I have been a member of Congress and to you, Joe Shannon, let me ask what did I ever do that you should bring this thing down on my head? I do not know whether to forgive you or not." But evidently forgiveness triumphed and they remained good friends.

Perhaps no more interesting and unpredictable character ever reached the halls of Congress than a young man from the state of Washington named Marion Zionchek. He was quite an athlete, exercised religiously and vigorously every day, and was tough and muscular. He had a combative instinct and when he got into an argument with a fellow member of Congress, he was quick to threaten the use of physical force. He got into all manner of scrapes, predicaments, and difficulties to the point that his colleagues entertained the thought that he should be committed to a mental hospital, but we did not quite know what to do. We knew, however, that something must be done, because a single member of Congress can bring the body into disrepute. Even Speaker Joseph Byrnes was deeply concerned. The press announced that Congressman Zionchek called a young lady in one of the governmental departments on a matter of official business and liked her voice and her courtesy. He informed her that he was infatuated and that he was coming down to see her and propose marriage. He did exactly that. The wedding was extremely informal and when it was all over he brought his bride to the House of Representatives and escorted her to a seat in the front row in the members' gallery. I remember so well that she wore a huge picture hat and looked like a Gibson girl. She was quite attractive. Her presence in the gallery was not lost on Speaker Byrnes and, having a deliciously old-fashioned southern sense of humor, he could scarcely refrain from directing the attention of the members to the fact that Mrs. Zionchek was in the gallery. Members of the House, who were on the floor, stood up in a body and gave her a great round of applause.

On the afternoon of that day they started their honeymoon and decided to drive south in Zionchek's new car. In Alexandria, Virginia, ten or twelve miles south of Washington, he was speeding through the town and was promptly arrested and hauled to the police station, charged with violating the speed limits of that community. He insisted on calling his lawyer, who arranged for a bond, so they could proceed on their honeymoon. His next arrest came in Charleston, South Carolina, and once more by telephone his attorney arranged for the bond. This state of affairs continued throughout the trip until he reached Miami, Florida. There the newly wedded couple took a ship to Cuba. When he arrived in Cuba he sent a cablegram to President Roosevelt. It was exceedingly brief and as provocative as it was brief. He simply said, "Send me a detachment of marines and I will take over."

All of this seemed as fantastic as it was funny, but it also had its serious side. The decision began to harden in Congress that something must be done with Marion Zionchek so that he would not carry on in this way.

As a result of this determination, a group of police officers was assembled at the great door of the Old House Office Building on the New Jersey side, knowing that this was the entrance Congressman Zionchek generally used. At long last he appeared and was placed under arrest. Then the fight began. At least a half dozen police officers were involved in that scuffle, and it took every one of them to subdue Zionchek, put him in manacles, and take him to St. Elizabeth Hospital for detention and observation. If I recall correctly, he had to be put in a straitjacket and kept there until he promised to behave himself. He was, of course, permitted to talk with his wife by telephone. She arranged for his release.

Evidently, they arranged for a tryst somewhere along the railroad tracks of the Baltimore and Ohio Railroad. She was scheduled to meet him in a car and they were then to start away from Washington, D.C., in the general direction of Washington, the state from which he had been elected. At long last, they arrived in Washington. There was no disposition to bring him back to Washington, D.C.

The whole matter was about to be forgotten when a few days later the country and Congress were fairly startled by newspaper headlines to the effect that Marion Zionchek had jumped from the window of his office on the fourteenth floor of an office building in Seattle. That was the end of perhaps the strangest and most fantastic career of any member.

During my tenure in the House, the Honorable Huey Long, one-time governor of Louisiana, was elected to the United States Senate. Here was another truly colorful character. It was my good fortune—and it *was* good fortune—to be on the platform with Senator Long at one place or another over a period of time. He was certainly good with an audience and had real talent for enchanting any crowd he addressed.

On one occasion he and I were on the program together at the national convention of the Veterans of Foreign Wars in Milwaukee, Wisconsin. We were sitting together before the meeting began and he asked whether or not I wanted to speak first or last. I said, "Senator, it really does not make any difference to me. If you prefer to speak first, I know you are going to spoil this audience when it comes time to introduce me, because I know your talent and genius for literally hypnotizing a crowd of people."

All this happened shortly after an incident at Sand's Point Country Club in New York, where it was alleged that Senator Long had gotten a black eye in fisticuffs with someone whom he supposedly had offended in the washroom of the club. I knew when this was supposed to have happened and I knew, also, that he had come directly from New York to Milwaukee. "Senator," I said to him, "the newspapers allege that you got a black eye in New York."

"Dirksen, take a good look at me and see if I have a black eye."

I took a very careful look and said, "Senator, I do not see the slightest discoloration nor any abrasion of either one of your eyes." And indeed there was no outward evidence that he had been struck.

As the national commander of the Veterans of Foreign Wars prepared to introduce Senator Long, the number of press cameras was almost bewildering. Every photographer was snapping away for dear life, and they were trying to get closer and closer in the hope that the photographs they were taking might disclose a discolored eye. This procedure eventually became a bit offensive, and Senator Long turned around to appeal to Admiral Koontz and said, "Admiral, do I really have to submit to all of these indignities?"

The good old commander looked at the crowd, made something of a feeble gesture with his hand, and then said, "Please, boys, I hope you will subside, you have gotten enough photographs. Do not harass the Senator any longer."

The pressmen made a partial retreat, and Senator Long began his speech. Very shortly after he began, the cameras were back again. He made another appeal. Admiral Koontz made a further appeal. It was then that the senator turned to the crowd. The hall was packed with men who had worn the uniform. Senator Long said, "Fellows, do I have to put up with this?" In an instant I saw veterans leave their seats, move into the center aisles in a solid phalanx, and start in the direction of the stage. They rough-handled every photographer there and proceeded to fling cameras on the hard floor. It became a real scuffle before tranquillity could be restored and Senator Long could resume his speech.

While on the subject of Senator Long, I should have mentioned one incident about him which really intrigued me. I had been designated to serve on a select committee to investigate the Bondholder's Protective Committees. These were committees that had been set up in all parts of the country to undertake the reorganization of real estate properties where outstanding bonds were involved, in the hope that both the properties and the value of the bonds might be preserved. It involved bondholder committees dealing with the reorganization of apartment houses, hotels, and other properties where, as a result of the economic depression, the properties had gone into foreclosure. Congressman A. J. Sabath was the chairman. That committee journeyed to many parts of the country to conduct investigations in the hope that legislative remedies could be found and enacted by Congress.

The committee enlisted John Carroll, a former Chicago banker who was extremely knowledgeable in this field. He and I became intimately acquainted. One day he came to the office and said, " 'Dirksen, you know Senator Huey Long quite well. I note he is on the Senate Banking Committee. I would like to talk with him and I would prefer to do it away from Capitol Hill."

I said, "John, I will try to set this up for you."

Consequently, I made an appointment for him to see Senator Long in his suite at the Mayflower Hotel. What happened is best related by Mr. Carroll.

"I pushed the bell and in a little bit the door opened and there was Senator Long. He was in lavender pajamas. He told me to come in and said he would be ready in just a jiffy. He washed his face, combed his hair, and then emerged from the bathroom.

"While he was arranging himself, I had a chance to look around the apartment and one of the first things I noticed was that there were half a dozen Bibles, large and small, all open and all open in different places. As he came out of the bathroom I said, 'Senator, what is the idea of all these Bibles?' He made something of a theatrical gesture and then said, 'Mr. Carroll, that is the Book of Law. I would not think of undertaking anything until I first found it in the Great Book.' To me it was amazing that this could happen and I wondered whether the country had not completely misjudged the character of Senator Long.

"The Senator then began to amplify. 'Mr. Carroll, mankind somehow has always had a penchant for crucifying their faithful servants. Did not they crucify the man of Galilee? Did not they burn Saint Ambrose at the stake? Did not they ostracize Joan of Arc and John Huss? That's been the tradition of mankind. You know, Mr. Carroll, I sometimes get the feeling that people do not want to be saved, but damn them, I'll save them whether they want to or not!' "

Few men have combined the politician's art with such faith, which I believe was sincere.

II

THE NEW DEAL AND I CONTINUE

I MAKE NO PRETENSE in this narrative of maintaining any kind of strict chronology. By that I mean I prefer sometimes to skip around the years. Had I kept a careful day-by-day diary I might have been able to maintain a continuous time pattern, but this I did not do. I find, however, that in going over the composition of the various Congresses, beginning with the Seventy-third, and in examining the biographies of members with whom I served, the mere sight of a name brings back some event or some personal item.

Perhaps at this point I should recall the state of the economy and what had been achieved in solving the pressing problems before the country. One thing is absolutely certain, and that is that we discovered that there were no royal roads to a solution.

The jobless population continued to rise everywhere and, in consequence, huge expenditures for relief and for projects which were, in some instances, of doubtful value had to continue. Notwithstanding what had been done in the field of agricultural legislation, the farmers were still struggling for a fair price for their commodities. I believe it is a fair appraisal to say that the New Deal was long on reform, much longer on relief, yet very short on actual recovery and restoration of normal conditions. But life continued to be an adventure and each session of Congress added new friends and new ideas.

It was my particular privilege to become intimately acquainted with former president Herbert Hoover. He came to Washington quite often, and when he did he would ask a half dozen of his friends to have an informal dinner, at which time they would reflect upon the condition of the country and also reminisce about the days when he had been secretary of commerce and later president. I was invariably invited to these dinners, possibly because of my long-standing friendship with Lawrence Richey, who for years continued as a secretary to President Hoover. I always referred to him as "Chief."

At one such dinner I raised a question concerning his relationship with the Honorable Henry T. Rainey, of Carrollton, Illinois, who was majority leader in the Seventy-second Congress and became Speaker of the House in the Seventy-third Congress. Mr. Rainey represented the district that lay south of mine. He was a man of striking appearance with an abundance of snow-white hair. He always wore a Windsor-type string tie and it became him very well.

When the tragic financial crash came in October of 1929 it was necessary for President Hoover to obtain legislation from Congress with which to meet acute problems. As he recited it to me from time to time, the real force behind the crash which led to the prolonged depression emanated from Germany after the failure of three of its largest banks. The effects of that failure had spread like wildfire throughout Europe and were bound to reach the United States sooner or later. President Hoover had an overall plan with which to meet the crisis and, accordingly, he outlined to Mr. Rainey his views on what must be done. Mr. Rainey, however, soon made it abundantly clear that a Democratic House of Representatives did not intend to give President Hoover the legislative aid that he had planned on, and he made it equally clear that they intended to bring about his defeat.

The result of the 1929 crash here at home triggered great economic dislocations that soon took on the dimensions of our worst depression. The end result was that this nation had to march through the valley of the shadows for a time, and what a long and dreadful journey it turned out to be. Even after many years of the New Deal, we were not very far along on the recovery road. Had Speaker Rainey and the Democrats heeded President Hoover's original recommendations, some consequences of the slump might have been avoided. But I am not attempting a history of the era. I prefer to think about the personalities I encountered and particular events worthy of remembrance.

I recall, for example, Congressman William Lambertson from Kansas. I had a great deal of affection for him. He was a farmer, and if there could be a typical Kansan he would have been it. He continued his farm operations after his election to Congress and gave particular attention to all matters relating to agriculture. He and I served on an appropriations subcommittee on agriculture, and our acquaintanceship ripened into a very warm friendship.

Bill Lambertson loved to play golf, and it was his custom to make up a foursome and go to one of the available courses early in the morning whenever the weather was mild. He had the odd habit of driving his car to the course without socks or shoes.

On one particular morning he was driving out Fourteenth Street in the direction of the golf course and, since traffic was light at that hour, he was moving faster than the speed limit permitted. Suddenly he heard a siren and perceived a motorcycle officer who was signaling him to move over to the curb. The officer quickly noted, on looking through the open window, that Mr. Lambertson had bare feet. There was the usual official conversation, the noting of the license, and then the instruction to follow the officer to the precinct station. When they arrived and brought Bill into the station, a number of other officers, who had been on night duty, were gathered in the station indulging in light banter and pleasantries. They noticed that the culprit, though well turned out, had bare feet. It really became an occasion for a great deal of levity and for Lambertson it was exceedingly embarrassing. When they requested his name for the police blotter, he gave the name of his administrative assistant. He was released after depositing a cash bond and went his way.

A hearing was set on his case, but the summons to appear went to the administrative assistant. It was then that the whole story came out and the congressman himself had to appear and plead to the charge of speeding. The magistrate castigated him and Lambertson had to apologize profusely to the court and to all concerned. He was then turned loose. Obviously the story quickly found its way to Capitol Hill, and members who liked to indulge in waggish appellations promptly dubbed him "Sockless Jerry Simpson," recalling a congressman of earlier vintage who used to attend sessions without socks or shoes.

I was always intrigued by Congressman Vincent Palmisano, of Baltimore. If there had been no other reason for my interest, it could have sprung from the fact that he was actually born in Italy and came to this country with his parents when he was but five years of age. He became an attorney in Baltimore and soon entered into the political life of the community. It had a heavy population of Italian extraction. Palmisano's election was actually a tribute to our democracy and to the fact that an immigrant could come to this country and, when he had completed his citizenship, gain high federal office.

The thing that intrigued me, however, was that, for reasons unknown to me, Palmisano never did lose his very strong Italian accent. It was very noticeable and it was not long before playful congressmen conferred upon him the title of Doctor of Broken English. I do not believe that good-natured title ever left him in all the days that he served.

I have mentioned the two men I met when I heard the call of the roll for the first time in March of 1933. One of these was Congressman Ernest Lundeen, of Minnesota. Years later Lundeen was elected to the United States Senate. He was killed in a plane crash as he was on his way to a speaking engagement in Minnesota. I came into the picture for a reason I certainly could not have anticipated.

Senator Lundeen had a secretary who came from my hometown of Pekin, Illinois. I knew her because we attended the same church. She came from a very fine family. After completing high school there and several years of college, she left Pekin, and for years I did not know where she was living. I was, therefore, astonished when she walked into my office a few days after Lundeen died and said she wished to talk to me about a very serious matter which was troubling her.

It appeared that one of the frequent visitors to Senator Lundeen's office was a man who could very well be described as a German agent. He was well known around Washington; and I remembered that on one occasion he had come to my office and, after a bit of pleasant conversation, had asked whether I would be interested in making a speech to the House of Representatives on the situation abroad for which he and his associates would prepare all the material. The speech would in effect justify German policy and actions in the war. I advised him flatly that I was not interested and that was the last time I ever saw him.

In view of this man's visit and of the tragic accident, I did go back and examine the *Congressional Record,* and there I noticed that some speeches made by Senator Lundeen had a certain cast which reflected the influence of the person in question.

When his secretary became aware of the crash, she had commandeered a taxicab to take her to the scene of the accident. On arrival she indicated to those who had taken charge of the matter that she was the senator's chief secretary and that she came to retrieve his briefcase and his wallet, because she had cashed a check for him just before he boarded the plane. She found the briefcase. Somehow the crash had broken the clasp and the papers had slid out all over the plane. She gathered up the briefcase and its contents and took them back to the senator's office.

Shortly thereafter she received a call from the Federal Bureau of Investigation. It frightened her, and that is why she had come to see me. She was advised not to leave the city and to maintain an address where the FBI could reach her. She followed this instruction, but nothing happened; she was never called. There were occasions when I wanted to query my friend, J. Edgar Hoover, the director of the FBI, as to what it was all about, but I never satisfied that curiosity and let it stand as a closed file.

Another interesting personality who was, in fact, one of the most colorful I ever encountered in all my Washington years was Congressman Francis H. Shoemaker, of Minnesota, who later became a candidate for the United States Senate. He was the editor of a small-town newspaper in Minnesota. It appears that a lady's husband had passed away and left a comfortable estate in the form of stocks, bonds, and cash in a safety deposit box in one of the largest banks in Minneapolis. The woman appealed to Mr. Shoemaker for help. She alleged that the good securities in the bank box were withdrawn and that other less valuable securities had been substituted. She insisted that it was an inside bank job.

Francis Shoemaker, with a newspaper man's instinct for a page one story, promptly dispatched a letter to the president of the bank and reiterated the allegations made by the widow. He made one slight mistake, however. On the outside of the envelope, which was addressed to the banker, he added, "Robber of widows and orphans."

Obviously this was a violation of the postal laws, and a complaint was quickly filed by the banker and then by the Post Office Department. All this resulted in an indictment by a grand jury and Shoemaker was sentenced to a federal prison. As I recall, the presiding judge gave him the option of a five-year sentence with an immediate suspension and a five-year parole or a year and a day in prison since it was a felony charge. Shoemaker preferred to serve the year and a day rather than be on parole for such a long period.

In prison he became rather intimate with his cellmates. He had a great sense of humor and, I presume, he would have felt at home anywhere, whether in or out of prison. At the time he was released, the Minnesota courts had invalidated the primary election law in that state so that all candidates for Congress had to run at large, which simply means on a statewide rather than a congressional district basis. Shoemaker managed to secure the necessary signatures to a petition and so became a candidate for Congress.

By that time his name had become well known throughout the state because of his indictment and prison record. The amazing thing is that he was elected. One of the first things he did was to contact his prison cellmate, who had been convicted on a charge of bank embezzlement, and bring him to Washington as a congressional secretary.

One of the first things a new congressman does is to prepare a short biography for publication in the *Congressional Directory*. Sometimes these are longer and sometimes shorter. Mr. Shoemaker submitted a biography of modest size, but at the end of it he wrote, "Where others go from Congress to prison, I came from prison to Congress." A California congressman was so furious about it that when the oath was administered he exercised his right under House rules to ask Mr. Shoemaker to stand aside. It was not until later that the oath was administered and only after the offensive sentence had been stricken from the biography.

The one person in the original cabinet of Franklin Delano Roosevelt who really looked every inch a leader, with his erect frame and white hair, was the Honorable Cordell Hull, of Tennessee, secretary of state. He was not merely a fine southern gentleman but a statesman in the finest sense of the word, and I say it even though I often disagreed with his views. He had served with distinction in the United States Senate, and it was not surprising that President Roosevelt chose him for secretary of state. It may have been sheer chance that I became acquainted with Cordell Hull, to a certain degree, or it may have been due to a certain brashness on my part. When I encountered New Deal dignitaries, I made myself known and sought to enlist them in whatever conversation might have a bearing upon points of interest to me.

I also developed a great admiration for Senator Alban Barkley from Kentucky. In later years he was to become vice-president. I have had occasion to pay testimony to him and to salute him for his service to our country. It may not be generally known, but Alban Barkley was a man of truly resolute courage. He showed it on many occasions, but the instance that comes to mind was when he was serving as a member of the Senate Finance Committee. Tax bills must, under the Constitution, originate in the House of Representatives and then go to the Senate for further consideration. The Senate is then free to modify or amend them in any way that it sees fit. Being on the Finance Committee obviously gave Senator Barkley an opportunity to modify tax bills in a way that he thought would be in the national interest. On one occasion he was at complete variance with President Roosevelt on a tax item. When the president vetoed the tax bill in which Senator Barkley had participated, the senator displayed his true Kentucky colors and resigned from the committee. It then became a test of strength between these two. His courage fascinated me and I entertained nothing but admiration for him.

Another lovable character came to the House from California. He was John Steven McGroarty. In 1933 the California legislature designated him as the poet laureate of the state. He was a master in expressing tender sentiments, and on special occasions like Memorial Day or Independence Day he would always find time to make a brief but scintillating speech on the floor of the House. I remember a day when we were in session a few days before the Sunday on which Mother's Day was to be observed. Congressman McGroarty took the floor and declaimed some very tender sentiments. I believe the House even applauded as he walked from the floor. Only a few minutes later he was back, his face was quite agitated and, in violation of the rules since another member had obtained the floor for some remarks, he brandished his fist and said, "Mr. Speaker, some vile wretch has defiled the holy name of his mother and stolen my brand-new topcoat." It got a resounding laugh.

Then, of course, there was "Little" Joe Hendricks, of Florida. "Little" Joe was more nearly a term of endearment than anything else. He was the author of the celebrated House Bill Number One, which embodied the so-called Townsend Plan. In brief, it called for levy of a tax on every commercial transaction, the revenues from which were to be used to pay so much as was necessary to bring every person's income at age sixty-five to thirty dollars per week. Sometimes it was derisively referred to as the "Thirty Dollars Every Thursday Bill." Townsend clubs sprang up all over the country like mushrooms. Immediately they undertook to exercise their influence in politics and to threaten any incumbent member of the Congress or any candidate for Congress who refused to support the plan. It had been before the Ways and Means Committee of the House for several years and, at long last, that committee, obviously to rid itself of this pesky measure, decided to report it to the House calendar without recommendation.

What seemed so incredible about this move was the fact that Congressmen Allen Treadway, the owner of many hotels in Massachusetts, and Frank Crowther, of New York, rockribbed conservatives, fell in with the idea and intimated they would vote for the bill. I could not understand it.

A day was designated for its debate and for a vote on the plan. But before that day arrived I had a visitor in my office. He was Dr. Francis Townsend's general manager and adviser. Our conversation began in a light vein and then he became very serious. What he said was, "Congressman, we find that the new members of Congress pay a good deal of attention to you and you have considerable influence on how they vote. I trust, therefore, that I can talk to you in strict confidence about our plan. We want a very substantial vote for the plan but we do *not* want it to pass. You can well understand that if it passes, the money will stop rolling into the Townsend treasury. We must keep these revenues coming in." As he talked I made some cryptic notes and, when it was over, I advised him that I would take the matter under consideration.

And so the big day came. The leadership decided that Majority Leader John McCormack, of Massachusetts, would make the concluding speech on the Democratic side, and that I was to make the concluding speech on the Republican side. The galleries were filled to overflowing. Our hope was to lay the Townsend Plan to rest once and for all.

I shall never forget that speech; nor shall I forget how tense the House was, with a full membership on the floor. I had been thinking so long and intently about our ultraconservative members on the Ways and Means Committee who had voted to send the bill to the floor, and it embittered me a little.

A line from Shakespeare kept creeping into my mind. I said, "Ladies and Gentlemen of the House, long ago Shakespeare wrote, 'Cowards die many times before their deaths; the valiant never taste of death but once.'" From that point on I built up some suspense by informing the House that I had had a visitor who had given me important information. He had told me that the Townsendites wanted a substantial vote for the plan, but they did not want it enacted because it would stop the flow of nickels, dimes, and dollars into the coffers of the Townsend organization. After I built this sentiment to a climax, I pointed to a man in the front row of the gallery and said, "There he sits. There sits Dr. Townsend, there sits Robert Townsend, his son, and there sits the field marshal of the Townsend Plan who came to see me and to suggest that it should not be approved, that there should be only a substantial vote for it."

The roll was called and that was the end of the Townsend Plan. I was tagged as public enemy number one for them, but that was neither here nor there. What did concern me a little was when I went to the Republican cloakroom for a cup of coffee, I found Congressman Crowther, of New York. He seemed rather shaken. When I entered he fairly snarled out of the side of his mouth, "Cowards die many times before their deaths."

It is strange how a seemingly uneventful happening can also be very pathetic. I am thinking of Arthur B. Jenks, of New Hampshire, a banker and shoe manufacturer who had been elected to the Seventy-fifth Congress. His margin of victory was rather small and his Democratic opponent decided to contest the election. Actually, the House Democrats could have ignored that contest in view of the huge majority they already enjoyed. They did, however, take the count in the election to Congress and had it fully and completely investigated. As a general matter the investigation of a contested election usually runs throughout an entire Congress, and the committee making the investigation does not report until close to the end of the session. So it was in the Jenks case that the report was filed in June and was accompanied by a resolution which said simply, "Resolved that the Honorable Arthur B. Jenks is not entitled to a seat in the Seventy-fifth Congress." It was on this resolution that the roll was called and, because of the heavy party line vote, the resolution was adopted. The practice is that the moment the result of such a vote is announced, the congressman in question whose seat has suddenly been forfeited, so to speak, is expected to arise and leave the floor since, by official action, he is no longer a member of that body. I shall never forget the day, while the House sat tensely still, that Arthur B. Jenks arose, walked down the center aisle, out toward the speaker's lobby and vanished from sight. It was truly a little pathetic, and the margin was only a handful of votes.

Strange things can happen in Congress. One would normally assume that out of 435 members anyone could quickly familiarize himself with every face, every name, and the characteristics of the other congressmen. It was not, however, the case with a man named Christopher Sullivan. The Tammany members from New York had arranged for a party at the Mayflower Hotel, where they and a few others might come for an excellent dinner and champagne and then for some poker playing and crap shooting for those who engaged in those sports. Only two Republicans were invited to the meeting. One was Congressman Joe Martin, of Massachusetts, minority leader in the House, and the other one was I. It was truly an enjoyable evening and, in the course of my visits with first one and then another, I saw what I thought was a strange face. I went up to Congressman Martin Kennedy, of New York, whom I esteemed as a friend and who had been very successful in the insurance business.

I said, "Martin, who is the chap standing right over there with the ruddy face and twinkling eyes who looks as Irish as Paddy's pig?"

He laughed long and loud and then replied, "Why, that's Christie Sullivan, the leader of Tammany Hall in New York City."

Then I asked, "What does he do?"

Kennedy replied, "He's a member of Congress."

I was puzzled and told Martin, "I have never seen him on the floor of the House."

Martin Kennedy's reply was simply, "Well, really now, Christie Sullivan doesn't have to come to meetings of the House as the boss of Tammany Hall.

We don't need his vote, and if some of the boys get restive and try to run out on the New Deal, Christie can always get them on the telephone. If they are too obstreperous, he comes down to Washington and administers the right kind of discipline." I thought it was quite amazing that Christie Sullivan came to Congress in 1917 and had been a member until 1941 and yet I hadn't any recollection of ever seeing him on the floor of the House of Representatives.

In looking over a picture gallery of senators who served through the early years of the twentieth century, I noticed many, if not all of them, wore beards. Some were truly beards of distinction both in size and in training. That was equally true of a great many congressmen, but the only bearded congressman who served in my time was George Holden Tinkham, of Massachusetts. He was about five feet six inches, as erect as a poker, and walked with a slight strut which actually made him look quite distinguished. Perhaps if I describe him as looking like one of the celebrated Smith Brothers of cough-drop fame that will convey a fair image of Congressman Tinkham.

When he became a member of Congress he entered into a lease for a suite at the Arlington Hotel, which was to run as long as he was a member of this legislative body. But the day came when Washington began to expand in amazing fashion and new structures were the order of the day. The federal government had bargained for the Arlington property in order to build an office building for one of the agencies, and notice was served upon all the tenants to vacate. All of them did except poor Mr. Tinkham, who decided to stay. I am not sure what he did about elevator service or maid service, but in any event, there he was in solitary splendor, amid the clank of machinery, absolutely determined that he would not move.

He served on the Foreign Affairs Committee of the House and liked to regard himself as a bit of an expert, but on those occasions when he made a speech on foreign affairs not too many members listened.

I, among others, thought he deserved far better attention because of his age, his seniority, and his dignified bearing. On one occasion we conspired to get members to the floor of the House and prepared to do full justice to Mr. Tinkham's remarks, whether they agreed with them or not. I had a hand in serving as the cheerleader on that occasion and had several points marked in the manuscript where I felt that there should be appropriate applause. As our colleague, Mr. Tinkham, began to read his manuscript, I broke into applause and other members followed my action. As the manuscript went along I thought it deserved something better than mere applause and, every so often, would not only applaud but shout, "Yeah, George! Yeah, George!"

The members caught the spirit of the occasion and it was almost like a college football game. When Mr. Tinkham had finished the speech, we rose in mass and really gave him the cheer to end all cheers. I am not certain, but I believe as a result of this incident the order was issued to the public printer that indications of applause and other loud and boisterous approbation must henceforth be deleted from the *Record*.

Often what at the moment seems an idle promise never to be kept turns out years later to be a solemn obligation. I am thinking now of the case of the Honorable Jack Nichols, of Oklahoma. He was bronzed and leather skinned as if he had spent his life in a saddle. He was variously a teacher and lawyer and began in his high-school days as a soda jerk. He came from the same town which produced Sherman Billingsley, the proprietor of the celebrated Stork Club in New York, and had a flare for flashy clothes. I recall one occasion in Denver, where we had gone as part of a funeral delegation at the last rites for Congressman Edward Taylor, chairman of the House Appropriations Committee. In view of the fact that we were in that part of the country, the House Special Committee on Air Safety, of which Jack Nichols was the chairman, decided to hold some hearings on that subject in Denver. I remember so well the morning Congressman Nichols appeared at the hearing. He was attired like a cowboy who had found time and money enough to dress up to match his wildest sartorial dreams; cowboy boots, a white silk shirt, a gay light blue bandana around his neck, and gray, close-fitting trousers were all topped off by a cowboy hat. His regalia would have frightened any cow pony or self-respecting steer. Our colleague was really in his glory.

Sometime after we returned to Washington, he became captivated by the idea that the committee, consisting of five members including myself, should make a tour of Latin America in the interest of air safety and air navigation. We journeyed to nearly every Latin American republic, and when we returned it became my duty to write the report. Many interesting things took place in the course of our trip, and the report had sufficient verve and color to beget the interest of several publishers who wanted to see it expanded and made into a readable and salable book.

But that is not the real part of the story. We were attending a cocktail party in Buenos Aires, in Argentina, and just why this subject came up I shall never know. In the noise and bedlam of that party, Jack Nichols turned to me and said, "Dirk, if anything should ever happen to me I want you to preach my funeral oration." I passed it off as cocktail conversation and forgot about it.

Jack Nichols came from a congressional district where he won each time by a margin of three hundred or four hundred votes, and he knew that sooner or later the proverbial ball would turn up with his name on it and that would be the end of his congressional career. When finally he was defeated, Trans World Airlines offered him a position as vice-president for international affairs because of his interest in, and knowledge of, the airplane industry. His duty was to examine the problems of the airline and see what might be done to secure cooperation from the authorities in other countries in developing facilities for Trans World planes.

While Jack Nichols was performing his duties as a vice-president of TWA, I had an opportunity to make a world trip. It was done with funds which the people in my hometown had collected and placed in the bank to further a possible campaign for the vice-presidency of the United States. Since I never ran for the office, the good home folks insisted that I make this world trip to broaden my own legislative horizon. On that trip I had an interesting session with the regent of Iraq; the king was only a boy, and a regency had to be established to look after the affairs of the country.

On the day I called on the regent he had with him an interpreter who was a colonel in the Iraqui army. At some point in the conversation, the colonel advised me that the regent was coming to the United States as the guest of President Roosevelt, and that he was not especially interested in looking at stockyards, tank factories, railroad shops, tractor plants, and similar dull things. What the regent wanted was a bit of American night life.

I told the colonel to advise the regent that he was talking to the right person and that when they arrived in Washington to call me at the Capitol. Sure enough, that call came, and I promptly contacted my former colleague Jack Nichols. He was delighted and said, among other things, that his company was deeply interested in landing rights in the regent's country and this would give him an opportunity to pursue it. When the regent and his entourage arrived, Jack Nichols had already made arrangements to take him on a plane to Chicago. As I recall, they spent a week there together and really saw Chicago night life. Then they flew to New York, where they secured a huge amount of space at the Waldorf Astoria. There they spent another week and saw New York night life as only Jack Nichols could show it to them.

When next I heard from him I said, "Jack, did you ever get your landing rights?"

His only reply was, "What do you think? And thanks a million for remembering me."

It was while he was doing duty at Payne Field in Cairo that he boarded a plane which crashed shortly after takeoff. At the time I knew nothing about it, and it required a good many weeks before the body could be returned to the United States. One day, out of a clear sky, Jack Nichols's sister phoned me. She said, "Ev, Jack's body has been returned and we are having a formal service for him at the First Baptist Church on Sixteenth Street here in Washington. In going over his effects we found a notebook and in it was this notation, 'If anything happens to me Ev Dirksen promised to deliver the funeral oration.' We have scheduled the service for next Tuesday afternoon, and we do earnestly hope that you can carry out the promise you made to Jack."

All I could say was, "My dear, I'll be there."

It is amazing how much economic nonsense the human brain can produce in time of crisis. Once a man, probably thirty years of age, in a very soiled shirt, carrying his jacket over his arm because the day was warm, managed to get by the secretary in my outer office, walk in on me, and nonchalantly perch himself on my desk. I was a bit abashed and said to him, "Mister, I don't know who you are, I've never seen you before, but people have been thrown out of this office for conduct far less rude than that you are exhibiting this minute."

My words did not seem to bother him particularly, and in a rather jaunty tone he said, "I am from Indiana. I am your neighbor. I have a scheme for solving the problem of the depression."

To that I said, "Where have you been all my life? We have been looking for you. Shall I call in a stenographer or would you like to tell me informally what this scheme is?"

He said, "It's very simple. You know that if you want to telephone you have to put a round nickel or a round dime or a round quarter in the slot. If you want a pack of cigarettes from a vending machine you put round coins in the slot. In fact, if you want to use any automatic vending device it takes a round coin. Now suppose you put a bill in the congressional hopper requiring that over a period of time all the round coins must be called back to the mint in Philadelphia or Denver or some other place and reminted with square corners—presto! You can't telephone, you can't get cigarettes or gum out of the machine until the telephone boxes and all the vending machines are rebuilt so they will work with square money. Now, Congressman, I figure there are twenty million people out of work. I figure also that it will take just about twenty million people to refit all these vending machines and coin boxes. So overnight the depression will be solved."

I looked at him slightly flabbergasted and then said, "Mr. Whatever-your-name-is, you're just a plain genius. You had better write your name, address, and background on a piece of paper so I can send it to the secretary of the treasury and have him interview you, because nothing but sheer and undiluted genius could come up with an idea like this." He went away quite content.

The incident also reminds me of a man from New Jersey who appeared before one of the congressional committees to protest the fact that there was no improvement in prices and that, as a tomato grower, he was steadily going broke. And then to the startled committee he said, "What we need is a darn good war to pep things up and raise the price of tomatoes." When I saw that report I began to reflect on it and thought what a weird and unhappy equation it really is: red blood, red tomatoes.

The square-money man from Indiana and the tomato grower from New Jersey were both reminders that, year after year, the economy continued to show few signs of recovery. Relief projects were not only kept alive but also were substantially expanded. Reform projects were being steadily put through the congressional mill but had made no appreciable dent in the situation. The mood was sometimes mean and bitter. We had the devalued gold, and we were buying silver until its ratio to gold in our monetary system would be sixteen to one. We were improving farm production but also piling up surpluses. We were confronted with constant pressure to give our surplus commodities to anybody who would take them, whether at home or abroad. If this had been done in our home market, it would have defeated the very purpose of the farm plan, to reduce acreage and surpluses and thereby raise prices. To distribute these commodities to other countries would only disorganize their whole agricultural economy, and their diplomatic representatives often protested the idea.

There were still millions without jobs, and their plight could not be remedied until they had regained sufficient purchasing power to purchase the goods which would make the wheels of industry spin again. This dislocation continued year in and year out, and I felt that perhaps time alone would be the healer.

In reflecting on this economic disaster that had beset the nation for so many years, I began to wonder anew why anyone would wish to be a senator. The problems and the headaches would be greater. Was there enough glory and prestige to offset it? I doubted it very much.

12

METEOR ACROSS THE SKY

B Y 1940 THE NEW DEAL was struggling with its promises and its lack of performance. It was the eighth year of Democratic power, and certainly the country expected far more than it got. What was true of the unemployment situation was equally true in the farm domain. What the New Deal offered were actually panaceas that were either modifications of old programs or certain new programs that seemed equally dubious. The farm surpluses continued to increase, and farm prices continued to be depressed.

I must say a word for at least one person who was connected with the general farm program. As administrator of the Farm Surplus Commodity Administration, Milo Perkins was able, knowledgeable, and had a far better concept of what should be done than most. Yet his task was simply too much for him. His endeavors were not readily appreciated by the New Deal leaders since he tried to keep our farm economy on a sound basis. He was ultimately relieved for his pains.

And so the New Deal chariot raced on and on. The favorite charioteer was Harry Hopkins, who commanded the ear of the president and received almost carte-blanche authority to carry on according to his likes and desires. He had a thorough understanding of public psychology, and his famous observation that the New Deal would "tax and tax, spend and spend, and elect and elect" was being carried out.

Much of the wave of good will on which the New Deal rode to victory in 1932 was, however, being dissipated. Hatreds were beginning to build and they were extremely intense.

It was only natural, therefore, that the political field was being carefully canvassed to find someone who at long last would be a fair match for Franklin D. Roosevelt and bring substantial modifications to New Deal plans. It was reasoned that a good Republican candidate with magnetism and campaign vigor who could speak in a forthright fashion might be able to encompass the defeat of the New Deal. Such a candidate would, of course, be armored, along with other things, with the so-called anti-third-term tradition which had been so zealously guarded and preserved since the days of George Washington. Surely an able candidate who could speak fluently and with fervor could win in November of 1940.

That year the Republicans met in Philadelphia to go through the agonies of a convention in the heat of summer in order to select candidates for the presidency and vice-presidency and to draft a platform with broad appeal for the entire country. Several candidates had for some time been presenting their views and their causes to the electorate in all parts of the country. One of these was Harold Stassen, former governor of Minnesota. A mutual friend once remarked to me that in a conversation with Mr. Stassen, the governor stated that he had staked out three precise goals in life: the first of these was to be elected as county attorney at age twenty-three, the second was to get himself elected as governor at age thirty, and the third was to become president at age fifty. Actually he had achieved the first two of his goals, and that inspired him to plan his strategy to achieve the Republican nomination for the presidency and then take his cause to the country. It must be said for Governor Stassen that he was extremely vigorous, highly articulate, and presented his case very well.

Governor Dwight Green, of Illinois, a very attractive personality who had been selected as the keynote speaker for the convention, also had presidential ambitions. Steps were taken to put the Illinois delegation behind him and that effort had the unremitting support of Colonel Robert McCormick, who was owner and publisher of the crusading *Chicago Tribune.*

I have but one comment to make in connection with the budding candidacy of Dwight Green, and that is in connection with his keynote speech. He had asked me to help in his preparation and specifically asked that I lay out my idea of such a speech. I devoted considerable time and effort to this undertaking, and when I had finished I thought I had done a very creditable piece of work. The speech was basic and fundamental and predicated on my evaluation of the New Deal, based on eight years in Congress, and on my estimate of what the country really wanted. I submitted this handiwork and heard nothing more about it. The keynote speech which he delivered I heard by way of radio in my room in the Bellevue-Stratford Hotel. Candor compels me to say that it was a distinct disappointment. Actually, he did not make one speech but rather three speeches rolled in one. It was terribly disjointed: there were no points of drama and appeal and the effect on the convention was like a sudden rain shower. It had not lifted the delegates as a keynote speech should do.

The real fighting speech that went to the very heart of the great issues was made by former president Herbert Hoover. It was, in my judgment, one of the finest he had ever delivered; and as I listened I thought that there in substance was the kind of speech I had prepared for Dwight Green.

Out of a clear Indiana sky like a blazing meteor along came Wendell Willkie to have his name presented to the convention. It seemed as if a full-blown campaign for his nomination had been hurled out of the sky like a thunderbolt. You might have called it a blitz. I remember the whole episode quite well, including the battles which took place prior to the convention meeting in Philadelphia.

On the train which carried many congressmen and senators who had been designated or elected as delegates were others who either occupied positions of leadership in the party or who had in years past been leaders and still exercised substantial influence. Among them was James Watson, of Indiana, who had served as majority leader in both the House of Representatives and the Senate. He was a conservative politician and a devoted Republican. He dropped his huge frame in a seat, and I took a place beside him and we struck up a continuing conversation over party affairs and what was likely to happen at the convention. I topped it off by asking him directly, "Jim, what do you think of Wendell Willkie as a candidate?" He fairly snorted and then began quite a harangue.

"Dirksen," he said, "I'm not sure whether Wendell Willkie has ever been a Republican or even an independent. I know of no time when he has manifested any interest in politics generally or in the Republican party. His sudden advent on the Republican horizon reminds me of nothing so much as a gal in Indianapolis who was the keeper of a bawdy house. She was very successful in her operations and finally got religion, but that, however, did not induce her to foresake her calling. She thought it might be well for her soul if she expiated her sins and joined a church. She marched down to see the minister and told him she was a sinner, wanted to join the church, and offered the preacher a thousand dollars as a contribution toward his salary and for the upkeep of the church. She showed up the very first Sunday and then insisted to the minister that she wanted to join the choir. She also appeared in church the next Sunday and then insisted that she become the leader of the choir. That's how I feel about Wendell Willkie. He no sooner joins the party than he strikes out to be the party's candidate for president."

Notwithstanding the feeling of Hoosier Jim Watson for his fellow Hoosier Wendell Willkie, the blitz really got underway. Telegrams by the thousands from all over the country reached the delegates, and it could well be in view of the number of delegates that the telegrams, telephone calls, special delivery letters, and other communications may have reached into the hundreds of thousands. There were also personal calls by interested parties who buttonholed all delegates on behalf of Wendell Willkie. Other candidates could not match this mass attack on the convention. As a result, in a surprisingly short time Wendell Willkie was nominated.

In some quarters there was great elation, but Democrats generally were not particularly dismayed by his selection. They knew, of course, that he was a corporate and a utility lawyer, and it was quite obvious that they intended to make the most of it. Great preparations were made to formally announce the nomination at a huge outdoor festival at Willkie's hometown, Ellwood, Indiana. After that, the campaign would get under way in high gear. A campaign train to start from Chicago and to swing westward was readied, and I was summoned from Washington to join the train. Actually, Mr. Willkie had been doing some campaigning before that; and when I reached Chicago and found a place on the train well removed from the end coach, occupied by the candidate, a messenger asked me to step into another coach to speak with Mr. Willkie's brother. He told me immediately that Mr. Willkie's throat was in very bad shape and, since he regarded me as a seasoned campaigner, he insisted that I go to the end coach to talk with Mr. Willkie and give him some advice. This I was reluctant to do because Mr. Willkie did not actually summon me to see him nor had he asked for advice. His brother, however, continued to urge and finally got me by the sleeve and pulled me along to Mr. Willkie's private car.

When I greeted him and he returned the greeting I knew at once what the difficulty was. Knowledgeable as he might be in many fields, and particularly in the law, he had never learned to use his voice properly. He spoke from his vocal cords rather than from his diaphragm. Sustained speaking, therefore, produced in him a condition somewhat like laryngitis, and his voice sounded like a violin bow drawn over tightly stretched baling wire. I waited for him or his brother to open up the conversation about his throat, but since they did not do so, I went back to the coach to which I had been assigned.

In a little while others on the train convened a kind of informal council to see what might be done. At that juncture I suggested that before the train departed from Chicago, they should contact a throat specialist, because the train would make at least three short stops before it arrived in Peoria, where it was anticipated that a large crowd would be on hand. I further suggested that still another throat specialist might be put in a speedy automobile, provided with a police escort, and hurried to LaSalle, Illinois, another stop on the itinerary. The suggestion, however, was not followed, and at long last they left the candidate to his own devices. I rather dreaded what I knew would happen.

Mr. Willkie would make his first short speech of the trip at Joliet, Illinois, the second speech would be in Ottawa, the third speech would be made at LaSalle, and the fourth stop would be at Peoria.

It was indeed a huge crowd that had assembled at Union Station in Peoria to receive the candidate. The first order of business when the train came to a halt was to usher Mr. and Mrs. Willkie to a platform that could be reached by merely stepping from the rear platform of the end coach. A little girl had been chosen to present Mrs. Willkie with a gorgeous spray of roses. The president of the Caterpillar Tractor Company was afforded the honor of introducing Mr. Willkie.

It is a bit difficult to describe the raspy, guttural whisper which came from Willkie's throat. It was ominous, and yet in that pitious condition he undertook to make a speech. I agonized through it with him for every word that he uttered. It appeared even more so in view of the fact that Wendell Willkie was a robust person whose whole being reflected a certain magnetism and virility, and it seemed almost incredible that this had happened to him at the very outset of the campaign.

From Peoria, Illinois, the train was to wind its way westward to Galesburg, Illinois, and from there on to other points until it reached Coffeyville, Kansas. I had no way of knowing what was happening to Willkie after the sad performance at Peoria, but I knew his voice would get progressively worse and could not possibly improve until there was a halt in campaign activities.

History has already fairly well evaluated the Willkie phenomenon, together with his proposals for "One World" and his proposal that the Tennessee Valley Authority and all of its properties be sold to private utility companies. The first of these items came as a distinct shock to those who still nurtured isolationist concepts, and the proposal to sell the TVA was like a bombshell to the devotees of public power.

At an early stage in the campaign, while Congress was still in session, Republican members of the Senate and House gave a dinner in Willkie's honor at the Continental Hotel in Washington. It was just a stone's throw from the Capitol. A substantial number attended the dinner, and on that occasion Mr. Willkie made a reasonably short speech and then agreed to submit to questions. The questions were in great variety but one in particular intrigued me a great deal.

It related to Mr. Willkie's then recent visit with Joseph Stalin, the Soviet dictator. The author of the question wanted to know something about Stalin as a person, his habits and eccentricities, and his general political philosophy. When Mr. Willkie got to an answer on Stalin's personal habits he said, among other things, that Stalin had a great many mistresses and that he liked them fat, tough, and frowzy. This shocked the lady members of the audience. I shall never forget how deeply incensed Clare Boothe Luce and Frances Bolton, both of whom were members of the House of Representatives, really were. They never quite got over it.

When the score was computed for the presidency on election day, we had gained some votes since 1936 but not really enough to be important. The total vote was 27,244,160 for Roosevelt and 22,305,198 for Willkie. The vote was so distributed that Franklin Roosevelt received 449 electoral votes and Willkie received 82. In the Senate the Republican party managed to increase its strength from 16 to 28 and in the House from 88 to 162. The period 1939–41, as everyone will recall, saw the war clouds grow darker and darker. It was marked by the deep distress in which Great Britain found herself as a result of Hitler's blitz campaigns, which threatened the survival of Great Britain itself. She needed help, and there was only one place to which she could turn; that was the United States. First came the so-called Destroyer Deal, in which we made ships available on a lend-lease basis. This was followed by requests for supplies of other weapons and equipment. All this precipitated the great neutrality debate which swept the country, as well as Congress, and inspired what became known as the "cash and carry" campaign. This simply meant that there were to be no weapons supplied by the United States to a belligerent country without payment in cash and delivery by the vessels of the recipient country.

It was in this period that the president summoned Congress into special session to deal with various aspects of the war problem in Europe. When I returned to Washington for this session, my office was fairly inundated with postcards, letters, and telegrams embellished with "cash and carry" slogans. There was a veritable deluge.

Insofar as I could spell out some kind of a pattern in these messages, as it related to my own constituents rather than those who were sending their entreaties and commands from other states, it appeared that there was an overlay of pro-German sentiment still vigorously expressing itself. Perhaps this could not be regarded as extraordinary because virtually every county in my congressional district had a very substantial number of people who were of German extraction, as I was myself.

For me, it was a phenomenon in the sense that it was a real pressure bath, and the question was how to meet it without incurring some enduring political damage. Suddenly I remembered that a former congressman—a Democrat who had served in the period of the First World War when Woodrow Wilson was in the White House—might have some timely advice for me, and I consulted him about it. He pointed out that our own security had to be the foremost consideration, and that our action with respect to the European conflict had to be such as to safeguard and augment security by giving friendly countries whatever assistance might be required. He was, therefore, of the opinion that we had no choice except to assist Great Britain in every possible way. This is precisely what took place.

One curious incident which I remember about that special session was that there might be a joint session of the Congress to receive a message from the president. As was the custom, there would be one gallery ticket available to each member of the House. On the morning of that session, I went to work reasonably early and as I moved down the corridor in the direction of my office, I saw a man and woman loitering outside my office door. When I approached, it was possible to identify them immediately, and I told them to come in. We had a short visit and then came the question of how they might be admitted to the joint session. I advised them that I had only a single ticket, but I would make it available to them. This I did.

Some weeks later when this couple returned to their home in Peoria, they sent a note of thanks and appreciation. The lady was thrilled that she was able to attend the joint session and see the officials of the three branches of government together with the diplomatic corps all under one roof.

By way of more tangible appreciation, they said that for a number of years they had been raising pedigreed terriers as a hobby and asked whether I would accept a puppy as a gift? I remembered immediately that our daughter, by now quite a young lady, had so often expressed the hope that she might have a pet dog, so I accepted. When at long last that little animal became a part of the family, Joy promptly bestowed upon it the name Licorice because it was coal black. I never realized how a friendly puppy could insinuate himself into the affections of a family, and when she was killed later by a passing automobile, it seemed years before the family grief was assuaged.

While reflecting on occasion on all the pressures, the mail volume, the dissident opinions expressed, and other factors which developed in connection with the growing war menace, I wondered why anyone would want to be a senator. Surely the pressures on a statewide basis would be enormously greater and keep one in a state of high agitation most of the time.

During that period when the country was becoming highly emotional over the war issue, the German ambassador was staging a series of what became known as "beer parties" or "beer nights" to which many members of the House and Senate were invited. I was invited and discovered that a warm fellowship prevailed even though I was not particularly fond of beer. But it was good to be on hand to listen and to learn. I detected at the very first of these "beer parties" that conversation almost invariably turned to the war in Europe and what the United States might do in case a serious situation developed, threatening our own security as well as the integrity of some of the countries in western and southern Europe. I noticed also that embassy officials and clerks, who were easily recognizable, circulated constantly through the crowd and made a special point of joining in the conversation whenever they found a group discussing the growing European conflict.

At one point in the evening, one of the embassy attachés joined a small group where I was present and began to express some rather firm convictions on the war. I began to wonder whether the German ambassador might not be misadvising Adolph Hitler as to what the United States might do.

After a moment, I tapped the young man on the shoulder and beckoned him to come off in a corner. I was quite certain that he was a member of the embassy staff and that the effort he was making to participate in many conversations that evening indicated that he had been told to try to build up some slight sentiment against any intervention by this country in affairs abroad. I then said to him that I thought since I was of German parentage only one generation removed from the old country I might tell him sincerely that if the ambassador was giving Hitler that kind of advice, he was deceiving his boss, and that events could easily overtake that advice. This is precisely what happened, and interestingly enough I was never invited to the ambassador's "beer parties" again.

As I have said, when I was first assigned to service on the Committee on the District of Columbia along with other committees, I uttered something of a groan and promptly took myself to the office of Joseph Martin Jr., of Massachusetts, who was the whip or deputy leader on the Republican side. I had learned from other members who had committee experience that service on the committee which looked after the affairs of the nation's capital was to be carefully avoided because it had no political value back home. But Joe Martin counseled me to be a good soldier and perform my committee chores and do my homework.

It turned out that service on this committee was productive of a great many contacts in the District of Columbia, and I think back to some of them with considerable amusement. Each year the Board of Trade staged an annual dinner to which congressional leaders, and particularly the members of the Committee on the District of Columbia, were invited.

It was at one of these dinners that I found my table companion was one of the law professors and, also, one of the bar examiners. In the course of the evening I mentioned my great disappointment that I had failed the District of Columbia bar examination. The colloquy with him was about like this, "Did you use a portable typewriter in writing the exam?"

I told him that I had written the exam in longhand. Then he asked, "Did you write long answers to the questions?" I told him that I was afraid I had. "The reason I ask about the typewriter," he said, "is that I and others have to read these examination papers, and usually there are as many as twelve hundred young men and women who take the bar examination at one time. That becomes quite a chore. The reason I asked you about long answers is that if in the course of such an answer you volunteer information that is wrong, even though not directly relevant to the question in the quiz, you get a zero for your pains." Some months later when I took the bar examination a second time, I followed his instructions and was successful.

One incident in connection with my service on the District of Columbia Committee has recurred over the years. It was my custom to go to work early in the morning, and my office was usually ready for business at 7:30. Early on a given morning the telephone rang and it was a congressman from a western state. He said, "Can I come over and see you right away?" Very shortly he appeared in the office with another gentleman whom he introduced as from his home state. This man had been the president of the State Federation of Labor. The story was then quickly unfolded.

The congressman's friend was a bachelor and had come to Washington to serve in the National Labor Organization. It was his custom on Saturday nights to spend the evening at a club to which he belonged where he could get a drink and play pinochle. Under the closing laws that existed in the capital, the orchestra, if any, played the "Star Spangled Banner" at midnight, the waiters gathered up the glassware, and the club then closed.

The congressman's friend may have imbibed a little too freely, and as he drove home a traffic officer on a motorcycle sounded his siren and pushed the car to the curb. He directed him to drive to the precinct station where he was booked on a charge of drunken and disorderly driving. If convicted of the charge he would lose his license to drive a car, so the query was to me, "What can you do about it because you are the ranking minority member on the District of Columbia Committee?"

I thought for a moment and then looked up the home number of the District corporation counsel. Fortunately, I caught him before he left home and asked whether he could drive by the office before he went to his own office in the District Building. When he came, the story was quickly retold. The corporation counsel went to the telephone and in a few minutes managed to get the name of the arresting officer and whatever details he needed. He then turned to the congressman's friend and asked, "Would you take a plea of plain disorderly conduct, because that does not involve losing your license?" The congressman's friend was more than glad to accede to that suggestion, and so the case was processed and dismissed on that ground.

The congressman's friend then turned to me and said, "You certainly are a decent guy, what can I do for you? How does labor treat you out in your congressional district?"

"Labor has not always been too friendly," I answered, "and I have seldom been invited to the annual Labor Day picnic."

His response was, "They should treat you better. How would you like to have an endorsement from my boss?"

I laughed a little and said, "I have a spotty labor record, because I just cannot follow all the demands that organized labor makes upon a public servant in Congress."

"We'll see what can be done," he said. About three days later my secretary brought an envelope marked "personal" to my desk. I quickly opened it, and there was an unequivocal endorsement from the State Federation of Labor for my reelection to the Congress.

I was invited to the annual Labor Day picnic that year. Public officials and candidates were always introduced. They saved me until last. The master of ceremonies addressed the crowd and said, "I have a very special pleasure today. I want to introduce our congressman, and before I present him, let me read to you a letter which I received from our national president in Washington." He then proceeded to read the letter of endorsement, and it was greeted with loud and enthusiastic applause. I have thought of that incident often and marveled at what can happen as a result of fixing a traffic ticket.

Another incident comes to mind in connection with my service on the

District Committee. The nation's capital has no racetrack, which is no great handicap because neighboring Maryland has an abundance of racecourses. It seems strange, nevertheless, that promoters in this field of sport have not undertaken to secure dispensation for the building of such a track.

One day a representative of a racetrack operator in another state dropped in on my office and, after some pleasantries, gradually warmed up to the subject of the need of the capital for such a racetrack. When he had finished his discourse, I said, "The answer is a plain and emphatic no. In support of that answer I'll give you a couple of reasons: in the first place, there is a huge government payroll and, knowing how strong the instinct for wagering money on racehorses is, I can envision a lot of government people spending money which they can ill afford. And I'll give you another reason: the small loan business enterprises find it difficult to do business under the restrictions imposed by the District ordinances. You will find, therefore, a great many of these small loan offices on the border in Maryland and Virginia. I have seen a good many queues of people in the morning after payday standing in line to pay off their small loan debts. That situation would become greatly aggravated if the lure of a racetrack caused them to go deeper and deeper into debt."

That ended the conversation, but word came that despite my opposition an effort would be made in any event to get a license for a track. The venture was not succeeding very well. After the lapse of several weeks, a stranger came to my office and renewed the conversation. Among other things, he said, "I am sure you know that there is a great need for jobs in the Washington area, particularly for manual labor. I have been thinking about a project that could generate a very substantial number of jobs, and I believe we would be well advised if we could get a permit for a racetrack. You look like a good sport to me. What would it take to remove your opposition?"

I arose and said, "My friend, I think you had better leave before you get yourself into deep and unhappy trouble." He left and that was the last time I ever heard of the effort to saddle Washington with a racetrack.

Sometimes service on the District Committee could lead to embarrassing situations. I well recall the case of a congressman who lost his wallet ostensibly in a taxicab. It contained a very substantial sum of money. His wife, who was quite intimately familiar with his habits and his deportment on occasion, telephoned me and complained bitterly that her legislator husband had been robbed. As a member of the District Committee I was expected to do something about it. It so happened that when he arrived at home in the small hours of the morning, she was waiting and went to the door to receive him and managed to fix in mind the license number of the taxicab. From there on the investigation was placed in my lap. I managed to locate the cab driver and asked him to come to my office. Over the years my relationship with the cab drivers in Washington was always very pleasant and friendly, and quite often some of them would come to my office and take counsel and sometimes suggest legislation and regulations that could be useful to them as cab drivers.

Without mincing words I said to him, "You had Congressman —— in your cab recently. It was late. His wife insists that he had a substantial sum of money in his wallet. When he reached home the wallet was gone, and she also insists that when you took him home you robbed him while he was in tipsy condition. Just what have you got to say about this situation?"

The cab driver did not lose his poise for a single minute and then said, "Dirksen, the cabbies know you quite well and they respect you. You often helped them to fight some of their battles and, because I know you'll be fair, I'll tell you the whole story. I picked up your colleague after midnight. He had a pretty fair package aboard even then. He wanted to find a place where he could get a pint of liquor and insisted, also, that I drive him there. Well, you know how it is with cab drivers, they do know a few things and most of them know where you can get a little whiskey after closing hours. I drove him to the place. He gave me some money and I went in and got a pint. I handed him the change and he said that I could keep it. He opened that bottle and took a kingsized swig of whiskey. I then took him home and that is the whole story."

I kept thinking about the lost wallet and finally I said, "Your story sounds straightforward enough but it does not sound very persuasive. I would hate to report you to the authorities but I do not know, under the circumstances, what else I can do."

He then began to lose a little of his cool and poise and his voice began to rise as he said, "So help me, I did not do it—I did not take his wallet! I know the district from which he comes. I'll write the newspapers and tell the whole story and tell them he's a drunk!"

There was little more to the conversation, and then I said, "I have your name and address and your cab number. Sometime later I may wish to talk with you again."

The following day I reported to the congressman exactly what had happened and then phoned his wife and advised her, also, of this conversation. After reflection, both of them said just about the same thing, "I guess we had better let the matter drop." There were quite a few such incidents while I was a congressman.

Although it was entirely unofficial, it was generally said that the chairman of the House District Committee was actually the unofficial mayor of Washington in those days. As such he was called upon quite frequently to welcome groups and conventions and was, in a sense, the official greeter. When I became chairman I was requested to extend greetings to a convention of surgical nurses. The largest ballroom in Washington was packed and it was said that at least five thousand nurses were in attendance. It just so happened that the opening day of their convention fell on the birth anniversary of George Washington. I had prepared no remarks and no suitable stories and was sitting on the stage ready to be introduced, all the while wondering what appropriate story I could tell, and then out of my mischievous mind came a story about Halloween. It had a certain relation to George Washington.

I remember uttering some pleasantries and then I decided to take the risk, and went on, "Girls, I should tell you at least one anecdote appropriate to the occasion, since this is the birth anniversary of the father of our country. It is a story about Halloween, when in small towns and villages it used to be the custom for youngsters not only to indulge in 'Trick or Treat' but also to become even a little more destructive. Once in my town that destructive instinct found vent, and they sallied through the neighborhood and undertook to upend what was politely known as the family chick sale—It was before the days of outdoor plumbing. It so happened that on the following morning the father of two boys called them in and said, 'Were you two among that group that was engaged in mischief in the neighborhood last night and took part in overturning some outhouses?' At first there was some reluctance to answer, and finally the younger of the two said, 'Dad, I'm sorry. I confess. I was in that crowd that did those things.' By then the father was quite a little enraged and said, 'I'm going to have to take a strap and give you a sound thrashing.' The younger was quick to reply, 'Aw, Dad, you wouldn't do that. Aren't you forgetting that when George Washington chopped down the cherry tree and told his father that he did it and said, 'I cannot tell a lie, I did it with my little hatchet,' George's father blessed him for not telling a lie and for confessing the truth'? To this the father said, 'My boy, that might be alright for George Washington's father, but he was not sitting in the cherry tree.'" I must say I was absolutely flabbergasted by the hearty response this George Washington story evoked from the surgical nurses.

Then there was a unique one-man hearing which I conducted as chairman of the District Committee. I embalmed the record of it by having it sealed and placed in the committee safe. I presume it disappeared a long time ago, but I wish it might be available to substantiate what happened at this one hearing.

One of the Washington newspapers had carried a series of stories about a young lady from Russia who had lectured to a teacher's college in Maryland and to a high-school assembly in Washington. What made her lecture a front page story was that she so vigorously supported the communist line. As a result there came a demand for an investigation. I was quite reluctant to make it a matter for committee action and thought, to save the committee members' time, I might investigate it myself and I did. I had had a former FBI agent, whom I knew quite well, there to give me assistance in the matter. I suggested that he call on this girl and ask her to appear at a scheduled hearing in the committee room.

He came back to report and said she demurred at the idea and wasn't sure whether she would appear or not. Along with his report, however, he stated that there was a husband who was a native-born American citizen and that they had two very young children.

At some point the lady changed her mind and sent word that she would appear. When she arrived for the hearing, she brought her husband and the two children with her. I thought it would be well to hear them one at a time and alone, and I asked her to testify first. The story went like this: She had been a teacher in the Moscow schools. She spoke fluent English. She had a girlfriend who was dating a young man from the American embassy. The friend called her prospective date on the telephone, but instead of getting him on the line she got another voice. Whoever the young man was, he asked in a rather bantering fashion whether he wouldn't do to fill the date, and she said he would. Accordingly, they arranged to meet in a park. When he arrived, he found not one girl but two. And our schoolteacher was the second of the two. It was through this meeting that she had met her husband. They had begun to see each other quite regularly and finally decided to find a little billet where they could live together. In due course the first of the two children was born. As a result the story came out and along with it a good many other things. The young man had been serving as a code clerk at the embassy, where his duty was to decode messages. It was a very sensitive position. Our ambassador in Moscow, therefore, had no choice save to send the pair home.

I excused her and called on the husband and his story soon came out. He had been in the army. When he was released, he came to Washington. There he took a civil service examination and rather quickly found a position in the

State Department. Evidently his work was quite suitable for, in due course, he had a chance for an assignment to the United States embassy in Moscow. His description of meeting the girl in question was substantially as she related it, and that when the first baby was born they had to be married before being returned to the United States. Sometime on I plied him with a whole series of questions about her family life, the questions which she would ask about affairs in our embassy, the kinds of answers he gave, and whether or not he was disclosing confidential information which she could have easily conveyed to the Soviet secret police. He did not seem unduly abashed by all this. But since there did not seem to me to be any applicable law under which he might be indicted for misconduct, the one-man hearing closed at that point.

All this might have been a good prelude to a series of front page stories. But one thing inhibited any disposition on my part to make disclosures, and that was the presence of the two youngsters who were cavorting around in the committee room while first the mother and later the father were testifying under oath. How easy it might have been to cast a dark and indelible mark upon the future of those two blonde children!

There were many more of these episodes. Whenever I reflected on whether or not I wanted to be a senator, I wondered, in case I was successful, whether the Committee on Committees, which had charge of assigning new senators to committee posts, might insist on having me take an assignment on the Senate Committee on the District of Columbia or on the Appropriations Subcommittee for the District of Columbia, which handled fiscal matters for the nation's capital. Would I undergo the same local experience if I were in the Senate? Would there be the same patronage problems and would senators undertake to bedevil me to find jobs for friends from home in the fire department or the police department or the District government?

All this has been changed since, and the District of Columbia has a greater measure of self-government.

13

DRAMATIC DEEDS

O VER THE YEARS the history books have fully told the grim story of the decade beginning about 1933. It included Adolph Hitler's rise to power at the very time that Franklin Delano Roosevelt was elected president of the United States. It embraced Benito Mussolini's invasion of Ethiopia in 1935. It included Hitler's annexation of Austria in 1938. It embraced, also, the takeover of Czechoslovakia by Hitler in 1939. It was Hitler then, and it was the Soviet Union thirty years later, who moved upon the Czechs. Also in this period came the invasion and subjugation of Poland in September of 1939. This task required only five weeks, and, subsequently, came the takeover of Belgium and Holland in mid-1940.

To us watching these developments from afar, it all seemed so remote at first. There was a rather general disposition to let the European nations fight if only they left us alone. And then came for us a dramatic and indeed a world-shaking moment. The day was December 7, 1941. It was Sunday. I am not quite sure what took me to Washington at that time, but I believe the Appropriations Committee was holding preliminary hearings on the independent offices appropriation bill. This measure embraced estimates for appropriations for the independent agencies of government. It included the Veterans Administration, the Tennessee Valley Authority, the Federal Trade Commission, the Interstate Commerce Commission, the Federal Communications Commission, the Securities and Exchange Commission, and a great many others. Customarily this was the first appropriation bill to be considered and gave both committee members and the House generally something on which to work at the very beginning of the session, which would get underway shortly after Congress convened in January. By beginning the hearings a month early, it was possible to hear the testimony of many witnesses and prepare the measure for consideration by the full committee and by the House.

I shall never forget that day. In the afternoon I was comfortably loafing in our apartment while listening to a professional football game. Memory dictates that the Chicago Bears were playing the Washington Redskins. They were really mauling each other. From my point of view, it was an excellent game. It was rough. The clacking of collarbones came like music to one who was fond of sports. Professional football was at the very top of my list.

Somewhere in the middle of that game the voice of an announcer intruded and said simply, "Stand by for a special announcement. The Japanese have bombed Pearl Harbor." That, as I recall, was all that was said. Brief as it was, it spoke volumes. It was laconic, so pointed, so unadorned, but all the implications were readily apparent to one who had lived through a similar period a generation before.

Suddenly I lost all taste for the football game. I got into my overcoat and walked down Connecticut Avenue. My thoughts tumbled, each one marked by anguish and turbulence of spirit as I walked along. It was so amazing that, even through the closed doors of apartments which fronted on the avenue and the side streets, one could hear Christmas music. It was the season when the hearts of people were lifted in anticipation of Christmas Day and all of mankind was attuned to Christmas carols.

It made no sense. As I walked I would catch a bar of "O Little Town of Bethlehem." I walked further. From another doorway came the strains of "Hark, the Herald Angels Sing." I walked further. I could hear that sweetest of all Christmas songs, "Silent Night, Holy Night." To think that this fell blow should come in such a season of the year. The anxiety would not be dismissed from mind. I could well anticipate what would happen the following day.

I went to my office on Capitol Hill at an early hour. Other members had also arrived early. Even at that early hour of the morning, people were moving in the direction of the Capitol. They would want to be on hand for what they knew was going to happen. Since my office was available and the door was open, other members looked in or paused for a moment to simply say, "What do you think of it?" Well, what was one to think but that the nation was in for a grim experience? Not the least of the strange thoughts which assailed me was the fact that two representatives of the Japanese government—Mr. Nomura and Mr. Kurusu—were in Washington and had been conferring with Secretary of State Hull. In addition, one had learned from press accounts that the president had sent a personal appeal to Emperor Hirohito to avoid war in the Pacific. That appeal was made the day before the attack on Pearl Harbor. All this merely confused one's thinking. When House and Senate met, they were quickly advised that there would be a joint session in the afternoon and that the president would appear. The president arrived early in the afternoon. As might be expected, the galleries were packed with government officials, the diplomatic corps, and any others who could find places there.

When the president actually appeared in the chamber, there was tremendous applause and it continued. His address took only six minutes, but it was punctuated throughout with thunderous cheers. Just before he began, however, a strange quiet fell on the assembly, and then came the voice of the president: "Mr. Vice-President, Mr. Speaker, members of the Senate and the House of Representatives: Yesterday, December 7, 1941—a date which will live in infamy—the United States of America was suddenly and deliberately attacked by naval and air forces of the empire of Japan."

He told us of the widespread Japanese surprise offensive, set in motion even as the Japanese ambassador replied to Secretary Hull with no threat of war. As commander in chief he had ordered our armed forces to take all measures for defense in this hour of national peril. He concluded:

"I ask that the Congress declare that since the unprovoked and dastardly attack by Japan on Sunday, December 7, 1941, a state of war has existed between the United States and the Japanese Empire."

When the president concluded his message, the applause was deafening. As soon as he departed, the Senate went back to its chamber, and both House and Senate immediately took up for consideration the joint resolution declaring that a state of war existed between the United States and Japan. The resolution was very brief and read as follows:

> Whereas the Imperial Government of Japan has committed unprovoked acts of war against the Government and the people of the United States of America: Therefore be it
>
> Resolved, etc., That the state of war between the United States and the Imperial Government of Japan which has thus been thrust upon the United States is hereby formally declared; and the President is hereby authorized and directed to employ the entire naval and military forces of the United States and the resources of the Government to carry on war against the Imperial Government of Japan; and, to bring the conflict to a successful termination, all the resources of the Country are hereby pledged by the Congress of the United States.

It took Congress only thirty-three minutes, after the conclusion of the president's address, to pass that resolution by a vote of 82 to 0 in the Senate and 388 to 1 in the House of Representatives. That one negative vote in the House carries with it its own little story. Fast and furious as the action was, the word got out almost immediately that there might be a vote against the resolution and it could possibly be Jeannette Rankin, who had been elected to the Congress from Montana. I knew her very well. She was a sweet, charming person and had deep and settled convictions on the subject of war. House leaders knew that Jeannette Rankin and I met and consulted very frequently on many legislative matters, and they therefore felt that perhaps I might be able to dissuade her from casting the lone negative vote. I sat with her in the chamber and told her how important it was to manifest to all the world that the Congress and the people were united and unanimous as never before in meeting the challenge which the Japanese assault had laid on our doorstep.

After I had exhausted every argument which I thought might be persuasive, she said, "Everett, I cannot do it. I cannot vote for a declaration of war. For my whole lifetime I have been dedicated to the cause of peace. War can only mean death for many young men of this nation, and I cannot subject them to this horror. My heart, my conscience, my conviction, compel me to vote no. I am sorry." And so the roll was intoned, and there was the one dissenting vote by Congresswoman Rankin, of Montana.

There was sheer bewilderment as members of the House gathered into little groups to speculate and to discuss what would happen next. One thing was quite clear: It would be necessary to prepare the nation for a war of unpredictable duration. There were, of course, a few who thought of Japan as a small nation and of the United States as a colossus, and that we could bring the war to an end in short order. But preparing the nation for war meant the acquisition of weapons and equipment, the expansion of the military forces, the imposition of restraints upon the business and financial economy of the country, the appropriation of huge sums, the development of propaganda and weapons, and every other consideration involved in converting a peaceful country into a war machine.

There came added burdens for individual members of Congress, for when you adopt conscription and undertake to bring the young men of the nation into uniform for purposes of war, inequities and complexities are bound to develop. One thinks of the students and those who are pursuing senior and postgraduate courses, particularly in professional fields like engineering, medicine, teaching, law, and others. The question was whether or not they could serve the country more usefully by placing them in uniform without partiality—or whether to permit them to pursue their studies because their professional skill and talent would be needed not merely in connection with conflict but for the benefit of our entire economy. These were not easy questions to answer. In addition there would be those who would seek refuge from conscription into the military service on the ground—and certainly a legitimate ground in most cases—of being conscientious objectors.

As induction and training of American manpower got underway, there came still other questions, such as why, during the training period, young men could not be assigned to camps which were close to home so that they might visit their families on weekends. If one undertook to meet all these requests, it could easily demoralize the whole military effort, and members of the Congress had to deal with these very human problems as best they could.

On the evening of December 8 when I returned to the hotel, the lobby was well filled with people, including some senators and congressmen, all engaged in conversation about the struggle in which we were to become engaged. Among those who lived at the hotel and who came to the lobby every evening to visit with friends was Joseph Tumulty, who had been private secretary to Woodrow Wilson when he was governor of New Jersey and later president of the United States. Manifestly our conversation turned to the subject of the conflict and what it would mean to the country and, particularly, the young men.

"Dirk," Tumulty said, "what happened today is such a strange parallel to what happened in April of 1917 when Woodrow Wilson delivered his message and his request for a declaration of war to Congress. I shall never forget it. Then, as today, the galleries were filled and Wilson's message was also greeted with tremendous applause. We left the Capitol and returned to the White House. As we were about to enter the White House door, the president turned to me and said, 'Tumulty, what an astounding thing that the people applauded my war message. It was a message of death for many young men. I presume mankind will always be that way and, when there is sufficient provocation, they will react in precisely the same fashion.'"

On the following day, and from then on, the grim business continued. Estimates were quickly supplied for war needs and the amounts involved were colossal. The planners and military tacticians were thinking in terms of thousands of airplanes and tanks, heavy artillery and ammunition for small arms, food and uniforms, medical supplies, and ships that would be needed to carry troops to distant shores. One needed only to name it and it took on the character of a vital commodity or supply needed for the war effort.

To students of this undertaking it was immediately evident that the vast funds to be made available would quickly find their way into the economic bloodstream, and that, of course, would produce an inflationary fever which might require the imposition of controls on wages, prices, and materials. Others were thinking also in terms of the negotiation of whatever war contracts would be let in order to make certain that there would be no profiteering. It would be palpably unfair to ask the young men of the nation to get into uniform and hazard their lives while their fellow countrymen were profiting unduly as a result of the conflict. There were also those who were thinking in terms of excess profit taxes to make sure that war profits would be taxed for the benefit of the public treasury. What it all added up to finally was the question of putting the entire nation into an economic straitjacket and devoting everything to the war effort until the victory was achieved. When later developments in Europe and the conduct of the European aspect of the war called for further declarations of war by the United States against Germany and Italy, it was certain that elements of freedom would have to be sacrificed until the job was done.

When controls are imposed upon a free economy, some strange situations develop. I think often of an intimate friend who was summoned to Washington to take a position of considerable authority in one of the war production agencies. Among other things, one of his responsibilities was to deal with the question of materials that might be deemed essential to the war effort. I recall his account to me, given not without some humor, when a group of sheep ranchers from Wyoming came to Washington to make a plea for corrugated steel sheets with which to construct lambing pens. They pointed out that it would soon be time for the ewes to drop their lambs and since the weather at that time was exceedingly severe, it was necessary to get shelters ready.

Their appeals to the government were emotional because they knew how serious this really was. My friend sat in on all those discussions and, in fact, had the final word as to whether or not this material would be released for that purpose. He had absolutely no knowledge, no background whatsoever, concerning what was involved. When the discussion ended he finally said, "Gentlemen, I am sorry, you will have to get along without the material you want, and the ewes will have to wait to have their lambs." One can well imagine the torrent of criticism that eventually developed as a result of that decision.

In wartime it was expected that the military experts would prevail. It was generally believed that the men who had been educated at the various military and naval academies over a long period of years would certainly know what they were about, and that their judgment would be based upon what was best for the nation. This was equally true where food was concerned. The cry quickly went out, "Food will win the war and food will win the peace."

In those times it was rather interesting to look at members of the House of Representatives, reexamine the biographical data on each in the *Congressional Directory,* and note how many had served in World War I. Obviously, their own war and military experiences would have a very definite impact upon their thinking.

In wartime so much of the business of government must, in the interest of expedition, be done at the administrative level. So many new people were brought into the government structure, and it was hoped that the very best administrative talent could be procured. The principal function of Congress, therefore, was to provide the authority and the funds and trust that the commander in chief would effectively employ those funds for the procurement of weapons and equipment and the imposition of policies which would best serve the nation. One factor intruded itself constantly; it was the classification of information and testimony that was not to be publicly disclosed. On many occasions, when military witnesses or those high at the policy level were summoned to testify before various committees, the official reporter's notes were often embalmed, so to speak, and placed in the committee safe so they would be secure from prying eyes. That, of course, meant that in the interest of keeping the senators and congressmen reasonably informed and happy, there had to be fairly close cooperation between the executive and legislative branches.

I recall one instance which, had it been fully disclosed in a newspaper, might have had an astonishing impact upon the thinking of our people. Members of the appropriations committees of the House and Senate were summoned to a completely off-of-the-record meeting in the Munitions Building on Constitution Avenue. Not knowing what to expect, everybody was punctual, and at the appointed moment George Catlett Marshall, chief of staff of the army, appeared for a discussion with the members. He did not keep them in doubt very long. The doors were closed and monitored and then, in substance, George Marshall said: "Gentlemen, I brought you here to acquaint you with something that is at the moment top secret. It will come as a distinct shock. We are now quite certain that Japanese planning calls for an assault on Alaska. If it should happen it can present real problems. We have developed a Pacific strategy that we believe is correct, and we cannot afford to detach troops from the Pacific Islands to establish an adequate defense for Alaska. This matter has been thoroughly canvassed by the staff. We are unanimous in the belief that, if Alaska is attacked and if the Japanese should succeed in capturing Alaska, we shall have no choice but to let them do so. Since we are looking down the long road to achieve victory, we must take this chance. I felt it my duty to advise you on this point so that it would not come as a complete surprise."

The members were quite thunderstruck. They knew full well that if this happened it would be on the front page of every newspaper in the land. Who could say what the public reaction would be? Not the least of the problems involved would be the impact on the morale of those forces already in the field. Since most of us regarded General Marshall as one of the great military men of our generation, I would be the last to quarrel with whatever strategy he had in mind to meet the tactical problems that would develop as a result of the war.

One other public servant of this period who was a member of the United States Senate was William E. Borah, from Idaho. His views were often at variance with those of the administration, but he asserted them with vigor and conviction and had a very substantial following throughout the country. Interestingly enough, he had been born in the small town of Fairfield, Illinois, and obviously I had something more than a casual interest in his opinions and convictions. I mention him not to make any particular comment on his service in the United States Senate but rather because, when a memorial service was planned to do him honor in his home city of Fairfield, Mrs. Borah asked me to come and deliver the memorial eulogy. I was not only glad to do so but I felt highly honored that I had been selected for the occasion. The people in the countryside in southern Illinois turned out in great numbers, and I felt proud that I could do my full duty to the memory of this great son of Illinois.

War hysteria was bound to blind the nation to all except making an end of the matter as quickly as possible. The army command was combed for someone to lead our forces in the European and African theaters, and the one who was finally selected to lead the expeditionary force was Dwight David Eisenhower. In the early stages of conflict, there was a presidential assurance to the nation that young men would not be called upon to serve on foreign battlefields, but how could it have been otherwise in a war with Japan, which was ten thousand miles distant from our shores? And how could it be otherwise once we had declared war on Germany and the Axis powers?

Because it had always been so and because the laws and the Constitution called for it, there would have to be a political campaign involving the presidency, one-third of the Senate, and all of the House of Representatives, as well as those who would be running for office at state and local levels. Not even during our embroilment in the Civil War had we failed to go through an election, and 1944 could be no different in that respect. If Franklin Delano Roosevelt, despite his infirmities, was to be a candidate for the presidency again, it would mean that he would be seeking a fourth term. Perhaps a fourth term would not be regarded as a real obstacle so far as people were concerned. Much had been made of the third-term tradition in 1940 but to no avail, and one had to assume that a fourth term, particularly with a war in progress, would make little difference.

I was impressed on this point by a single experience I had in North Dakota, though I am sure it might have happened in other parts of the country. In the course of addressing a huge campaign meeting, one of the first things I observed was that there was a preponderance of women present. I had to conclude that they were in large part mothers of young men who were either in the military service or who might be summoned for that purpose in due course. After the meeting was over, one woman, who freely confessed that she had one son in the service and another nearing induction age, said to me so very simply, "Mr. Dirksen, if the country should elect a Republican president, is it fair to assume that he would select his own cabinet?"

"That, I believe, is a fair assumption," I said. "The president, as commander in chief, could also select his own particular military leaders and advisers if he chose to do so." She said nothing more but the implication was unmistakable. As a Republican, her disposition was to vote for a Republican candidate, but she had grave doubts about swapping horses in the middle of the stream. That, to me, was an early indication of how the campaign of 1944 might end.

The Republican party felt that Chicago was the appropriate place to hold its national convention, and speculation began early in the year as to who might be nominated to carry the standard of the Grand Old Party. There was a rather substantial group supporting John W. Bricker, the senator from Ohio, who served for a number of terms as governor of the state. Senator Bricker was a distinguished-looking, tall, erect person with white hair who comported himself with great dignity. Governor Thomas Edmund Dewey, of New York, also had very solid backing, and the fact that New York had such a substantial number of delegates and electoral votes made him a formidable candidate. Harold Stassen, the former governor of Minnesota, who had been a candidate for the nomination before, was still nursing the belief that perhaps, at long last, the lightning of good luck might strike him.

As for the vice-presidency, there were quite a number of hopefuls. In my home city of Pekin there were friends who undertook to erect billboards on the main highways leading into the city carrying this legend, "Pekin, Illinois, home of Everett McKinley Dirksen, next President of the United States." This was indeed high flattery. Perhaps they did not fully believe that I might be nominated for the presidency, but they did rather fondly hope that I might be a vice-presidential candidate.

This hope was based, in part at least, upon action taken by my colleagues in Congress. They drew up a petition which read as follows:

> Of the thirty-one men who have occupied the Presidency, eighteen previously served in one or both branches of the Congress, ten of the thirty-one served only in the House of Representatives. One man who has served in the Congress and possesses knowledge of and familiarity with the structure, functions and processes of the Federal government would lend strength to the Republican National Ticket in 1944 from intimate and close association with Congress—Everett McKinley Dirksen of Illinois.
>
> We know his diligence in the public welfare, his devotion to sound and balanced government, his broad grasp of Federal functions and his capacity for dealing with national problems.
>
> We, the undersigned Members of the House of Representatives, do, therefore, urge him to submit his name through appropriate channels for consideration by the Republican National Convention for nomination for the office of President of the United States.

This petition was signed by thirty-six members of Congress, mainly from midwestern states, and, of course, I felt highly honored by this action on their part.

When news of the petition reached the public, invitations for appearances developed almost overnight by letter, telephone, and telegram. I was quite bewildered, for in response to that petition I was expected to make appearances in different parts of the country and let the voters see what I looked like and what my views were. It would obviously require money; in addition to the necessary expenses for myself, provision would have to be made for an assistant to travel with me. I had such an assistant in mind. He had been identified with political life at the local and state level, and his advice was frequently solicited because he was a temperate person who had the capacity for analyzing political situations and coming up with the right answer.

I sought him out at the first possible opportunity so that we might consider the prospect of a tour through the western states, even though it was still winter and traveling would not be too pleasant. Having determined on a course of action, I then turned my thoughts to how and where to develop some campaign funds. The assistant to whom I refer was Harold Rainville, a newspaper man, a publicist, and a real student. He had some ideas about raising money that envisioned a rather substantial sum to be derived from wide solicitation. I, however, had a different idea. In Chicago there was a very wealthy man who for long years had been engaged in the manufacturing business and whom I had come to know quite intimately. Now and then he had a problem on which I was asked to help and I always undertook to oblige. Quite often I succeeded. One of those occasions involved the settlement of a strike at several of his plants. It was taking on rather ugly and dangerous dimensions, and reaching a settlement and strike adjustment was no easy undertaking. I did, however, make suggestions, and when next I saw this man he took out a checkbook and undertook to reimburse me for services rendered. I steadfastly refused to accept even so much as a five-cent piece. This only impressed him more deeply because of his experience with certain other persons in public life.

I decided quite some time after this strike was over to go and lay my cards on the table. This I did. I told him of my plans. He listened very intently and then said, "How much do you want?" I replied that it was not how much I wanted but only how much I needed, because I would certainly not want to raise more money than was absolutely necessary to conduct a preconvention campaign. After a few moments' reflection he took out a checkbook, scrawled a check, and handed it to me. It was for ten thousand dollars. As he gave it to me he said, "If you need more, come back, and don't be bashful or hesitant. I want you to have as much as you need."

Frankly, this measure of trust and esteem really overwhelmed me and I was profuse in my thanks. The first burden upon the new campaign checking account was to buy two air tickets, which in the aggregate totaled about four thousand dollars to cover the trip we had planned. It was also necessary to think about some literature that would be useful to fix my name and qualifications in the minds of those who would be attending the meetings to which I had been invited. Accordingly, we prepared a very modest booklet with a reproduction of the United States Capitol and my photo on the front page stating that I was a candidate for the Republican nomination for president of the United States in 1944. On the next page was a reproduction of the resolution adopted by Republicans in my home county. This was followed by a statement that I signed and then a copy of the petition signed by the thirty-six members of the House showing their signatures and their states. The booklet also contained a brief biography, a series of pictures, and a number of quotes from the press from different parts of the country. That was the one and only piece of literature that we felt we could afford, and we had it printed in large quantities in order to secure the benefit of mass production.

The first meeting on that tour, as I recall, was a luncheon meeting on Lincoln's birth anniversary at Lincoln, Nebraska. It was to be followed by early dinner with the Honorable Dwight Griswold, governor of Nebraska, later to be a fellow senator and our ambassador to Greece. We were to leave Lincoln, motor to Omaha, and take a train or plane for Portland. The governor was kind enough to provide a police car from Lincoln to Omaha. About halfway on the journey the police radio announced that a blizzard was coming and that, from all signs, it would be a fine example of this species of weather. It was indeed. When we reached Omaha we were hopelessly winter-bound for two solid days and could not get out by train, plane, or automobile. As a result we missed the Portland meeting but did get to Boise, Idaho, on schedule and then to Spokane, Washington, and Helena, Montana. When we landed in Helena, the pilot alighted from the plane and with a broad grin said, "End of the line." I asked him what he meant by that. He said, "Blizzard should strike here this evening." I wondered whether this would be our luck throughout the trip, but we were not dismayed.

After a speech in the hotel dining room in Helena, I accosted the governor about transportation to Billings, Montana, which I figured was about one hundred fifty miles away. At Billings I expected to catch a morning train in time to arrive in Sheridan, Wyoming, for the next meeting.

When I made this point-blank request to the governor, he looked at me rather sheepishly and said, "I am afraid I cannot let you have a police car and a driver for political campaigning. Four years ago I did so for Wendell Willkie when he was in this area, and I was roundly scolded by a lot of people—and I have to remember that I also am a candidate for office."

Just then I saw a chap moving through the hotel lobby wearing a cap that indicated that he was probably a cab driver. I left the governor summarily and accosted the man in the cap. "Do you own the cab line?" I asked him. "No, sir," he said, "the owner lives out on the highway west of town. I just work for him."

"How far is it to Billings?" I asked.

He looked at me with some astonishment, "You're not going to try to go to Billings tonight, are you?"

"I will if I can find somebody to take us," I said.

"Have you looked outdoors?" he asked. I said I hadn't. "There's a blizzard going on," he added.

My reply was, "Who cares? Call up your boss and find out what the fare is from here to Billings." When he returned he said the cab fare would be seventy-five dollars. I said, "My friend, seventy-five dollars for your boss and a twenty-five dollar tip for you if you get me to Billings in time for the seven o'clock train. Let's drive by your house and pick up a pillow and blanket so I can curl up in the rear seat of the car. My administrative assistant will ride up in front and entertain you to keep you from falling asleep."

That's the way we started the trip. After the first fifty miles there was not the slightest hint of snow or any evidence of a blizzard. From then on, we had no difficulty. We arrived in Billings by 5:30 in the morning, proceeded to a Chinese restaurant, and indulged in a solid breakfast after which we drove to the station in ample time to catch the train. I settled with this obliging young man and wished him well on his return journey.

And so the initial campaign trip went on—Sheridan, Casper, Cheyenne, San Francisco, Los Angeles, and many other places, and a stimulating and educational journey it proved to be.

Meanwhile the good citizens of my home city of Pekin began to take more than an ordinary interest in what was going on in the struggle for the Republican nomination for the presidency and the vice-presidency and decided to help the cause. I was quite sure that, in the main, they still thought that any effort on my part to seek the presidency was aiming rather high but that there was something of a chance to drop into the second slot. Traditionally that is about the way it works. Accordingly, they made up a fund of five thousand dollars. One morning when I was at home, the editor and publisher of the *Pekin Daily Times,* Mr. F. F. McNaughton, who was indeed a tried, true, and enduring friend, came to see me. He told me what had been done and laid a bankbook and a checkbook on my desk. When he told me how and from whom the five thousand dollars had been raised, I scarcely knew how to thank him and could only hope that I might merit this trust and esteem on the part of my fellow citizens at home.

I kept up with my congressional duties but continued to make appearances in different parts of the country until it was time to journey to Chicago to attend the convention.

It is quite strange how sources which can be so remote and unrelated can give color and also direction to a campaign. It was fairly clear when the Republicans met in Chicago that the nomination would probably go to Thomas Dewey, and that the real issue might be in the selection of his running mate. It so happened that all through the convention period Mr. Gerald L. K. Smith, who was something of a crusader and who was quite often referred to as an unrestrained rabble-rouser, had been holding meetings several times a day in the basement of the Stevens Hotel, now known as the Conrad Hilton Hotel. Reports of these meetings came to the attention of Herbert Brownell, who was the active manager of the Dewey campaign. These meetings gave him a deep concern and inspired more than ordinary interest in the selection of a vice-presidential candidate who might offset the labors and efforts of this militant rightist group.

As he expressed it to me, it was Mr. Brownell's opinion that probably Senator John Bricker, of Ohio, who had such a solid reputation for character, stability, conservatism, and devotion to constitutional principles, would be the answer to the problem; but the question was whether he would forsake the campaign being conducted in his behalf for the presidency and accept a second spot on the ticket.

It was on the night of Governor Dewey's nomination that a selected group was summoned to meet at the Blackstone Hotel at midnight. I was in attendance at the meeting. When the matter of the vice-presidency was discussed, Mr. Brownell asked whether I would bow out of the race if they contrived an understanding between Governor Dewey and Senator Bricker. The same question was addressed to Governor Stassen. I readily replied that my interest was in the party and in a Republican victory, and that I would gladly stand aside in order to achieve this larger objective. The effort was then made to bring Governor Dewey and Senator Bricker together on the telephone to see whether conversations could be quickly initiated. The effort succeeded and thus a Dewey-Bricker ticket came out of the convention in Chicago in 1944.

Once more I must salute a wise wife for her excellent intuition. When we went to Chicago, she said, "It would be just as well if you left the checkbook and the bankbook that the home folks gave you right here at home. You can be pretty certain that when the tumult and the shouting is over and someday I step out of the front door in a new dress, somebody, not meaning particularly to be catty or petty, will surely say, 'I note Mrs. Dirksen is wearing a new frock. We helped to buy it for her.'" So, the money was never touched, and when we returned home after the convention, I called upon

Mr. McNaughton and asked him whether he had time to run in for a visit. When he came I said, "Mac, here is your bankbook and your checkbook. I was certainly honored by this very generous gesture on the part of the home folks and by your devotion to the cause. I didn't touch it and Mrs. Dirksen will tell you the real reason why I didn't." When I gave him the details, he laughed a little and then remarked that he might have some other ideas about that fund and would come in and see me within the next several days. In about a week he returned. He had contacted every contributor to the five-thousand-dollar fund and only three or four very modest donors, whose total contribution was less than three dollars, felt they would like to have the money returned. It was then that he fully disclosed what he had in mind. The money was to be used whenever I was ready for a world trip to broaden my horizon in the field of foreign relations, and I advised him that I would see when this could be done.

The November election came and Franklin Delano Roosevelt won with a plurality in excess of four million votes of his fourth term. The ardent efforts of my party were of no avail. In the House of Representatives the voters returned 242 Democrats and 190 Republicans; in the Senate the score was 57 Democrats and 38 Republicans. So Congress still had slightly lopsided majorities.

As I contemplated the election result, I wondered whether the mood of the country was such and would remain in such a state that, henceforward, we could expect only a Democrat administration in the White House and substantial Democrat majorities in both branches of Congress. If that were to be the case, what virtue would there be in going to the Senate if it could be done? It would mean only trading a smaller constituency for a much larger one. My congressional district consisted of only six counties where I was very well known indeed. It would be a different dish if I undertook to win a seat in a constituency consisting of 102 counties, including Cook County and the city of Chicago, where the population was well in excess of three and a half million and which embraced nearly one-half of the entire population of the state. The compensation would be no greater. The official chores for an entire state would be enormous. To be sure, one might regard a place in the Senate as more prestigious than a seat in the House of Representatives; but on balance was it worth it? And did I want to be a senator after all?

14

BROADENING HORIZONS

G RATEFUL AS I WAS to publisher McNaughton and his associates for
making possible a world trip through the generosity of my own
constituents and not at public expense, such a trip entailed many problems,
particularly at a moment when the war was still going on. When should I
start? Where would I go? Who would I see? What clothes did one take? How
best to arrange transportation? What about weather? These and many other
questions promptly presented themselves, and I spent many days speculat-
ing on these things and making notes.

There was still another important matter to settle. Could I get any special
credentials which would prove useful and timely on such a trip? I went to see
Congressman Clarence Cannon, chairman of the Appropriations Committee of the House, and also Congressman John Taber, the ranking Republican
member of the committee, and placed the matter before them. They had
sufficient confidence in my sense of responsibility and provided me with
a letter which I was free to use in any circumstance. That letter began
as follows:

> My dear Mr. Dirksen:
> By virtue of the authority invested in me as Chairman of the Committee
> on Appropriations and with the approval of the ranking Minority Member,
> the Honorable John Taber of New York, I hereby designate you as a Subcom-
> mittee of one during your journey abroad in Europe, the Middle East, the
> Orient and elsewhere for the purpose of inspecting and reporting on Federal
> activities and functions which properly come within the jurisdiction of
> the Committee.
> You are authorized to make full inquiry concerning personnel, administra-
> tive expenditures, travel items, the efficacy and economy with which Federal

functions including those of the national war agencies are discharged and to make a full report thereof to the Committee.

That letter was dated February 19, 1945. I needed nothing more than this to meet every possible situation and get every possible attention. A diplomatic passport would be issued me, which commanded very special consideration from all our diplomatic representatives in every part of the world.

It was my good fortune about that time, through a very close personal friend, to be introduced to one William Stevenson, generally referred to as "Colonel." Whether he was actually a military colonel or not I did not know, but I quickly learned that he was in charge of British Intelligence for the Northern Hemisphere and maintained an office in New York. He advised that he wished to be helpful in every possible way and that he was quite certain that he could open a good many doors which might otherwise remain closed to me.

Mrs. Dirksen could not go with me in wartime, of course, so I weighed the possibility of having an aide accompany me. That almost solved itself when the general details concerning this trip were publicized in the Washington press. The news inspired a good many calls and callers, including a man who was in the naval reserve with rank of commander. His name was John Young and he had played a role in the world broadcast of His Holiness, Pope Pius XII, at Christmas. I was impressed with John Young, but he indicated there was one hitch, and that was that he was due for promotion to the rank of captain and was not sure, therefore, that he could leave as early in the year as I had indicated. We finally agreed that I would start the journey alone in the hope that somewhere enroute, most likely at Tel Aviv, he might catch up with me. That disposed of the matter for the moment.

In determining when to leave, I was thinking about the election in 1946. I would certainly be a candidate for reelection and would want to time this trip so as to score maximum benefit from whatever observations I might make. I decided, therefore, to leave quite early in the year so as not to be rushed.

I sought advice on the matter of weather, knowing that Europe can be cold and dismal even in early spring. This inspired the idea of making a brief stop in Britain and France first, and then going on to Africa, and thence to the end of the line in Ceylon. I would work back after that to take advantage of the warmer weather that would prevail at that time.

Then came the question of transportation. Finally I decided to take a train from Washington to Montreal, Canada, thence to Newfoundland, and from Newfoundland to fly in a British Lancaster bomber to Prestwick, Scotland. The State Department proved extremely helpful in arranging this.

The United States consul general in Montreal was at the station to meet me and take me to lunch. He was a capable, jaunty, and uninhibited person. I found very quickly that I could talk to him on most any subject without reservation and that he could do likewise. Oddly enough—or perhaps it was not so odd after all—we got around to the question of allowances for our diplomatic and consular representatives abroad. I asked him a number of questions, including the amount of the so-called representation allowance which Congress had set for the station in Montreal. Then I asked him about those out-of-pocket expenditures that he was called upon to make in order to effectively discharge his responsibilities and observe the proper social amenities. I said, "I presume you belong to certain clubs and organizations and that you must receive quite a number of visitors, including congressmen and senators and governors whom you feel should be taken to lunch or dinner."

"That's quite true," he began, "and offhand I must say that club dues and other necessary expenditures each year exceed the representation allowance many times over." I reminded him that when the State Department appropriation bill reached the floor of the House of Representatives and the membership finally reached the item in the bill dealing with these allowances, that they are commonly referred to as the "whiskey allowance," and it became the signal for all manner of cynical and jocular remarks. I told him I was glad to have his point of view because I expected to do something with it when I returned to my duties in Washington.

Prestwick, Scotland, was only a brief stop before boarding another plane for London. In London I learned that Ambassador John Winant was suffering from influenza. I did, however, pay him a very brief courtesy call. When I found him he was having a discussion with the Soviet ambassador, Mr. Gusev. I embraced the opportunity which presented itself to tell Mr. Gusev that I expected to visit Tehran in Iran and that would bring me rather close to the Soviet border. I had no visa for the Soviet Union and thought perhaps Mr. Gusev could help that cause. We indulged in some pleasantries, but he gave no assurance that it could be done. I was to learn later when in Tehran that it might be worked out if I remained there patiently for six months until I could be thoroughly investigated. Obviously, this was out of the question, so I forgot all about the prospect of going to Moscow and other Russian cities.

One of my most interesting visits in London was with a number of secretaries to Winston Churchill. As I recall, they were all men. When asked if I wished to see Winston Churchill, I frankly stated that I would rather talk with a number of his secretaries to get some idea about his habits. I discovered that they were about as extraordinary as those of any man I had known. He seemed to like nothing so much as to get up at an awkward hour, say two o'clock in the morning, summon a number of secretaries, and dictate speeches, articles, and chapters for his books at a wild pace. After several hours of this he would return to bed and, sometime in the forenoon, he would go to Downing Street to his office to discharge his responsibilities as prime minister and make important decisions. Then came lunch, some relaxation, and then perhaps another rugged tour of several hours with his secretaries. He would, on occasion, nap before dinner and then address himself to all manner of matters engaging his attention. From their running freehand account of how his days were passed, I realized that it was an amazing routine for a man of his bulk and his age.

One enlightening visit that I had was with Malcolm Macdonald, the secretary of colonial affairs. We had some desultory conversation and then I asked him this pointed question; "Mr. Secretary, why does not Britain give to Ireland its complete freedom and let them hew out their destiny according to their own lights?"

He looked out of the window and paused for a sustained period before returning an answer. Then he said, "Whenever we satisfactorily dispose of the status of India so she can have complete freedom and still remain in the Commonwealth, and if we can then solve the problem of Palestine in view of the assurances which were given in the declaration of Prime Minister Balfour, we shall then be ready to address ourselves to the question of whether there could be a free and undivided Ireland." There was more conversation on all three of these points, but it added up to the same thing, and it was so very evident that, in the secretary's opinion, the Irish question was the most difficult of all to solve.

During my sojourn in London, I became fully aware of what it meant for a huge city or a country to have been subjected to rocket attack. The Germans had perfected the so-called V-1 and V-2 late in the war. It must have been a ghastly experience to awaken in the night and hear the whine of the V-1 before it reached a target. The damage, of course, was astounding. The V-2 rocket was more deadly than the V-1 because it traveled faster than the speed of sound and gave no warning until it exploded on reaching its destination. It was to these menaces that the people of Britain were subjected for a long time. One could only marvel at their patience, their ruggedness, and their sacrifices in the interest of a principle and, also, in the interest of their own survival.

There were many things to which I addressed my attention while in London but I recite only one other experience. I was rather anxious to visit the secretary of the British Trades Union Congress and ascertain from him how they handled their labor difficulties. I had noticed in going around London that there were a number of industries on strike, but I saw no picket lines, and this was the one question I addressed to him: "I note a number of plants that are strikebound, but there are no picket lines whatsoever. How do you manage this and do it effectively?"

His reply was quite to the point. "Long ago we contrived an understanding with plant management to the effect that we would not do any picketing if management was willing to respect the fact that a strike had been called. Accordingly, all we have to do is to tack our strike signs on poles and place them at the gates of a plant and, thereafter, no attempt is made to break the strike or to operate the plant unless and until the strike has been settled."

I followed this observation by asking, "Then your strikes are not attended with violence?"

His answer was, "We try to avoid all violence and, generally speaking, I believe we have succeeded." This attitude is certainly worthy of the stolid British temperament.

Much more time might have been spent in London, but I was anxious to resume my journey and equally anxious to maintain the timetable I had set for myself. Accordingly, I flew to Paris and from Paris to Algiers. I did not expect to stop in Algiers because I had a plane connection to take me on to Tunisia. It was a night flight. By that I mean it took place in the early hours of the night and, as I recall, we expected to land in Tunisia around midnight. I never realized until then how frightfully cold it can get in the desert. I was the only passenger abroad and most of the cabin space was occupied by sacks filled with mail. The flight encompassed mountainous country, and it became evident that the pilot was either off the beam or he was lost. In the course of that uneasy flight, the sergeant who served as a steward on the plane came to tell me that we had lost contact with Tunis and could only hope that somehow it might be reestablished. Meanwhile I should prepare for any eventuality.

He deposited a quantity of the softer mailbags on the floor of the plane, had me lie down, and then proceeded to cover me with a great many other bags to cushion the shock if there should be one. There are occasions when there is nothing to do but review one's life and utter fervent prayers. Fortunately, contact was established and when we flew into the capital of Tunisia, I was about as completely frozen as I have ever been in my entire lifetime.

Even at that weird hour the American consul was on hand to greet me and take me to his home, where I was to be billeted for two days before resuming the journey. It took a fair share of bourbon and hot water to thaw me out, and all the while I was encased in several heavy blankets and my teeth chattered like a trip hammer. But circulation returned and, after a good sleep, I felt as good as new.

I was intrigued with Tunisia because it was the site of ancient Carthage, which under the great leader Hannibal and his predecessors had developed an advanced civilization and become one of the outstanding trading nations of ancient times. In the discussion I had with the American consul about the history of ancient Carthage and her military victories before she was vanquished by the Roman Empire, he alluded to Hannibal's use of elephants in wartime. Without endeavoring to be facetious, I merely commented they were the precursors of the modern tank, and he thought the point was well taken.

One place I wanted to see was the amphitheater of ancient Carthage. It was some distance from town, but there were no structures or even rubble of any kind remaining to attest to the great civilization which was once there. I located two fair-sized fragments of granite that seemed to be the only true evidence of that ancient culture. I sat down on one of those and began to reflect on what I remembered of this earlier civilization and how much of it had completely disappeared.

Two little boys saw me and came up to show me some coins and to say in their best pidgin English that they were ancient coins and perhaps I might be interested in buying them. I had no interest, however, and fell to musing all over again about the eventful things that had happened in this very spacious bowl that was once the site of an amphitheater. Incidentally, it was in this bowl that Churchill addressed the troops of Great Britain who were serving in Africa and inspired them to an even greater effort in the war.

During my brief sojourn in Tunisia, the distribution of clothing and commodities from the United States was under way, and I went to the central point in the city with the American consul to watch this proceeding. The first thing I noticed, however, was that there was no evidence on the packages and crates that all this was made possible through the generosity of the United States and its taxpayers. I thought it surpassingly strange that we got no credit whatsoever for our assistance, but as the journey unfolded, I discovered that much of the same thing was happening in other countries.

Egypt was also something of a way station for me. The one incident that always comes back was when the commanding officer of our forces at Payne Field in Cairo came to advise me that it was necessary to entertain a Soviet major general and his staff, and that by his estimate of the protocol involved I should serve as host at the luncheon.

The general spoke no English and I spoke no Russian. But, subsequently, there was available a fine-looking sergeant in our army who had been born in Leningrad and who spoke Russian fluently, and when he sat down at the table with the general and a staff of nine people, I advised the sergeant that he should present my conversation and my questions to the general exactly as I framed them. A Syrian mess sergeant in our army prepared the luncheon and, I must say, he certainly did himself proud—not only with the food but in the way in which the luncheon was served.

When we had reached the dessert stage, and I can still recall that the mess sergeant had prepared a delicious parfait, I said to Alexis, the interpreter, "Ask the general why they have three hundred fifty people in the Soviet embassy in Cairo." The sergeant turned to me and said, "He might be offended by that question."

To that I answered, "Sergeant, ask him, anyway, exactly as I presented the question." He did precisely that. Color came into the general's face and in a somewhat guttural voice he said, "How do you know that we have three hundred fifty people in our embassy here?"

To the sergeant I said, "Tell him I went there and counted them."

The general placed his spoon in the plate; so did the rest of his staff. He arose and they all arose with him. He bowed from the waist, walked out of the door, and that was the last I ever saw of the Russian general.

I was not anxious to loiter in Egypt because it was still a long way to the end of the line, and I carefully observed the timetable and went on to Calcutta. It is a huge, dismal place, and one of the first things to impress me and emphasize a feeling of distaste was when I watched women coaling a vessel in the river. There seemed to be hundreds of them, each one carrying a basket. They would go to dockside, fill a basket with coal, place it on their heads or shoulders, and with measured tread walk up the gangplank and upend the basket in that part of the vessel's hold which was the coal storage. It seemed to keep up hour after hour, and I could not escape the feeling that it was indeed a degrading chore for women in India, or anywhere.

I advised the commanding general in charge of that area that I wanted to move on to Ceylon and then work back. I did not, however, want to use a military plane and consume so much fuel unless a plane was going in that direction. He laughed uproariously and said, "Congressman, you asked for it and you shall have it." What he meant was that an official plane was already loaded with lumber to the point where there was scarcely room for more than one passenger to sit. The lumber was to be transported to Bangalore, and I would go from there to Ceylon. Sure enough, the next morning I climbed aboard and must admit I then had some second thoughts about this arrangement. I wondered what would happen if we encountered heavy weather and the huge load of lumber shifted forward in the plane. Certainly I would be crushed as if I had been flattened out with a steamroller. But at that point I could scarcely welsh on the bargain I had made, and so we took off and safely and uneventfully negotiated the journey to Bangalore.

Word had been sent ahead that I was aboard, and the colonel in command of that station was there to greet me. He was quite delighted that I should be there. He said, "You know, Congressman, way down here we are off the beaten path and get to see very few of you fellows. I don't know what your plans are, nor do I care. You are going to stay here as my guest for a few days because I do not propose to let you leave until we have enjoyed a few meals and had a lot of conversation."

I was quite agreeable. As we drove to his billet, I said, "Colonel, what is this hideous noise that continues without interruption?"

"Those are airplane motors on the testing block. You see, the planes which have been flying the hump in this China-Burma-India theater are all reexamined and retested when they return from those flights. This is the official repair spot, and I presume you have observed the many facilities we have for that purpose." I had observed them, and it was amazing how much of our technical skill we have exported to India for this purpose and how many thousands of Indians representing virtually every caste were working in this repair plant.

When the time arrived for a drink and some dinner, the colonel said, "Of all the people who could have come this way, if I had had my choice I would have picked you, and you will never know why until I tell you. Some years ago a select committee of the Congress came to Detroit to investigate the bondholders' protective committees which had been set up to protect the holders of bonds in apartment and commercial buildings that were on the verge of bankruptcy as a result of the depression."

I am sure my face lighted up as I said, "Yes, Colonel, I remember all that quite well. It was known as the Sabbath committee and I was a member."

"I know you were," he replied and then added, "the committee came to Detroit and held public hearings for nearly a week. My business, before I got into the military, was that of attorney and counsel to a number of those bondholders' committees, and you subpoenaed me to appear and testify. I remember as if it were yesterday the kind of grilling I got at the hands of the committee, including you, and now I have you for my very own, way off here in Bangalore, India."

We enjoyed quite a laugh as some of those events were reviewed, and then it was my turn to ask him all manner of questions about the extraordinary operation that had been established at Bangalore. I asked him about his work, and one incident he told me has remained in my mind.

"I had a real labor problem," he began, "but I got on top of it without too much trouble. One problem you have in India when you have thousands of employees performing highly delicate and sensitive work, such as repairing radios and communications systems on the planes that fly the hump, is this question of castes and subcastes in the plant. We have all of them, from the so-called untouchable caste to the cultured Brahmins. One day it happened. A member of the untouchables walked by a Brahmin when the latter was eating his lunch. The shadow of the untouchable fell athwart the lunch basket, and immediately the Brahmin refused to eat his lunch and quit his job. Other Brahmins followed suit, as did members of the intermediate castes. It appeared that I was about to lose the entire work force on this station. I sent word that there would be a mass meeting at a large recreation area that we have, and I set it for nine o'clock the following morning. They all very dutifully assembled, and it was a huge crowd. I made them one of the shortest speeches I ever made in my life and the substance of it was about like this, 'Workers, starting today your pay will be doubled. Go back to work and don't let me hear anything more about the difficulties you have one with another as a result of any differences of caste.' That was the speech. They turned to each other and there was buzzing and noisy conversation for only a little bit, and then the group dispersed and went back to their jobs. I have never since had any trouble because an untouchable shadow fell upon a Brahmin during lunch."

He told me they had had one other incident that might have been extremely serious, and that was an epidemic of bubonic plague. He had conferred with the medical officers who advised that rats were the carriers of the plague and that there should be a real extermination effort. Once armed with that information, he organized a rat-catching and rat-killing enterprise covering the entire community. Before they were through they had fairly decimated the rat population for the area, were on top of the epidemic, and had not been bothered since that time.

There was much other interesting conversation but at long last I said, "Colonel, I must be on my way. I have a timetable to keep. How good it was to see you again so far away from Detroit. What I need now is a plane to take me to Ceylon, and I trust you have a vehicle handy and available for that purpose." He was most obliging and shortly after I was the only passenger on a plane destined for Colombo, the capital of Ceylon.

Ceylon was an intriguing place, and who of all persons should meet me there but Lieutenant General Raymond Wheeler, the deputy supreme commander of the area under Lord Louis Mountbatten, the supreme commander. The peculiar fragrance of the cinnamon trees was in the air, the parks were so lovely and inviting, and everyone was extremely hospitable. Two things intrigued me immensely. The first was that as we drove around we saw a small patch of corn. Tacked on a post was this sign, "Doff your hats, you are passing an Illinois cornfield." There was imagination for you.

What intrigued me most, of course, was that General Wheeler was from home. By home I mean that the Wheeler family lived in a small mining community called Orchard Mines only one mile from my home city. Some of his family were still there, but I remember "Speck" Wheeler from long ago. It added so much to the pleasure of the trip.

In the course of our conversations, we talked about Lord Mountbatten and the fact that his wife was quite ill and in need of major surgery. To this General Wheeler added, "Lady Mountbatten insisted that the operation must be performed by surgeons from the United States and this was done." I thought what a great tribute that was to the whole medical fraternity of our country. The visit in Ceylon was all too short, but I remained long enough to find and bargain for a star sapphire ring because the star sapphire is found in some abundance in that area. I felt that this would be a fine memento for my wife of my visit in Ceylon. From there I journeyed to Bombay, then still in British-ruled India. The British commander in Bombay wanted very much to be my host at cocktails and lunch and I was quite willing. He had assembled an interesting group of military men and Indian merchants and businessmen. All of them spoke flawless English. While chatting over a cocktail, a number of the native businessmen were putting their heads together, and one of them raised his voice loud enough so that I could hear. To his associates he said, "We must be very, very nice to our guest. He is on the money committee of Congress, and you know what that can mean." They knew, and so did I.

From Bombay I went to Delhi, which was the capital and also then the home of the viceroy. I had heard it said that if you wanted to know how royalty should live you should go to Delhi. I found out for myself how true that really was. When the plane landed at Delhi, the chief of our mission, since we had no embassy in Delhi at the time, was there to meet me and arrangements were made for me to stay at the United States mission while I was there. His name was Ira Nelson Morris, and he was a bachelor. He had brought his sister with him to India to do the honors, and I must say that both of them were the soul of courtesy and grace. Almost immediately he handed me an invitation. It was from the viceroy, Lord Wavell.

When I went to the viceroy's residence for dinner that night and saw for myself the appointments, I was frankly overwhelmed. I had never seen anything like it in my life. It was a huge palace, beautifully decorated, and it seemed as if the personnel to maintain it ran into hundreds, all of them in resplendent and colorful uniforms.

Lord and Lady Wavell and his son were there to greet me. There were six or seven other guests for dinner and it proved to be an extremely pleasant affair. After coffee and brandy, the guests were preparing to leave. I thought I should go with them but the viceroy's son came by to tug my sleeve and say, "Don't leave, I hope you and I can have a talk." I had to ask, of course, whether this was proper protocol so far as Lord and Lady Wavell were concerned and he said it was. Shortly after the guests departed, Lord and Lady Wavell took their leave and that left the son all alone with me. We went to a corner of the living room, which seemed to be as large as an acre field, and there sat down in comfortable chairs to visit and reminisce.

The first thing I noticed was that he was minus a hand, and I said, "How did that happen?" He then told me that he had been in the army and that a Japanese sniper had caught him in the hand, making it necessary to have an amputation. (His father, too, had lost an arm.) He was anxious, among other things, to ask about Lord Halifax, who was then the British ambassador in Washington. I brought him up to date on Lord Halifax's son, who lost both legs as a result of a land mine explosion in the war, and about his efforts at walking after he was equipped with artificial limbs. I expressed unbounded admiration for his grit and courage in surmounting this great obstacle and how well he had succeeded. It was late when I left the palace. I thought perhaps the door of our mission might be locked and that I would have difficulty getting in unless I disturbed the chief of the mission, but a guard had been posted to await me and there was no difficulty.

One of the things about Delhi that stood out in my mind was my meeting with Dr. Ambedkar. He was the leader of the seventy million so-called untouchables, who were members of the most depressed caste. He was indeed a fine gentleman and a graduate of our own Columbia University. Yet he had been rigidly brought up in the caste system from which there was no escape. One remains in the caste into which one is born. Yet he had a delightful personality and was doing his best to help free and rehabilitate his country and its teeming millions of people.

I never ceased wondering about the caste system and how it could so envelope an entire country and all of its people, placing them in rigid categories from which there simply was no escape. In this modern age it seemed incredible, but it was so then and, insofar as I know, it is so even now.

My visit to the Indian Congress in Delhi was indeed a delightful adventure. So many of the members were dressed in colorful uniforms, but the amazing aspect of this was that virtually all of them, including the Speaker of the House of Parliament, were in bare feet. It was true of nearly all the members of Congress. I listened with great interest to the debate, which was entirely in English. At the time they were discussing a bill relating to the civil service system. How familiar it all seemed, and after greeting the Congress and receiving the greeting of the Speaker, I was asked to convey his respects and good wishes to the Speaker of our own House in Washington.

When I left India, I flew to Abadan on the Persian Gulf in Iran and was prepared to take a train ride of nearly a thousand miles from the Gulf to the capital city of Tehran. Iran is oil rich, but at that time few improvements in the cities and in the public facilities had been made, and primitive conditions often obtained.

Before I left the States, I had a message from our pharmaceutical manufacturers stating that, despite our best efforts, they were making no progress in securing some of the Iranian drug trade. I pursued this matter with some vigor and finally discussed it with a member of the cabinet whose particular domain was the field of health. I not only discussed it but, in fact, made some complaint that the United States, despite all it had done for Iran, was not being treated very fairly when it came to the purchase of drugs, and that by far the greater part of this business was going to British manufacturers. He gave me a curious explanation, and to this day I do not know whether what he said was entirely correct.

In substance he said, "Although we are rich in oil, we are nevertheless a poor country and the government of Iran does not have money to spend such as you have in the United States. When a person is selected for a cabinet post he does not expect to be paid a salary. There is a tacit understanding that he must obtain his compensation as best he can from arrangements he may be able to make with foreign and domestic firms that do business with the central government of Iran."

I puzzled over that answer for a moment and then said, "Am I to believe that it works on the principle of the old Ottoman Empire under which the sultan designated his provincial governors and they were expected to compensate themselves from all business that was done in their respective domains?" He said that was a correct estimate of the situation, and I knew then the kind of answer I would have to give to the pharmaceutical people when I got back home. Since then, of course, the shah has changed things materially.

The railroad on which we made the journey into Iran was built by German engineers over the most difficult terrain, and it is said that thousands of people perished on the job before the line was completed. Arrangements had been made well in advance, and the train that made this journey consisted of two diesel engines, one dining car, and a sleeping car that was the private possession of the shah of Iran. The passenger list consisted of four United States colonels and myself, and I thought what a spectacular trip this could be. It turned out exactly that. After we got under way, the colonel in charge of the party asked whether I would have any objection if the train stopped now and then at a number of places en route. I said that I had no objection, but I was not quite ready for what was going to happen.

Word went through the Persian Gulf command that I was aboard and that all troops from Illinois at the various stations in Iran would be supplied with necessary transportation to get them to the railroad station when the train arrived.

At the very first stop on that trip, I suggested to the colonel in charge that I might like to step down from the coach for a bit of fresh air and he thoroughly encouraged the idea. Then I saw there was a great gathering of GI's waiting, and when I alighted they gave vent to a really gusty cheer. I went among them to shake hands and to ask where they were from and I began to receive replies in quick succession, "I'm from Galesburg," "I'm from Quincy," "I'm from Chicago," "I'm from Rock Island," "I'm from Peoria." All of them were from points in Illinois and, frankly, I was amazed that they had gone to the trouble to comb the command and find every Illinois GI who might be available and have him at the station to greet me when I arrived.

When we went into the next station it was precisely the same. Troops from Illinois were on hand, and I never felt so honored in my life. They were far from home and eager to extend the hand of fellowship to the congressman from Pekin.

I was not unduly impressed with what I found in Tehran, particularly the meager facilities we had for diplomatic purposes. We had acquired a building next to the embassy to be renovated and used as a chancery building. Immediately before the time set to hold the three-power meetings, between Britain, the United States, and the Soviet Union, it appears that a heavy rain caused the ceiling in the chancery to collapse, and virtually all of the ceiling plaster fell to the floor. Along with it, the entire electrical system became inoperative, and the problem of finding a plasterer and an electrician to remedy the damage in time was difficult indeed. I felt that the United States of America should certainly do better by its diplomats than it was doing in Iran.

During my brief stay, General Booth, a fine young officer, arranged for a party in my honor at the officers' club. When I arrived everyone present was the very essence of fellowship and hospitality. It was in the course of that party that an extremely attractive Iranian girl came up to introduce herself. She was faultlessly dressed in a gown of cut lace. There was dancing at the party and she was aggressive enough to ask if I would dance with her. I quickly discovered that she was a superb dancer. As we danced she said, "I want to go to the United States. I work for General Booth as a secretary. I am told that you are a very important and influential person in your country. I am told also that you could help me obtain a visa. I hope, therefore, that you will help me to get to your country."

I slightly shrugged off the suggestion and then said, "I am afraid it is not quite that easy to obtain a visa, but let me make an alternative suggestion. There are many fine-looking men of our army up here, including so many corporals and sergeants. You are pretty and I am sure you would have no difficulty developing an attachment for one of them. If you married him, your entry into the United States would be easy enough."

She stamped her foot with some vexation and said, "I do not want to go that way. I want to be free when I go, and I am sorry if you cannot help me."

I thought no more about her until quite some time after I had returned home. One afternoon out of a clear sky she walked into my office in Washington. It was my turn to be absolutely astonished. I could only say, "How in the world did you get here?"

With a small, wry smile she said, "There are ways, and I am here." After a little more conversation she disappeared, and I never saw her again, but I felt I had indeed underestimated feminine willpower.

When I left Iran for the air journey to what was still called Palestine, I was the only passenger on a British plane. The pilot found time to leave his seat in the cockpit quite often and come back for visits. On such occasions he pointed out various things of interest in the landscape and could identify for me distant sandstorms, which were so common in the desert. The plane finally came to a ridge, including some small mountains, which separated Palestine from the adjoining countries. He pointed out that almost directly below us was a mountain called Mount Nebo, on which Moses stood after his forty-year quest to reach the promised land. At that point I said to the pilot, "Do you know the rest of the story?" He said that he did not and so I supplied the rest, "The Great Book says that when Moses stood on Mount Nebo the Lord spoke to him and said, 'I have caused thee to see it with thine own eyes but thou shalt not go over thither.'"

How lush and green it all seemed after the flight across the desert. It looked for all the world like an entirely different land. It was my privilege while there to examine its many attractions, such as the Sea of Galilee, the Jordan River, the place where Samson brought down the pillars of the Temple, the village of Nazareth where the Christ lived and moved and worked in the carpenter shop, the village of Bethlehem where he was born, the Garden of the Agony at Gethsemane, and so many other places which heretofore were only places on the map. Now it was all coming to life, and I made the most of this opportunity.

I also explored the agricultural and industrial regions of Palestine. On one occasion I made some special inquiries concerning tax collection methods and was given to understand that they had no rigidly enforced system like that which prevails in the United States. You paid your full measure of taxes only if you were caught and if the officials could prove how much you really owed.

It was my special fortune to be in Jerusalem on Easter, and I looked forward to the Easter morning service in a tower which stood across from the King David Hotel. Word had gone out to tourists and, in fact, to anyone interested, that the services would begin at precisely a given hour and that when that hour arrived the door would be locked. Unfortunately, I was late and the door was actually locked when I arrived. I began to beat on it with my fist and kept it up until finally the door opened. I made my apologies and told them who I was and they showed full sympathy with my difficulties and permitted me to enter. As a rule, one reason for being so meticulous about the time was that this special service was being broadcast to all parts of the world, and I could fully understand.

One other incident occurred which seemed worthy of note. I was supplied with a car including an Arab driver who spoke Yiddish and Hebrew very fluently. While motoring around to see the places I had in mind, I suggested that we drive to the bridge that crosses the Jordan River. When we arrived, there was a sentry on duty who proudly informed me that unless I had a visa to enter Jordan he could not permit me to cross. After some discussion and my emphasis on the fact that I really was a one-man congressional committee, he finally relented and said that if I came back the same way so that he would not get into trouble he would permit me to venture into Jordan. It is possible that we drove fifteen or twenty miles when the driver turned to me and said, "We are coming to the summer home of Abdullah the emir of Jordan. There is a visitor's book on a stand under a tree along the roadside where a visitor can write his name, the name of his country, and other things he feels should be included." I very dutifully entered my name in the emir's guest book, and then it occurred to me that if the emir was at home, there was no reason why I should not see him. The driver protested and said, "Without a proper introduction it simply is not done." That, of course, was the height of formal protocol. I was far from home and I did not want to forgo the chance. While discussing this with the driver, I heard a clanking noise and it proved to be the captain of the emir's bodyguard, who was summoning the members of his command. I appealed to him, and the captain escorted me into the presence of the emir, who later became King Abdullah.

The driver served as an interpreter until the emir's own interpreter arrived, and we carried on a wide-ranging conversation. He wanted to know where I had been, what I had seen, and what I thought of world affairs. I tried to give him good, responsive answers. It might well be that I spent an hour with the emir, and then I heard what sounded like the clank of a saber. It turned out to be a high-ranking British officer, Colonel Glubb, who was on duty, training the Jordanian army. It was quite evident that somebody had phoned him to advise that an itinerant American congressman had suddenly descended on the emir without warning, and that this might have some significance for the country. He was soon placed at ease when I explained who I was and what my general mission was.

In Lebanon I made a special point to visit at length with the foreign minister whom President Roosevelt had invited to San Francisco for the initial meeting of what was to become the United Nations. He was an extremely interesting man with a kindly face and white hair. He was actually a professor of electrical engineering at American University in Beirut. He spoke excellent English and made a long inquiry as to where I had been and what my conclusions were.

He then ventured to say that he had some doubts about accepting the invitation to San Francisco because he had never been on an airplane, and this would involve a journey across the Atlantic Ocean, as well as across the United States after he arrived in our country. I undertook right then and there to give him a sales talk on how little real hazard there was in flying anywhere in the world and particularly in the developed areas. I suggested that he could probably get a twin-motored plane to take him to Egypt, where we had such an excellent air base in Payne Field, and that a four-motor plane with great power could pick him up at that point and fly him across the Atlantic. Observing that he was still in doubt about it, I continued to recite for him my own experiences. I told him how much I had flown all over Latin America, as well as in Europe and Asia, and that the very best of pilots and navigators would be available for a journey of this type because he would be catalogued as a very important person. At long last my sales talk succeeded.

I was anxious to go to Damascus in Syria if for no other reason than to see the little prison where the Apostle Paul had been incarcerated. I had underscored his comforting words in the khaki-clad Bible that I carried with me during World War I, for Paul had stated, "For I have learned whatsoever state I am in therewith to be content." Truly those were words to serve one's purpose all through life.

One of the highlights of the visit in Damascus was a lunch with the president and his cabinet, and an interesting lunch it turned out to be. There were no chairs or tables. A suitable cloth was spread upon the ground and the food served in such fashion that all could sit cross-legged and reach for whatever he wanted. There was little or no protocol, and I noticed that no one was particularly bashful in reaching for whatever food appealed to him. An excellent interpreter was on hand and the luncheon conversation covered a great many subjects that were of particular interest to the officials of Syria.

I noticed while going through our embassy facilities that on the mantel in a large reception room was the photograph of a very attractive young lady. It was done in color, and that but enhanced her real beauty. I said nothing about it, but when the ambassador and I were preparing to drive across the mountain to Beirut, the first secretary of the embassy came rushing out of the door. The ambassador stopped the motor, got out, and went to see what the trouble was. He said nothing for quite a while after we started our journey, and then I mentioned the photograph on the mantelpiece and what an exquisite person she seemed to be. He turned to me and said, "That was the reason the first secretary was so upset. He is engaged to that girl. She is Russian and was born in Leningrad. He wishes to marry her and that presents something of a problem nowadays, in view of the general suspicion which seems to obtain with respect to all Russians and whether or not they would be under obligation to report to Soviet authorities matters of interest which might come to their attention."

I puzzled for a little over the whole matter and finally said, "Mr. Ambassador, even if I was Solomon I don't think I could give you an answer." Later I heard that the young man had married her—and left the foreign service.

Next I went to Turkey. I planned to visit both Ankara and Istanbul. Turkish officials were ready for my visit, having been alerted well in advance of my arrival.

In Ankara there was a loud knock on the door of my hotel room one morning about seven. I couldn't imagine what it could be until I opened the door and a maid in fairly good English advised me that Franklin Delano Roosevelt had died and they wanted me to know without delay. Obviously the news came as a real shock. For a president to die while the nation was still at war would be a shock to the entire country and to the whole world. My spirit drooped but I decided that I must go on with the trip and complete my timetable. The embassy advised me early in the morning that a memorial service would be conducted for the late president and that Turkish officials, the diplomatic corps, and others would all be on hand. It was an invitation affair, and a seat would be reserved for me.

I am not quite sure why it was that an official identified with the YMCA was called upon to deliver the memorial eulogy. It could well have been that a regular ordained minister serving a church in Turkey was not immediately available, but in any event, that is what happened. In the course of that eulogy the speaker was building up to a climax in his oration. I still have a vivid image of what happened. He began his peroration and said, "We honor the great humanitarian beloved by people throughout the world; that great speaker whose voice brought such singular comfort to all who heard him, that great chief of a great nation, Theodore . . . " There he stopped. A hush fell upon the audience. The speaker's face flushed with embarrassment and then he resumed, "Franklin Delano Roosevelt." I have encountered a great many incidents that might be called life's most embarrassing moment but this is still at the top of my list.

The Turkish cabinet and parliament undertook a cocktail party in my honor. When I was advised of the fact, I was quite astonished because I had never realized that the cocktail hour had caught up with Turkish society or that Turks by and large were given to the use of alcohol. Actually this cocktail party did not differ essentially from cocktail parties given back home. The alcohol which was served was substantially the same—bourbon, scotch, gin, manhattans, martinis, and for all I know, there may have been others. After the usual pleasantries and the handshaking, a middle-aged man stepped forth from a group and reached for my hand. He spoke excellent English. He gave me his name, which I have since forgotten, and then said, "I am a member of the Turkish parliament, a congressman like you. I'm an electrical engineer. Believe it or not, I studied electrical engineering at the University of Illinois at Urbana and there received my degree before returning to Turkey." He still remembered the names of some of the professors and the president of the university and inquired how they were and whether the school was still growing by leaps and bounds. In the visit which ensued, I thought what a small world it really was. There must have been three or four cartoonists at the party, all of whom were very busy sketching me in various postures, and I wondered what it was all about. Someone advised that there were eight morning newspapers in Ankara, mostly of the four-page variety, so that three cartoonists in a city with eight newspapers did not seem unduly strange. I did not appreciate at the moment what a useful service those cartoonists were going to render, but I found out a day or two later when I ended my visit and prepared to board a plane at the airport.

Prior to that, however, I enjoyed interviews with a number of very important people, including two or three Turkish admirals and generals. We sat on the porch of the hotel in Istanbul and indulged in desultory conversation covering many subjects. Finally I said, pointing across the water, "I have noted what looks like a rather large manufacturing plant over yonder but it seems so devoid of windows that I thought it could be a prison."

The admiral who responded said, "That is a government-owned factory where they manufacture matches." "What kind of wages do they pay in a plant like that?" I asked. He told me, and it was very little. I said, "That's a terribly cheap wage. I'm quite sure that I would not work for wages like that."

"You probably would not be asked whether you would work for such a wage or not," he replied.

My response was, "I would quit my job."

The admiral laughed a little and said, "We should haul you back." I said I would continue to quit. His reply was, "You probably would get over that in a hurry because we have a way of dealing with people who become difficult.

There is nothing that so quickly persuades a person to go back to work as to shave the top of his head until it's very smooth, place one bedbug on that smooth area, and then strap a glass or a cup over the bug so that he cannot escape. You would be surprised what a persuader such a little bug can be."

To get back to the cartoonists, I picked up all the morning papers to take with me and then our counsel general escorted me to the airport. Sure enough, the cartoons were in several of the newspapers. Despite the fact that I was traveling on a diplomatic passport, Turkish customs officials were more or less insistent on going through my baggage. I uttered a protest but they did not understand. Finally I turned to the consul general and said, "Tell them to stop. I'm on a diplomatic passport."

His answer was, "I can't. I've only been here a little while and I know only a few words in Turkish." My ire was rising, and then I happened to think of the newspapers in my pocket. I took out one in which the cartoon appeared on the front page and spread it out where the customs officials could see it and could also read the text. They looked at each other and without more ado closed my bags, bowed from the waist, and muttered something which could have been an apology. It all helped me to realize the value of visual aid in communication when no common language is found.

When I arrived at the airport in Athens, a colonel in the Greek army, representing the prime minister, came to meet me and as we prepared to load the bags and start for the hotel, he tendered a package which was done up in multicolored ribbon. As he handed it to me he said, "Accept this with the compliments of the prime minister." I felt the package and could not guess what was in it. He noticed the puzzled look on my face and then said, "It's a million drachma for spending money." I could scarcely believe my ears. I said, "I'm rich."

The colonel smiled and to put me at ease said, "You might be able to buy one good shirt in an Athens department store with that million drachma." My dream of riches was quickly dissipated.

Here in the ancient cradle of democracy I wanted to see practically everything, and it took time to do so. Here were the Acropolis and the Parthenon; here was sculpture from the Golden Age. Everything seemed to stem from the pages of ancient history as I had studied it in high-school days. The one thing not so recorded was the terrible destruction occasioned by the Red forces during the civil war in 1944–45.

When I went to Italy I saw our commander, General Mark Clark, who told me one of the most hilarious of his experiences—hilarious yet serious enough in its beginnings to threaten a real international incident. As the story comes back to me, the Yugoslav forces were intent on moving into the city of Trieste as the war ended. It was one of General Clark's duties to see that this did not happen and yet to take care that the Yugoslavs were handled in such a way as to create no real incident of international proportions. All the while Clark's forces were gradually pushing the Yugoslavs back, a British broadcasting service was covering a substantial area of Yugoslavia and reciting the fact that both the Yugoslav troops and their officers were being pushed out of the way as if they were so many paper soldiers. The Yugoslav commanding general was furious. Finally some bright member of General Clark's staff hit upon an idea that not only could be conciliatory but also might conceivably settle the whole matter. It was to invite the Yugoslav general and his staff to dinner and to make it a real affair. When the invitation was accepted, the best cooks in Clarks' command and the finest connoisseurs of wine were set to preparing the dinner. Nothing would be omitted; nothing would be overlooked. The day for the dinner came and there was good fellowship and jollity. When the dinner was over, General Clark raised his glass to salute the Yugoslav general, his officers, and his troops and to tell them what a great people they really were and that their courage, stamina, and competence was simply unmatched.

The Yugoslav general replied amiably to this toast and then, for good measure, General Clark stated that he had already contacted British broadcasting and that starting in the morning they would remain on the air all day, just to tell the world over and over what superb soldiers the Yugoslavs really were and what a capable commanding general they really had. This completely changed the situation, and before they left the dinner table that night, the Yugoslav general turned to Mark Clark and said, "I will not attack you anymore."

I arrived in Paris on May 7, the day before victory in Europe was announced. After getting properly settled at the hotel, I waited to see what would happen. It was not a long wait. Pandemonium broke loose in Paris. It was simply incredible how many people jammed the streets of that great city and gave full vent to their pent-up feelings. It was fully understandable. For years the city had been in darkness because of the danger of air raids; now suddenly on the night of VE Day the lights came on. The suffused pink lights on the Opéra would have stirred any heart. The Champs Elysées was jammed as people surged up that wide thoroughfare and through the Arc de Triomphe. Headquarters advised that a victory service was to be held in the cathedral in Rheims and that General Eisenhower and many of his staff would be on hand. I thought it appropriate that I attend the victory service, which was deeply impressive. I had learned that General Bedell Smith, Eisenhower's chief of staff, had set up temporary headquarters in Rheims, and I felt reasonably certain that when the service was over, he probably would go to his headquarters, where I could see him. That is precisely what happened. It afforded me a chance for a visit. After some conversation he said with quite a laugh, "I suppose like all congressmen you probably want to take a souvenir home in the form of a Luger or some other German pistol?"

"General," I said, "of all the things in which I have no interest whatsoever, number one on the list would be a Luger or any other kind of weapon. I notice on your desk a short ceremonial sword probably taken from a German officer. If I took any memento at all of my trip I would rather have that." "It's yours," he said.

Then I asked, "By the way, what's in that bottle on your desk?"

"That's vodka."

"I'll take it," I said, and he handed over the vodka. The sword came back with me but the vodka did not.

Just watching the crowds in Paris was enough to fatigue the spirit, but that was not quite the whole story. By this time I was tired of traveling and wanted to go home. I had a conference with my aide, Commander Young, and told him that I thought I would make a brief stop in London and then get aboard the *Queen Mary* and go back to the States. That's the way it worked out, and the first order of business, when I had returned, was to make a rather lengthy report to the House of Representatives on some of my observations.

Among other things, I devoted considerable attention to our war agencies and how they were functioning and, particularly, to the Office of War Information. Elmer Davis, a well-known and highly respected newspaperman, had been selected to head up this agency. Some of the members on Capitol Hill thought he was entirely too liberal. He may have been, but I had got a different impression of him when I went to visit at his office before leaving on this trip. He felt rather hurt by this attitude on Capitol Hill, and he gave me a bit of information that struck home. He had lost a son in the war, and I could not imagine the father of a son killed in battle who was not a thoroughgoing patriot. Moreover, in examining the various offices of OWI in so many parts of the world, I learned that it was more than a competent operation, and I felt duty bound to note that fact in my report.

A few days later I went down to breakfast in the Mayflower Hotel and there I found Senator McKellan of Tennessee, who was all alone. I joined him and we talked about many things. Suddenly he got on the subject of the

Office of War Information. "I read what you said about this outfit. I was appalled. I cannot believe they were worth much with the kind of leadership they had."

There was much more to his tirade but I was in no mood to answer. He had no first-hand knowledge and had not examined those facilities, but I had and I had no choice save to report what my conscience dictated. Another thought kept crossing my mind; if that was a good example of the Senate's attitude, why should one ever want to be a senator?

15

A CRISIS IN MY LIFE

I BELIEVE IT WAS Henry David Thoreau of Walden Pond who first re-marked that most people lead lives of quiet desperation. I have thought of that observation many times and I fancy there is a lot of truth in it.

For in every life there are those factors that easily lead to desperation, frustration, and despair. One cannot easily ignore them or the causes of this neurotic attitude toward life. There are the money problems in many families and especially the fact that there never seems to be enough to go around. There is never enough to adequately enjoy a summer vacation, or for the education of the youngsters, or for a new car, and obviously this leads to quiet desperation. But there are other reasons as well. At the head of the list I would probably put the question of health. When people are afflicted with some kind of physical impairment or disease, it is easy to become desperate and wonder precisely what to do.

This leads me to what happened in June of 1947 when I journeyed to Illinois to address the alumni dinner at Bradley University in Peoria. It was the usual dinner. I doubt very much that my speech was world shaking. I am quite certain the food was good. I believe there was a cocktail party prior to the dinner, but it was very quiet and restrained. I recall also that the dinner ended at an early hour and it was possible for me to go home. When I arrived home in Pekin, the lights seemed rather dim. There seemed to be cobwebs in my eyes. I passed it off as some transient thing and I was sure it would disappear after a good night's sleep. But in the morning the cobwebs were still there. It was not a matter of deep distress, but I could not help being somewhat concerned.

The cobwebs remained even after I returned to Washington, and I let this condition persist for several weeks. Then I became truly worried. I felt I needed some good professional advice but I had never had contact with any specialist in the medical profession. I sought out a friend who was born and reared in Washington and had a very extensive acquaintanceship with many people including physicians. I related what had happened. He said, "I think you should see my doctor."

I took his advice and without delay called on this specialist. He was a physician and surgeon who had a very extensive practice and had performed a great deal of eye surgery. After a thorough examination, we had a heart-to-heart talk. He said, "I believe your right eye is afflicted with chorioretinitis. You have those tiny hemorrhagic streaks on the right eye and that may account for it. It may not be serious, but on the other hand there is always the possibility that the condition of the eye could prove malignant." I left with that diagnosis ringing in my ears, together with his suggestion that I should not depend entirely upon consultation with any single doctor. He had stated very frankly that where eyesight is involved, it was always well to consult with others who had expertise in this field.

After some days I boarded a plane and went to Chicago to consult with another eye specialist who was regarded as one of the top men in this field. He came up with substantially the same opinion. I returned to Washington and paid the first doctor another visit. I said, "I suppose it might be a good idea if I were hospitalized for a few days and you treated me for this malady."

To this he replied, "The sooner, the better."

And so I was hospitalized and various kinds of treatment were administered. One of these was extremely rugged. I am not certain that I can accurately describe it, but it called for muscular injections. I was ready and willing to be a guinea pig. When that first injection was administered it had a truly astonishing effect. There was no pain, but it caused me to lose control of my nervous and muscular system to the point where the contortions and gyrations fairly threw me out of bed. It was really ghastly. I thought perhaps it was in the nature of a shock treatment that could do some good.

The following day I was to receive a second treatment, but it was complicated by the fact that Mrs. Dirksen had come to the hospital. Knowing what would happen, I suggested that she leave before they administered this second injection and gave her a hint of how it affected me. She refused to leave. I argued politely and said, "Mother, I am afraid you will be sorry that you stayed, because the physical agony that one must endure until this drug runs its course is not very pleasant to behold."

But it was administered and she remained. The agony soon began. I was not merely a writhing body, but a writhing spirit as well. To this day I am not sure whether it actually did some good or not. It would be difficult for a layman to say. Doubtless it was successfully used with some patients, but I could discern no particular improvement in my vision.

Meanwhile, I consulted other eye specialists, and before I got through I believe I saw five in all in Washington and Chicago. One day, arrangements were made for a conference call, with all of these doctors on the line to discuss my condition. They left it to Dr. Benjamin Rones in Washington to convey to me the results of that conference. The whole group suggested that I go to Johns Hopkins Hospital in Baltimore for further consultation with a distinguished professor and surgeon named Dr. Wood. He was rated as one of the top specialists in the entire country.

I lost no time, and the following morning I took the train from Washington to Baltimore to see this great man. When I arrived he said very simply, "I understand there was a difference of opinion among the men whom you consulted as to whether or not you have a malignant condition. If that is the case, then I suppose we should consider an enucleation." That, of course, was the professional term for the removal of the eye. He went on, "That is a decision, Congressman, that you must make based upon the available medical testimony."

I had been thinking a great deal about this. I said, "Dr. Wood, I do not believe so, and I shall have no removal of my eye even if a majority of the physicians whom I consult think the condition is malignant."

"Why then did you come here?" he asked.

My response was, "I came at the suggestion of the other doctors who discussed my condition in a conference call." And then as a kind of afterthought I said, "I have enlisted another doctor."

To that he replied, "How could you, you were on the train coming from the capital?"

"I found him while on the train," I replied. "I am referring to a big doctor, to the Great Physician. He's way upstairs. I found him when I got on my knees. From him I got a message that satisfied me, and I'll keep my eye."

Dr. Wood looked rather incredulous. "So you believe so completely in religion?"

"Yes, Doctor, I can be quite a rough person, but at heart I am a country boy, and I still believe in religion and that's how I got in touch with the big doctor. His response to my prayer was sufficient and I presume that's the whole story for the moment."

"Well, while you are here I can make an examination and perhaps take a few photographs, but you will have to make up your mind now because I will be leaving in the morning for California and I expect to be away for a rather extended period."

To that I answered, "Well, Doctor, I mean no offense, but under the circumstances it would make no difference to me how long you remain in California. I shall keep my right eye."

How strange all this seems in the light of hindsight. It turned out that the same affliction beset both eyes before I got over it. Stranger still is the fact that the right eye, which some thought should be removed, turned out to be my good eye in which I now enjoy virtually normal vision and that the left eye, which at first was not afflicted, finally developed beclouding scar tissue that ultimately resulted in my having only peripheral vision.

But all this is hindsight. Actually my vision was not clearing, and I had to conclude on the basis of further consultations that only a complete and protracted rest might finally restore my eyesight. Mrs. Dirksen and I discussed it at considerable length a good many times. I was by then completing my eighth term in the House of Representatives. The work of the Appropriations Committee was extremely heavy. My time was further burdened by the fact that I was serving as a vice-chairman of the Republican National Congressional Campaign Committee, and I was asked to go to many places to make speeches not merely at political meetings, but at virtually every other type of meeting or dinner that brought people together. So long as I remained in office it would be impossible to escape these chores. Moreover, the people in my own congressional district had a deep proprietary interest in me and wanted me back home frequently so I could keep up with the affairs of the six counties in the district.

We were back home in Pekin when Mrs. Dirksen and I finally arrived at a decision. I would quit Congress at the end of the current term. Then the question arose as to how the news should be released. It was only fair and proper to do it well in advance of the election so other candidates for my seat would have an opportunity to get their candidacies under way. We decided to prepare a release and give it to the local press and the wire services on the day we left by car to return to Washington for the second session of the Eightieth Congress. By leaving early we would avoid the telephone calls that would inevitably result from the announcement. I was certain that what I was doing was the right thing and that rest and relaxation would yet prove to be the best remedy.

Mrs. Dirksen drove us to Washington at a comfortable speed; the weather was ideal. It was winter, but it was bright and there was no snow at the time. It was possible to drop the windows of the car and get some of that bracing winter air. As we left Illinois and moved across Indiana, the radio brought us the first hint of the impact of my announcement. All morning over first one station and then another came a repetition of the text of the release together with comment by the announcers. How glad we were that there were no telephones, no interviews, no explanations.

But then came another problem, and that was how to convey properly this message to the House of Representatives. It was my clear duty to advise them without delay so that my retirement could be regarded as official. I finally decided to break the news by way of a speech. Actually it would be little more than an announcement. I would leave it to others to discuss my retirement.

There came still another complication. The Republicans in the District of Columbia were preparing for a banquet to observe the anniversary of Abraham Lincoln's birth. They had gone to Joe Martin, the Speaker, to have him prevail upon me to make the major speech. I went to his office and when he told me what they wanted, I gave him some additional details concerning my eye condition and frankly told him that I did not believe I could do it.

He responded by saying, "They want you and I want you to do it. Take a rest, get away from this business for a few weeks and condition yourself for this important address. Since you are retiring at the end of this session, I know of no reason why you and Mrs. Dirksen should not go to Florida and enjoy the sunshine and the warm weather. It will be a tonic for you."

I finally agreed, and very shortly thereafter we went to Palm Beach, hoping to enjoy good weather for several weeks. As everyone knows, Florida weather can be unpredictable, and that proved to be the case almost from the day we arrived. It became chilly, rainy, and miserable. It was necessary to turn on heat in order to make our quarters livable. This inclement weather continued for at least ten days. At the end of that time, we felt it was not doing us any good to remain there longer so we returned to Washington.

I had hoped during that Florida sojourn to put a suitable speech together for the Lincoln dinner, but my mind seemed like a well which had run dry. When we arrived back in Washington I had not committed a single line or a single thought to paper. Moreover, the time was getting short and it then became a case of isolating myself from all contacts until I had developed whatever speech I could contrive.

I shall never forget that dinner, not so much because of the speech but because of a comment which was penciled on the last page of the dinner program. Seated next to me was the Reverend Peter Marshall of the New York Avenue Presbyterian Church, chaplain of the United States Senate. He had written something on the program, folded it, and said, "Put this in your pocket and read it when you get home." I almost forgot about it until I began to take off my evening clothes and found the program. I unfolded it and there Peter Marshall had written, "Dear Congressman, God and Lincoln would have been proud of you this night." That one line was more than generous compensation for whatever misery and agony attended the development of that speech.

I knew, of course, that friends and well-wishers back home, and particularly those identified with my party who felt that I had rendered sound and conservative service to the district and to the country, would use whatever instrumentalities were available in order to persuade me to change my mind. But the conclusion had been reached only after long, painful, and prayerful consideration; there could be no retreat. I was still confronted with the prospect of impaired vision and even blindness, and this thought hardened the conviction that we were pursuing the right course.

I shuddered at the very thought that sometime I might become blind. I wondered how I might live if my eyes, those "windows of the soul," would no longer let in light and I would be deprived of the images of the world, pleasant and unpleasant. Could I bear it if everything was blotted out and I was left stumbling about in darkness? It was now a case of finding such labors and escapes and such exercise as would bring comfort and healing to the body and particularly to the eyes.

It was my good fortune to have grown up close to nature. I had always taken an abiding interest in everything that grew from the earth, and particularly flowers. I did not want to become a professional in horticulture but remained an amateur with an interest in all kinds of flowers, plants, and shrubs. It was not a case of trying to grow prize roses, but I liked to find comfort in marigolds and in zinnias, those hearty annuals with their rugged colors which seemed to absorb all the heat and the glory of the sun. The bright marigolds were closest to my heart and I felt their massive blossoms could add inspiration to the darkest day. And then, of course, there were those delicate petunias—whether in solid colors or candystriped, whether singles or doubles—how lovely they really were. One thing that flowers could do for me was to reaffirm my faith in the creator and his works. He had given man dominion over all things and not the least of these were the diverse color, beauty, form, and structure of flowers.

But my interest was not confined to flowers and shrubs. I found equal delight in the diversity of trees one could have almost for the asking. What a gorgeous sight it was in spring to contemplate a graceful weeping willow or a stately birch with its white bark. What a delight to see the flowering crab or flowering cherry in full bloom. Then, of course, there was our American dogwood to fairly delight the eye. In all this I found comfort in convalescence.

But the efforts to have me reconsider the decision did not relent. All manner of suggestions were made. Why not take a long leave from congressional duties to retrieve my fading vision? There were assurances in endless letters, telegrams, and telephone calls that after sixteen years the people of my district would not expect too much until my efficiency as a public servant was restored. But we clung resolutely to our decision and I felt that this course was in the public interest.

This was in 1948, the year in which Thomas E. Dewey, governor of New York, and Earl Warren, governor of California, were the candidates for the presidency and the vice-presidency on the Republican ticket.

After the Republican National Convention had selected the Dewey-Warren team, I was asked by Herbert Brownell, the chairman of the Republican National Committee, whether I would come to Albany, New York, to be part of the campaign team. I thought it would be a novel assignment that I could discharge and still find relaxation, and so I took myself to Albany where the participants were quartered in the DeWitt Clinton Hotel. There were at least a dozen or more ardent Republicans there who served as a speechwriting and strategy team. It included Mr. Brownell; Elliott Bell, who was serving as banking commissioner for the state of New York; Senator Henry Cabot Lodge; Edward Jaeckel, of Buffalo, who was the New York State chairman; Stuart Beech, the editor of a weekly magazine; Stanley High, who was on the editorial board of *Reader's Digest;* and a few others. The group was supposed to work out the perfect approach to campaign strategy and to victory. During the day each man was left to his own devices with an assignment which he was expected to whip into the form of a speech. This, of course, took abundant research to make certain that facts were carefully tested, that the argument was suited to the issues, that the proper appeals were made to the different segments of our voting population, and that the speech material had the kind of interest to hold audiences and to generate the right kind of press coverage. At six o'clock in the evening these labors came to an end as all of the staff gathered in a large reception room to observe what was facetiously referred to as the children's hour. Drinks were poured as each one contributed some items to the general conversation. Thereafter came dinner, and after dinner came a consideration of all the material that had been put into shape for examination by the entire team.

I shall never forget the initial speech that Governor Dewey was to deliver in the little town of Dexter, Iowa. It had been very carefully prepared and was to be read aloud to this assembly of strategists for comment and criticism. As I recall, Stanley High read the speech, and then Elliott Bell, serving as chairman of the meeting, began to go around the table with questions in order to elicit our views and comments. I believe I was next to the last person to be asked for my comment. I recall also that the New York chairman, Ted Jaeckel, was sitting next to me. Elliott Bell said, "Everett, what do you think about this speech for an opener in the campaign?"

I thought for a moment and then said, "Frankly, I think it is marvelous. I think it is perfect. There isn't a comma or a semicolon or a period out of place. There's not a single surplus preposition or adjective. It's in every respect a perfect speech except for one thing."

"And what's that?" he interjected.

I said, "There is no blood in that speech. It is to be made in a small town in Iowa and rugged, hardy, vigorous people from a large area will be on hand to hear it delivered. They will be expecting something that is warm, something with teeth. They want lots of hemoglobin and you give them ice water. In that respect the speech falls flat."

You can imagine what that did to the assembled group; they had labored so long and so earnestly to contrive what they thought was the last word in oratorical perfection. Chairman Jaeckel, sitting next to me, whispered in my ear, "I wish I had your guts."

Years later, I had occasion to discuss that speech with Senator Bourke Hickenlooper of Iowa and asked just what the crowd reaction was. He quite concurred in my estimate of how that initial speech had been received. He was present when it was delivered, and classed it as a great disappointment.

While I was serving on the strategy team in Albany there came a call from Washington. The Republican national chairman, Mr. Brownell, had gone to the capital and there received a phone call from the vice-presidential candidate. Governor Warren seemed a bit put out and felt neglected. He needed a few people for a strategy team of his own to assist in putting speech material together for the various places where the vice-presidential train was expected to stop. He asked Mr. Brownell to recruit and send him the kind of help he wanted. My name seemed to be close to the top of the list for this assignment. The trip to California appealed to me and I thought, among other things, that the weather would add to a mood of relaxation. I therefore agreed to go.

It took only a day to make preparations, pack a bag, and board an airplane for San Francisco. From there I had to find my way to the capital of the state at Sacramento where I would find the governor. A car was waiting at the San Francisco airport and I thoroughly enjoyed the drive to Sacramento. I arrived there on Labor Day and stores and shops were closed for the occasion. I went to a modest hotel across from the state capitol, got myself oriented, my bag unpacked, and then went down and walked to the capitol building. The first person I encountered was a uniformed guard.

He said, "What do you want?" It did not seem like a particularly cordial greeting, and I answered, "I would like to know where I can locate the governor."

To that he said, "This is a holiday."

"Yes, my friend, I know it is a holiday. I also know that a political campaign is about to get underway and I know the governor has asked me to come out here to assist him if I can. That's why I would like to locate him without delay."

Still not quite satisfied, the guard said, "And who are you?"

"If you get the governor on the phone, tell him there's a very humble member of Congress from Illinois who has come across the country to see him and to help him at his request."

From that point on the guard was all energy and alertness, and in just a moment he had the governor on the line. Shortly after, the governor arrived at the capitol and we went into consultation without delay. We had a long conversation concerning issues and the strategy of the campaign, and then I became rather specific.

I said to Governor Warren, "I'll need a well-oiled typewriter and plenty of white paper and then I'll try to do what I am supposed to do and that is to assist in the preparation of some speeches. Your very first speech will be made in Salt Lake City, Utah, on the seventeenth of September. Does that mean anything to you?"

He puzzled for a moment and then said, "As far as I know, the date has no special significance."

To that I said, "Governor, September 17 is the anniversary of the signing of our Constitution. In my book it is a great day since that document is the charter of freedom and liberty. But coming as it does at Salt Lake City, it inspires still another thought. You'll be in the heart of the Mormon country. These are rugged people who trekked across the country, after the outrages perpetrated on them in my own state of Illinois, to set up a veritable new civilization of their own. Had they been less robust and had their devotion to their own religion failed at any point, who shall say what might have happened to the Mormon people? They have proved to the world and to our own country that people can be self-sufficient and need not be dependent upon the largesse of the federal government. There you have the essentials of a speech that I believe would be very appropriate for Salt Lake City."

After some reflection he said, "That should make a great theme. When will it be ready?"

I said, "There is not too much time, and I'll have to labor early and late to put this in proper form for you. I rested pretty well today, and I presume I'll have to remain here late at night and hope the muse will stay with me. You'd better supply me with a key and advise the guards so that whatever the hour I can come and go. Sometimes I work through the night if I'm in the mood to do it."

As a matter of fact, I believe I did labor virtually all night on that first speech, and when I got through about six o'clock in the morning and took time to reexamine my handiwork, I felt reasonably satisfied with the result. Sometime before noon I went back to see about lunch, after which we could discuss the speech.

The governor read the script and said, "I note that your style is entirely different from mine. You use shorter and choppier sentences. And I also note that you weave a good many pungent sayings into your speeches. My style on the other hand is to use long sentences that run on and on, and so I presume I should turn this over to one of my speechwriters and let him see what he can do with it to make it conform to my usual style."

"Governor," I said to him, "I hope you will make it plain to the person to whom you assign the speech that he can take whatever liberties he wants with it. If he feels it has no quality, he can strike out whatever he does not like, and for that matter he can strike out the entire speech if that's his best judgment."

The history of that campaign indicates that this was precisely what happened. I listened to that speech only on the radio since I had to leave Sacramento before it was delivered, but I fairly wept because I recognized so little of what I had written. However, I had not offered my services out of pride, and I should not feel offended if what was finally delivered did not conform to my views. After all, I was not the candidate.

I then raised the question about the governor's next major meeting in Boise, Idaho. I suggested that out there in the western country something had to be said on the basic problem of public works. After some reflection he said to me, "I conceive of public works as a capital investment rather than an expenditure."

I asked, "Are you suggesting that perhaps there should be separate budget treatment for whatever is expended on public works so that it will not actually appear in the annual expenditure budget?"

On further reflection he said, "I believe that is the way I would treat it."

It was my turn to puzzle for a moment over the implications of his statement, and finally I said, "Governor, do you mean that we can expend any quantity of money by simply appropriating it to a capital account or to a trust fund and then spending out of such fund and it will be considered as a wholly separate budget item? I am afraid that you will have a hard time persuading me about this type of federal bookkeeping. Franklin Roosevelt tried it but never succeeded, and if that's the kind of a speech you think you must make, somebody else will have to prepare it."

We went on to discuss other things and tempers were rising just a little. Finally he said, "Don't get sore."

My answer to that was, "I'm not sore, but I would be less than candid if I didn't say I am a little upset at some of the views you have expressed."

He stood up then and said, "Put on your hat. There are some people out on the edge of town who want us to come early for one of those backyard parties. But before we go let me tell you that Mrs. Warren and the children are down in Pasadena and I am expected to leave the airport not later than seven o'clock." I said I'd try to see that he was on the plane at seven o'clock.

We drove to a beautiful home where the site was entrancing and where there was ample acreage to set off the house and the landscape to its very best advantage. As we walked up the front sidewalk toward the front door of the home, the door opened and the host and hostess were there to greet us. Governor Warren said, "Let me introduce the congressman from Peoria, Illinois, who has come to assist me in the campaign."

"Peoria, Peoria," the host echoed. "I'm from Peoria. Greetings to you, sir. You are like manna from heaven. How honored we are to have you with us." And with that we proceeded through the house into the garden where quite a number of people had already gathered for a late afternoon party. Of course, everyone rushed up to greet the governor and express the hope of a very substantial victory. I preferred to be left to my own devices and joined first one group and then another to make conversation. At the right juncture I had my share of succulent steak.

All the while I kept watching the time to make sure that my self-assigned mission of putting the governor on the plane by seven o'clock would not fail. At about quarter to seven I sidled up to the governor and said I thought it was time to say farewell to the host and hostess and proceed to the airport.

He was jovial but said, "Get away from me—have some more steak. Have a drink. Go and visit."

To that I responded by saying, "Look, Governor, you assigned me a mission and that was to see that you got on that plane by seven o'clock. Your family is expecting you. Either you come along or I'll have to get the chauffeur and between us we'll put you in that car." After a little more scolding, he finally subsided and to the car we went. Nor did I leave him until he was safely aboard the plane, after which I felt free to have the driver take me back to the hotel.

The next morning he returned and by then I deemed it necessary to have some conversation with him about my returning to Washington and perhaps later to Albany. I said, "Governor, very frankly I do not believe that I am making any progress here. My technique and form have no particular appeal to your personal speech assistants and ghostwriters. Under the circumstances I think that I ought to get back to Washington tomorrow. If you can supply a car to get me to San Francisco, I'll leave you to your own devices."

He seemed quite surprised and said, "You can't leave me." But I insisted and it was arranged that we would drive toward San Francisco the following morning taking two motorcars. The governor would accompany me halfway back and then let me proceed to the airport in one car and he would return to Sacramento in the other.

About halfway between these two cities there was a huge shady nut tree close to which some enterprising young man had set up what might be called a "juice bar" where light refreshments could be obtained. Under that tree, the governor and I drank orange juice and talked of the future and of our families. I feel reasonably sure that not once in the course of that delightful conversation did we get back to the subject of politics and the campaign.

I did not think that I would see him again on the campaign trail, but a Pennsylvania congressman broke an ankle and sent up a Macedonian cry for me to come and give him some assistance in his campaign. After several meetings in his congressional district, I discovered that the vice-presidential campaign train was coming through that area the following day, and I was asked to join him for a swing through New England and back in the direction of Maryland and West Virginia.

I shall never forget my conversation with the governor before I left him in Maryland. He said, "When I get to West Virginia I presume Senator Revercomb will join the train. I do not know what to say about him. I have familiarized myself with his record on refugee legislation and on other matters and frankly we do not see eye to eye."

That statement really astonished me, and my response was, "Governor, 'Chappy' Revercomb is running for reelection. He is our guy. When he boards the train you have to take him to the end coach and present him at every stop. You put your arm around him and tell the people of West Virginia what a great guy and what a good senator he really is."

His only answer was, "I don't see how I can do that." That ended the conversation, and I was frankly sorely distressed by his attitude toward one of our own senators, whether he agreed with him or not.

And so election day came. There was a general feeling that the Dewey-Warren ticket would win. I had some doubts, which I did not express to anyone except to the closest intimates. My views were predicated entirely on observations made during the campaign and it was my belief, notwithstanding the general sentiment to the contrary, that our party might lose. As everyone knows, when the vote count had been completed, President Truman had a popular vote of 24,105,812 and Governor Dewey had 21,970,065. This gave President Truman 303 electoral votes while Governor Dewey received 189. Anyway, at long last I would now be privileged to go home and convalesce.

But there were some things to be done before I could separate myself from Washington ties. For one thing, the office files had to be stripped and packed in filing boxes. Just what was to happen to them from there on I did not know, but as an afterthought, it occurred to me that perhaps this accumulated correspondence might be useful to my successor, and I decided to leave it. There were some farewells, and not the least of these would be to the president and his family.

I had observed over the years that when a session came to an end, most members were packed and ready to leave at a moment's notice. In my case, it was a little different. I would not be coming back, and so everything had to be made shipshape by the day of departure.

I called the White House and reached Matt Connelly, the president's appointment secretary. "Matt," I said, "I am leaving Washington. I am leaving Congress, and I would like to come and say good-bye to the president."

"He is very busy," Matt said.

To that I replied. "That's all right. I can wait as long as necessary. If he cannot see me this week, perhaps he can see me next week, but certainly I will not leave Washington without saying good-bye."

We went through the usual routine, and suddenly he said, "Wait a minute." He examined his appointment calendar and then came back to the phone to say, "The president could see you Tuesday morning at eleven o'clock."

At eleven o'clock on the appointed morning I was there and was ushered in to see the president. He was extremely cordial. Moreover, he did not seem overly busy. Nor was his desk cluttered with a great many letters and papers. We started off in the most friendly fashion and enjoyed a long, amiable conversation. He was from Missouri, and I was from next-door Illinois. We talked about many subjects, and finally he said, "You should not have quit. We need people like you in Congress. You've been a good public servant."

"Mr. President, coming from you this is generous indeed, and I appreciate it immensely." I jumped up with something of a start, for the watch indicated that I had been visiting the president for one whole hour. I concluded our visit by saying, "Mr. President, I wish you Godspeed. I trust all of life's blessings will come to you, and I hope you will give Mrs. Truman and Margaret my very best wishes and also those of Mrs. Dirksen." And on that happy note, my last piece of official business in Washington ended.

The car was serviced. Mrs. Dirksen was at the wheel. We picked up U.S. Route No. 40, and I knew that after sixteen years we were really going home.

On that three-day motor journey to Illinois, which we undertook in the most leisurely fashion, a certain nostalgia came over me. I was leaving a great many people for whom I had developed a singular attachment, and I would think of them often. In fact, I would miss them. There was Richard Nixon, with whom I had become very well acquainted. There was Lyndon Johnson, who later moved to the Senate to become majority leader and then became successively vice-president and president. John Fitzgerald Kennedy, too, was a member of the House, and I came to know him quite well. John Lodge, who was later to become governor of Connecticut, was also in the House. Subsequently he became our ambassador to Spain and then to Argentina. George Smathers, of Florida; Caleb Boggs, of Delaware; Norris Cotton, of New Hampshire; Carl C. Curtis, of Nebraska; J. Glenn Beall, of Maryland; Thruston Morton, of Kentucky; Margaret Chase Smith, of Maine—all were my House colleagues. I was to meet them often again later.

But as we drove home, I could not help brooding over the eye condition and just how the future might unfold. In a moment of near despair I thought: Why should I want to be a senator after all? Perhaps the Lord had other work for me to do—or perhaps he had no work for me at the moment. My ardor over any future quest of a senatorship began to cool. I was going back home, and I wanted to make the most of it.

16

"BUT YOU MUST BE A SENATOR"

IN 1948 THE LEADERS of the Democratic party in Illinois were casting about for candidates to lead the state ticket in that year. In due course they presented a very formidable team consisting of Adlai Ewing Stevenson for governor and Paul Howard Douglas for United States senator.

At forty-eight, Adlai Stevenson was in his prime. He had been educated at Harvard and Northwestern Universities. He had had considerable experience in the federal government. For a period of three years he had served as assistant secretary of the navy and then moved to the State Department as an assistant secretary. He had also served as an adviser in 1945 when the United Nations charter was drafted.

Paul Douglas was an economist and a professor of political science at the University of Chicago. He entered politics when he was elected as an alderman in the city of Chicago in 1939. During World War II, he enlisted in the marine corps, was wounded twice, and ultimately reached the rank of lieutenant colonel.

Just how or why these two were slotted in these particular places on the ticket has often been discussed and has been the source of much speculation. Rumor had it that Stevenson preferred to run for the Senate because of his experience in the federal government. Whether this was true or not, I am not prepared to say. I do recall that during one of my visits to Springfield after his election as governor, I said "Adlai, are you happy in your present job?"

He laughed a little and replied, "Why bring that up?"

The Stevenson-Douglas victory over the Republican candidates that year was truly massive. In fact, their majorities were in the range of one-half million votes and for a state regarded as normally Republican, that was indeed a king-sized victory.

Such then was the state of political affairs in Illinois when I retired from Congress after sixteen years of service to convalesce and nurse the hope that my vision might be fully restored and the eyes made whole again. Yet almost immediately a campaign of persuasion began with visits to my home from first one group and then another. They included county chairmen, county officials, state legislators, ardent party supporters, and others. The reason was quite obvious. With Governor Stevenson in charge of the state political machine, with Mayor Daley in charge of the Chicago machine, with Senator Douglas serving as senator in Washington under a Democratic president, it was clear that Republicans in office, whether at the local, county, state, or congressional levels, were thinking in terms of political survival.

Strangely enough, nearly all of them who called sang the same refrain, "You've got to run for the Senate. Of course, you can't win against Scott Lucas, the majority leader, but you owe it to the party to hold it together and to try to energize it in the 1950 campaign." How often I have thought of what they said. Perhaps those who said it never took too seriously its possible impact on me.

Here was the state of Illinois stretching from the Wisconsin line to the Ohio River for a distance of 350 miles. It embraced an area of 56,000 square miles and had a population of about ten million. The city of Chicago with its fifty wards contained roughly one-third of the population of the entire state. The state was both industrial and agricultural, and as I thought of the sentiment, so frequently expressed, that I couldn't win, I wondered how any human being with that kind of an advance fixation could ever undertake such a task. Could there be a more negative approach?

Moreover, a campaign under the conditions that confronted any candidate in 1950 would drain away every ounce of energy. Campaigns, after all, had only a few simple techniques and objectives. One was to give the party a clear-cut image with the voter. Another was mass exposure of the candidate to the entire electorate. Still a third goal was to energize the party workers and keep them on their toes through election day. All this meant that one must thoroughly cover the entire state many times and that meant work.

It was probably at this juncture that I received some real encouragement about my vision. It came from Dr. Derrick Vail of Chicago, a recognized eye specialist. It was suggested that I see him, and I did so when the Christmas season was approaching. He made a thorough examination and then said, "I have a Christmas present for you." In an instant my heart fairly thumped with excitement and I sat upright in the chair. How eagerly I waited for him to continue, and then he said, "You do not have one bad eye, you have two."

I slumped in the chair. I was almost speechless. Finally in what must have been a whisper of despair I said, "Doctor, did you say a Christmas present?"

"Congressman," he replied, "in my experience when *both* eyes are afflicted with chorioretinitis as in your case, only once in a million times could it be malignant." I had great faith in Dr. Vail and as I returned to my home in Pekin, I uttered a prayer of thanksgiving to God, not merely for this good news but for the comforting message which he gave me that day on the train from Washington to Baltimore when I refused to consent to the removal of my right eye.

People continued to come to see me, and I knew that sooner or later I must make a decision and give them a reply. I owed it to the party to make that decision and to any others in the party who might be harboring the idea of being a candidate. There were probably not too many who were anxious to seek a Senate seat in the light of what had happened in the election of 1948, but there might be some, and they were entitled to know how I felt about making such a race. My eyes were better, no doubt about it, but would they stay that way? I had to think it all over and decide quickly.

As if anything had to be added to my dilemma, the word had already gone forth that Senator Scott Lucas, the majority leader of the Senate, would be a candidate for reelection and that he would have the solid support of the governor; the junior senator from Illinois, Mr. Douglas; the Chicago machine; and the Truman administration. Surely that formidable team should strike fear and trepidation into the heart of anyone who undertook a senatorial campaign after the colossal defeat in 1948.

But despite this a decision had to be made. One interesting characteristic of all the delegations that came to see me was that not one had suggestions to offer with respect to what one might use for funds. Obviously it would require a great deal of money to operate, to pay campaign expenses, to engage television and radio time, to purchase newspaper advertising, buy literature, recruit workers, purchase billboards from one end of the state to the other, and do all those things that seemed indispensable if there was any hope of victory.

I was not forgetting still another fact, and that was that Scott Lucas was extremely popular throughout the state. He lived in the town of Havana, only forty miles from my hometown. We knew each other quite well. Years before, he played as a first baseman in the minor Illinois-Missouri baseball league. He was not only an excellent player but a great favorite with the fans. Both he and I had been active in the American Legion and in due course he became the national judge advocate of that organization. He was a very intimate friend of former governor Henry Horner. He was elected to Congress from the adjoining district and was, therefore, my congressional neighbor. We had served in the Congress together before he was elected to the Senate and became the majority leader.

Who shall say what our national political destiny might have been if Senator Lucas had been reelected to the Senate? Surely his senatorial colleagues would have continued him as the majority leader and that would have meant a term of six years in this very responsible position. In that event, Lyndon Baines Johnson, who was elected to the Senate in 1948 and to the leadership in 1953, might never have become a leader and might not have made so deep an impression on the political destiny of the country.

In mulling over my physical problem and my political dilemma, it occurred to me that other members of the family might have some suggestions concerning the prospect of my running for the Senate. After all, they were entitled to be consulted. One night at home when we had finished dinner, I said, "Kids, give your Grandmother Carver a lift with the dishes, and then let's gather in the study and consider a problem which calls for a decision." When my wife and Joy convened in the study, I reviewed the general political situation for them, summarized the number of callers I had had from all over the state who urged me to be a candidate for the Senate, and then said, "Suppose we discuss this one question under the rules of the House of Representatives. We each get five minutes to present the case for or against my running. Joy, suppose you speak first and let us have your views."

"Pop," my daughter began, "I think you should run. The newsmen in Washington always ask me whether I was a member of your staff in the House, and I always say I was your only uncompensated assistant and that I've never been on the public payroll. But I always enjoyed it and I think it would be great fun to be a receptionist in a senator's office even without pay. Just think of the important people I would meet and the telephone calls that I would handle. I think you should run for the Senate." There was some amplification, of course, before her five minutes had expired, but that was essentially the extent of her argument.

"Mother," I said to my wife, "it's your turn."

She knew pretty well what she wanted to say. "I could give you many reasons why I think you should run, but I believe I'll content myself with emphasizing perhaps two. First, let me say that someone is going to get that nomination for the Senate and whoever it is will be calling you even before the primary election day is over to say that he wants your active support, and you'll have to campaign for him. I have lived with you a long time, I believe I know you, and I fancy you'll be like an old fire horse who has been put out to pasture. When the fire bells ring, you will let out a snort and suddenly come dashing up to the pasture fence wondering why you're not racing off to the fire. That is exactly what you will do, and in that case, why don't you do it for yourself rather than for some other person who is not nearly so entitled to this nomination?

"But there is another reason," she continued, "don't you remember the many times we walked from the House to the Senate chamber where you wanted to take a look, since as a congressman you had the privileges of the Senate floor. I would wait for you and when you returned, you would give me an account of who was speaking in the Senate and what matters were under consideration. Then you would say, 'I hope someday I may graduate from the House to the Senate before I complete my political career.' You've said that not once but a great many times. For years and years to come you'll be very unhappy if you do not make at least one try, and if whoever receives that nomination should succeed, your unhappiness over a lost opportunity would know no bounds. I guess I could add other arguments but these will do. If I were you, I would run."

With due formality we actually took a vote, and we agreed in advance to abide by the majority decision. Mrs. Dirksen and Miss Dirksen voted that I should run. I felt that I should vote no, but when the moment came I said, "Kids, I do not run for the Senate. *We* run for the Senate. This time it will be all of us running. It will be like the Three Musketeers. Maybe it will be three against the gods. We'll have to start right away on the campaign."

So it was decided. I called Harold Rainville in Chicago and asked him to take a plane in the following morning and come to see me. I would be at the airport in Peoria to meet him. There was much to discuss. We had to pick a date on which to make the announcement and perhaps the best day of the week would be a Sunday, when people were at home. The second thing to determine was a place for the meeting at which the announcement should be made. I thought a place called Exposition Gardens south of Peoria would probably be the ideal spot. Then came the question of a speaker for the meeting. My preference was Senator Karl Mundt, of South Dakota, if he was free and if he would come. There would be releases to newspapers, radio, and TV. It should be a short statement that could be published in its entirety. Then came the question of letters to be sent to every county chairman in the state and perhaps to the ten thousand precinct committeemen. And then the billboards: What they would cost, what text should there be, and where would we go to find the necessary money? And finally we must settle the question of our approach to the campaign.

It could be done in several ways. One approach was to caravan the entire state, and that meant going from town to town after advance announcements and going up and down the main street, shaking hands with merchants, gathering a few people on street corners, and making brief speeches. My own feeling was that an adequately energetic campaign could not be carried on by the caravan method. What was really required was to build up meetings in all of the key spots in the state whether this included one county or a combination of two or three counties. It was only by getting substantial groups together that we could really give hope and inspiration to the workers and to the county committees who would be expected to carry the campaign load.

It would be necesary to stage these meetings from one end of the state to the other. I knew full well that the voters in the southern areas of Illinois for many years had complained that candidates for state and national office would come to their area early in the campaign and then disappear to the other more populous sections and not return again during the campaign. We agreed on a series of build-up meetings to which substantial crowds could be attracted.

The primary election campaign was of no immediate concern, mainly because there would be candidates who were more or less perennial and who made no real effort to obtain the party nomination. I might mention one character who appeared on the ballot as a candidate for some state or national office at virtually every election. In the campaign he would dress himself in an Uncle Sam suit, which consisted of red, white, and blue jacket, trousers, shirt, and a tall stovepipe hat to match. In this garb he circulated over the state, and his candidacy became a harmless perennial joke.

On one thing we all agreed, so far as the primary campaign was concerned, and that was that billboard advertising should be used if the money was available. If there was no great demand for billboard space after the primary election, there was always the possibility that the billboard posting service would leave our posters on the boards for a longer period than the one month for which we would contract. That way we would really get our money's worth.

When it came to fund raising there was, of course, the so-called hundred-dollar dinner which was coming into vogue in different parts of the country. It was the easiest way to raise funds because there were so many who were willing to buy a ticket and attend a dinner. This is where my friends, who enlisted in the cause, proved to be helpful.

As the campaign unfolded, I realized it would indeed be "three against the gods." Our first act in the campaign was to buy a new automobile, knowing that transportation must be certain and that any at given time we must be on hand for a scheduled meeting.

One of the early meetings in the general election campaign has always stood out in my mind. When it was over I was not sure what its real result would be. Attending that meeting were about seventy-five leaders of Negro organizations in Chicago, most of whom had been in Washington some weeks before to attend a rally in behalf of a civil rights bill which was pending in a committee of the House. The measure in which they had particular interest had been introduced by Representative Mary Norton, of New Jersey. I was quite familiar with it. When the dinner was over, the bishop—a huge man with a rich and rolling voice who served as chairman of the meeting—arose and, after some introductory remarks, suggested that I speak briefly to this group with special reference to the so-called civil rights bill and tell them what I proposed to do about it if I should be elected to the Senate. I said rather bluntly that I could not support the Norton bill unless the provisions relating to the use of subpoena powers were removed. If not, I felt that I must oppose this proposal. That came as quite a shock for this group and they very noticeably became agitated.

The bishop arose once more with some concluding thoughts. "Young man," he said, "you're rather abrupt, are you not?"

He paused as if to await a reply from me, and so I arose and addressed him once more. I said, "Reverend, I have a deep conviction on this matter, and I am opposed to the use of subpoena powers in a field of activity which is attended with so much racial emotionalism. It could do more harm than good and, in my considered judgment, would not solve the problem at which the Norton bill was aimed."

The bishop turned to the group before him and then in slow, studied phrases he said, "Ladies and gentlemen, in years gone by so many candidates for high public office have come before us with their glib promises and pledges which were never kept and which they did not intend to keep. In short, they came and lied to us. This young man has come here and bluntly stated what he would or would not do. Surely he must know that we believe the power of subpoena in dealing with civil rights is absolutely indispensable to their enforcement. I, for one, applaud him for his candor and honesty and it occurs to me that if we can persuade him to our point of view he could indeed become a valiant crusader for our cause."

My concluding response was simply to say, "If you can, persuade me." When the meeting was over everyone present came up to shake hands in the most friendly fashion, and I thought perhaps I had done some good after all.

In the campaign I discovered what a powerful force women voters could be if they resolutely set themselves to it and if a particular candidate had appeal for them. If women voters organize and conduct an effective campaign, they can determine the outcome of any election. By way of proving the point, it was during the campaign that the annual meeting of the Grand Chapter of the Order of the Eastern Star was to be held in Chicago. I was asked to attend and to participate. The invitation came because I was a member of our local chapter and because I was a candidate for the Senate.

The meeting was certainly a very impressive affair. It was held in an auditorium in the near north side of Chicago and lasted for most of a week. The place was filled to overflowing. The "girls," as I liked to refer to them, were beautifully gowned; the ritual was flawless and perfect. As orator, I was careful to remain nonpartisan and nonpolitical in my remarks. There was enough humor in the speech to make it appropriate for a midmorning meeting and the members were indeed responsive. Since they came from all sections of the state, it required no expert to measure the value of such a meeting in an election year.

Not long after the meeting, some of the "girls," who were ardent Republicans, suggested a dinner in one of the south-side wards to which they would invite their husbands if I would come and deliver a speech. The prospect delighted me. The dinner was held and about four hundred persons were in attendance. It gave me an excellent opportunity to discuss the issues of the campaign. What happened thereafter was something that I did not quite expect. The "girls" organized a club of Republican volunteers, and when next they were called to make a report on their activities, they had enrolled fourteen hundred working members, in a single ward—and that can account for some very impressive results.

But that was not quite the whole story. Later in the campaign, when only two of the Musketeers could be on the road because Mrs. Dirksen had other chores to perform, we were in Randolph County in the lower end of the state and were scheduled to leave there and proceed to Benton for the next meeting. It was while driving to Benton that a storm broke. It was attended by an incredible electrical display and rolling peals of thunder. Joy was driving and suggested that we skip the meeting at Benton because nobody would be on hand as the rain was coming down in sheets.

I listened patiently but demurred over this change in plans. The Benton rally had been set at our request; moreover, the storm might not be too bad in the Benton area and certainly I did not want to disappoint a substantial group of voters. When we arrived the area around the county courthouse was literally packed with cars, and when we entered the courtroom two things impressed me at once. The first was that the audience was, in large part, composed of women, and the second was that I had seen many of them at the Grand Chapter meeting in Chicago.

In saluting the power of women in an election campaign, I should pay my respects to the Federation of Republican Women, who operated on a national scale and had an actively militant organization in Illinois. They did their homework exceedingly well. They knew how to win elections. Their conventions were really spirited assemblies, and what they learned was translated into real action on election day.

There were so many other groups who became interested in the election of 1950. They included the Poles, the Baltic groups (the Lithuanians, Latvians, Estonians, Germans, and Scandinavians), the farm groups, the dairy groups, the labor groups, the professional organizations, and the business groups.

Let me record one special sentiment about the Ukrainians. Many thousands of these hardworking, frugal, and thrifty people had found their way to Chicago and became identified with industry and business. Their real interests centered in the church and also in the very modern school they had built without any public or outside aid whatsoever. Their spokesman was a man named John Duzansky, who was in the dairy business. Never did I have a more dedicated friend than John, and he was constantly watching for a chance to show me to his people whether in church, in school, or in their other assemblies. Once when a Ukrainian holiday was approaching and they had arranged for a meeting in the large hall in West Chicago, I was asked to come and make a speech. It occurred to me that such a speech should be done in the very simplest language and that the Ukrainians had not forgotten their ancestral home. This speech should be tied to a homeland sentiment. Yet a third aspect of the matter was their intense devotion to freedom. They had left the Ukraine under great difficulties to come to this country where all the benefits and blessings of freedom were available to them. I thought also that at some point in life they had performed some kind of military service and this should be kept in mind.

When I arrived for the meeting on a Sunday afternoon, the hall was filled to capacity. The audience consisted almost entirely of men. My speech was simple. By way of a foundation I began with a description of their homeland and what it would be like about this time of the year. There were the billowing fields of wheat since the Ukraine was really the breadbasket of that area. I talked of the blue sky and directed attention to the fact that their flag was blue and deep yellow, symbolic of clear skies and the Lord's blessing. I spoke of their military service sometimes for a cause in which they did not believe, and finally of the glory and majesty of their adopted country where any and every man and woman could go so far and rise so high as talent and diligence might take them. They understood, and when I spoke of their ancestral land I saw that some of them wept. At the end I was sure that the Ukrainian-American voter would be quite friendly on election day.

Despite all the resources and influences that seemed to be working in my favor, I got the feeling that the campaign was not catching on quite as well as it should. Lincoln on occasion used the word "scour"; when he wished to convey the idea that a policy or a speech or a candidacy was not having appeal, he would say that "it somehow did not scour." Obviously, this could only mean that it needed some stimulation, and all too often, as I had observed in other campaigns, it required some charge or statement that was not merely "nice" or obvious to utter.

I remember the occasion on which my campaign began to scour. It was at an afternoon and early evening picnic that the Republican women of Kane County were holding that I proposed to say that my estimable opponent Senator Lucas was a "faker" and then in one or two paragraphs to state why. Those paragraphs I carefully prepared, and I made copies for release to the press to make certain I was correctly quoted. The reaction was about what I expected. The statements appeared on the front page of all papers in the state. It placed the Democratic candidates for state and national office on the defensive. They promptly began to belabor me early and late, but it had the desired effect and those few paragraphs not only stimulated the campaign but interested the voters everywhere.

Perhaps it is appropriate that I include here a postscript to history. Long years afterward—and Senator Lucas and I had become exceedingly friendly notwithstanding those campaign differences—Senator Lucas developed a clot in the circulatory system of one leg. The doctor who was attending him called me one evening at my home. He said, "Senator, I presume you know that Senator Lucas is in the hospital? We have concluded that there must be an amputation of his leg. He knows all about it. I believe it would be a great boost for his morale if you called on him in the morning before we proceed with the operation."

I said, "Doctor, it will be my first order of business tomorrow morning to the exclusion of anything that might be on my calendar."

I found Senator Lucas very cheerful and amiable. His morale was excellent. We talked about so many things, including our days together in the American Legion, in Congress, and in politics; and it was then that I confessed to him a sense of shame that I had used a harsh epithet in the campaign of 1950. I found some comfort in the fact that campaign speeches are transient and pass away and that it was not this incident which finally influenced the outcome.

It was in the last week in June of 1950 that President Truman ordered General MacArthur to move troops into Korea in what was referred to as a "police action," but people knew instantly and instinctively that to move into another country with troops, tanks, planes, bombs, and all of the associated equipment simply meant war whether in a larger or smaller dimension. It meant that young men of our country would fight on battlefields far away in order to resolve the serious situation which had developed between North and South Korea. It meant anxious parents, wives, and sweethearts back home. As an issue it addressed itself to the very instinct of self-preservation, and that was doubtless the most impelling motive in the life of any individual.

Certainly Korea would be on the front page everyday. One could try— even as I tried—to generate interest in other issues related to agriculture, to labor, to our fiscal affairs, and to our economy generally, but always the people and the news media would come back to the fact that we were at war in Korea.

But we Three Musketeers, now together again, continued with the campaign timetable. The first campaign car was showing signs of wear. Funds had become available and so a new automobile was acquired. Every day, portable typewriters, stationery, and accumulated mail went with us, and the two unsalaried secretaries—Mrs. Dirksen and Miss Dirksen—were either driving or taking dictation and would transcribe their notes in a motel room. Thus, we kept abreast of correspondence and posted letters from virtually every post office of any consequence throughout the state.

About the last week in October there was to be the major meeting in the little town of Vienna in southern Illinois. Here the Republicans were staging their annual afternoon fish fry. It had become a traditional meeting place for a great many years and attracted not only all the candidates but the press corps as well. They came from everywhere. Among those who attended was a reporter for the *Wall Street Journal* named Vermont Royster. He subsequently became the managing editor. I can do no better than to produce the article he wired to his newspaper and which appeared on the editorial page. He captioned it "Gideon at the Fish Fry." There follows his account of what happened at that meeting on October 24:

Under the hot sun of a southern Illinois Indian summer the crowd was mostly in shirt sleeves and galluses. They had come from all over Johnson County to eat catfish, to talk, and to listen.

The men had come from the fields in the early afternoon, for many were not shaven and nearly all were in their working clothes. The women were aproned, for they had to fry the fish and set the long tables inside the big frame meeting hall, but beneath the aprons they wore bright printed dresses mindful of the festivities. The passel of children were in T-shirts or simple pinafores save for one youngster in a white shirt and his Sunday suit.

The evangelist came, appropriately, in a rush and a cloud of dust. Besides his own car, there were two carloads of followers and the inevitable pickup truck equipped to take his voice and spread it loud around the countryside. Spread it loud and spread it far was what he asked. Everett McKinley Dirksen had come to wrestle with a very live devil as he has done some 1,500 times traveling 200,000 miles along the Illinois roadways. And he wanted the countryside to pay attention.

The countryside has certainly paid attention. Whether Mr. Dirksen can pin down his personal devils, who in this instance are the Democrats and especially U.S. Senator Scott Lucas, up for reelection, is a dubious matter. But there is no doubt that here for once is a Republican who is putting on a fighting campaign of evangelical Republicanism. To one exhausted observer it appears that if Mr. Dirksen can't do it, nobody could have.

In the space of two days Mr. Dirksen tore through the southern counties of Illinois with the militant fervor of Gideon pursuing the Midianites. Pinckneyville, Murphysboro, Anna, West Frankfort, Benton, Marion, Cairo, Vienna— the roll call of the south. Then with a whisk he disappeared in the direction of Kankakee, far to the north. And all this in only two days. The Dirksen crusade has been under way for nigh onto two years and in that time he has been many times to every county in the state, at least once to practically every hamlet and crossroads where he could find a handful of people. Three speeches a day has been his average since midsummer, with four or five not unusual.

Sometimes his audiences are friendly, sometimes hostile, for he shuns no Democratic castle. He exhorts the faithful, cajoles the dubious, and charms the "wicked." But everywhere he sounds the trumpet and smites his enemies as one man. He is no prophet of complacency, of me-tooism, of compromise.

Mr. Dirksen charges in where—at least of late—other angels have feared to tread. He defends the Eightieth Congress, Mr. Truman's "worst" Congress. He upholds the Taft-Hartley Law. He attacks extravagance in civilian spending of the government right down to some Democratic-proposed projects for southern Illinois where he speaks. He lambastes the Democrats' foreign policy that made the Korean War necessary and builds a war camp for a bigger one. He withholds no fire from Democratic promises of bigger gifts to farmers and new gifts for the townsfolk.

Here in Vienna the afternoon took on all the aspects of a revivalist camp meeting. It began quietly enough with a few words by the local candidates, from the school superintendent to sheriff. Mr. Dirksen, dressed in a worn but presentable business suit, started with a soft voice, a voice either naturally husky or made so from so much talking. The people sat expectantly, the women particularly intent. From here on Mr. Dirksen was a study in technique—the technique of the crooner, the vaudevillian, or even if you will, of the arouser. Bing Crosby could not have been more suavely folksy, Raymond Hitchcock more skillful with the local references, Billy Sunday more astute at playing on emotions.

But on subject matter there was no talking down to the audience. Mr. Dirksen spread out a big map and with it took his country audience to old Vienna, to Czechoslovakia, to Poland, and the Far East. His argument was that Russia had not won but had been given; and he tried to make what had happened in the past to the Old World pertinent in the future to new Vienna, Jackson County, Illinois.

By and by the women's fans came out and Mr. Dirksen's coat came off. As the farmers began to see "where your boys are" there was a stirring along the benches. As the map became "a testimony, if I ever saw one, to disaster and failure," there was applause and one old woman moved up front the better to see. As the rhythmic voice slipped into sarcasm quoting Truman's "I like old Joe—he's a very decent fellow," the applause was mingled with laughter.

Smoothly the preacher swung from far-off places to the country grocery store, evoking memories of OPA and shortages and rationing, the things that come with a war. In a few minutes the women were helping him out and he picked up the impromptu cues with ease. Soon he was ready to shout: "This great administration has got you right back where you were in 1943! They've turned the clocks back!" And by this time he did not shout alone.

While the hour wore on it grew clear that the spirit had come upon Gideon and his trumpet blew louder. The people saw—even if they did not believe in—the devils with whom he wrestled, and they could see too that they were strong devils because his tie slipped away from his collar and his hair grew ruffled as he wrestled.

After it was all over and the fish fry proceeded, one could not be sure that he had licked his devils. Everywhere Mr. Dirksen goes he blows a lonesome trumpet; there is no chorus from the GOP soldiers who should be with him. Here, in Vienna as in Israel, the twenty and two thousand were busy elsewhere and the faithful were not more than three hundred.

But when sundown came on a weary day no one could say there had not been a battle. And if it should come to pass that on election day his enemies, surprised, should have to ask, Who hath done this thing?—the answer in the book of Judges will be that Gideon alone hath done this thing.

Just a few days before election day Joseph Alsop, the well-known columnist, came to the Oak Park Arms in Oak Park, Illinois, where I was speaking to a luncheon meeting, to interview me on the state of the campaign and what I expected would happen. I asked him where he had been, and he told me he had been in a great many states and had arrived in Chicago only a day or two before. He had contacted various people and particularly the mayor and his associates at the city hall in Chicago. Finally he said, "Dirksen, it's too bad that one of you has to lose in the election. You made a good record in the House and Senator Lucas made a good record both in the House and in the Senate. I am quite sorry you are the one who will lose."

I said, "Joe, how long have you been in the state?"

"Two days," he said.

Then I said, "I am really not a wagering person, but as an evidence of my confidence, here is one hundred dollars even money that I'll win."

"Sorry, but I would rather not bet," he persisted.

"Here's a hundred dollars even money that I shall win by one hundred thousand votes." He could not be beguiled. Then I made him one further offer. I said, "Joe, here's a hundred dollars even money that I shall win by two hundred thousand votes." He was still unpersuaded, and so we left it at that. He returned to Chicago still fully convinced, I'm sure, that I would lose the election.

On one Sunday night before election, we were at home when the telephone rang and a man, who gave me his name, which I identified in my mind and whom I knew had been connected with some petty racketeering, asked me whether I expected to win. I answered by asking, "Why are you so anxious about the outcome of the election?"

"Well, I'll tell you. I am sitting here in Springfield with eight thousand dollars in green money, and a fellow sitting here with me will give me odds of two to one that you'll lose. What I want to know is whether you think you are going to win, and if you tell me that you will win, I'll make the bet."

To that I said simply, "Tell your friend that I shall win."

A day or two after the election a car drove up before our home and the occupant honked the horn furiously. He continued to do so until I opened the door and walked down the sidewalk to the curb to see what all the commotion was about. In that car was the huge, fat, petty racketeer. I had seen him before. When he turned down the window, since it was clear he could not extricate himself from that small car, I said, "What's all the commotion about?"

He said, "I drove up here from Springfield to tell you that I made that bet and I collected. Thanks for the hunch. I am sixteen thousand dollars richer."

"In that event," I said, "you should feel generous, and if I have a campaign deficit I'll know where to come for a contribution."

He fairly snorted and said, "I wouldn't give you taxi fare."

During the last week of the campaign when we were in the very shadow of election day, I was beginning to succumb to the excitement of the campaign and the prospect of victory. There came back to me again the content of the letter that Abraham Lincoln wrote to his friend, Lyman Trumbell, in appeal of 1860. It was the letter in which Lincoln said, "As you request I will be entirely frank, the taste is in my mouth a little." And so it was with me.

17

JUDGMENT DAY

I T WAS THE NIGHT BEFORE election day. The final meeting of the campaign was scheduled for Rock Island, Illinois. Actually it was not a meeting in the campaign sense. The television station located there was to make its initial presentation that night, and the time had been purchased by the Rock Island County Republican Committee and the local Republican candidates.

This TV presentation had been generously advertised, and it was quite certain that there would be a very substantial audience of viewers and listeners. The telephone had been used freely by a battery of devoted girls who called up families throughout the area, and this helped to ensure a real audience.

A three-piece "cowboy" band had been engaged for the occasion. They were all young musicians and dressed in cowboy regalia. The announcer was quite new to all this and was rather timid. When I fully observed this fact, I undertook the responsibility as master of ceremonies and from then on managed to introduce all candidates for office and to intersperse these introductions with music from the band. I reserved the last few minutes of the program to make a brief statement on my own behalf, and when the clock indicated that the time was up, the campaign ended.

Mrs. Dirksen and I drove home. We had seventy-five miles to go and during the course of our return journey there was a chance to relive a good many of the highlights of the campaign. One fact stood out; compared with earlier campaigns youth had played a much larger part. It was so very evident, and perhaps the many meetings which I had had with high-school student bodies and in small colleges contributed in some measure to this growing youth interest.

At some point in the ride home, I was certain that my wife would ask the question and she did, "Now that it's over except for the result tomorrow, you must have some inner feeling as to how it will all come out."

I was ready for that. "Mother, do you recall our first campaign in 1930 when we turned off the radio and went to bed about two o'clock in the morning with the announcement still ringing in our ears that we were forty-four hundred votes ahead and only one county left for the final vote?"

She said she remembered it only too well and I continued. "You remember, as we ascended the stairway I told you not to set your cap too high because I did not get the 'feel' that we were going to win, and we didn't and we were counted out in Bureau County the following day. This campaign is different. I get a distinct 'feel' that we'll win, and if I were really a wagering person, I would venture a bet on it."

While driving along it was quite natural to philosophize on the general subject of politics and political campaigns. Why does one do it? How does one do it? How does one summon enough energy to do it on a statewide basis? If a man devoted an equal amount of time, energy, and concentration to any business or profession, I felt he would be bound to succeed, but there was a lure, a fascination in politics that had appeal to certain people and I knew I had placed myself in that category.

It was well after midnight before we arrived home. After we had enjoyed a leisurely snack, sleep came and it was indeed sound and rugged sleep induced in considerable measure by the immense reaction to the campaign. On election morning, my first thought was what the weather would be like. It happened to be good. One might have called it a good, typical November day because it was bright and there was just enough chill in the air to make it brisk and to add to the excitement of the day. It was an assurance of a great voter turnout everywhere in the state.

The very first visitor on election morning happened to be a young lady reporter. She found me in the yard in the rear of our home. She was indeed very brusque, "You don't really believe you're going to win today, do you?"

It was the kind of observation I expected. I said, "I not only believe that I shall win, I go a little further. I *shall* win." To her, obviously, that seemed incredible but she evidenced no desire to pursue the matter any further.

Early in the forenoon, we went to the county courthouse to vote. The press had called to ascertain when we would be there, and press and TV cameras were on hand to cover the momentous event. Many people were on hand. We had an opportunity to visit at length with a great many of our fellow townsmen whom we saw so seldom. There was the usual small-town banter with old friends and neighbors and when we returned home, a number of automobiles were already parked in front, and I could tell in an instant that these were the radio, television, and telephone people with an endless amount of gear that they expected to install in virtually every corner of our home to provide very thorough election coverage. In addition, telegrams, letters, and telephone calls began to arrive in quantities, most of them wishing me well. There were, however, a fair share who not only did not wish me well on election day but said so very bluntly and in scarcely complimentary terms. That, however, was usual in a campaign.

With a house filled with reporters, television announcers, radio announcers, and others, it was quite natural that there would be endless questions concerning the campaign and its highlights. I recall one reporter's asking what I thought was the most whimsical incident in the entire campaign. It took a minute to comb something out of memory and then I recalled a meeting one Sunday afternoon at Galesburg, in Knox County, Illinois. Preparations had been made for a huge Sunday afternoon campaign rally and Senator Taft had agreed to come and deliver a speech. He was favorably known in this area and very highly regarded. His presence was the best assurance that there would be a huge crowd and there was. It was my pleasure to introduce him, and he proceeded for about thirty minutes to make a truly rugged Republican speech. He came to the end of it abruptly and then sat down. Someone next to him cupped his hand and whispered to Senator Taft, "You forgot Dirksen. You forgot Dirksen." Actually he blushed in his embarrassment and then stood up and reached for the microphone once more. "Ladies and Gentlemen, I am sorry that I almost forgot the main purpose of my mission here and that was to urge a substantial victory for my friend, Everett Dirksen." That concluded the rally.

Another newsman reminded me of the unpleasant developments at our Illinois state fair in the month of August. The state fair ran for an entire week and the attendance every day was enormous. One day in that week was designated as Republican Day and one day as Democratic Day. The two parties were privileged to present a program about ninety minutes in duration prior to the horse raking and the festivities of the afternoon. On Democratic Day, Governor Stevenson and the state officers and Democratic candidates did the honors, and on Republican Day this responsibility rested on the shoulders of the Republicans, with the principal speech as my portion of the program.

Perhaps at least one thing I said on that occasion might have been regarded as in bad taste, but a political campaign is "for keeps" and whatever might be regarded as legitimate ammunition can be used. It was on that occasion, therefore, that I directed the attention of the people to the communist issue, to the identity of Alger Hiss with that issue, and to the fact that Governor Stevenson had made a character affidavit in behalf of Alger Hiss. I had carefully explored this and had secured an attested copy of the court record in which this affidavit was filed. The whole matter was thoroughly publicized on the front pages throughout the state.

The following Sunday one of the ministers in a Springfield, Illinois, church undertook in the course of his sermon to pay his respects to me in anything but complimentary terms. An account of that sermon was widely publicized. Among other things the minister referred to me as a deacon in the Presbyterian church in my home city of Pekin. The fact of the matter was that I was not a deacon in the Presbyterian church. I was, in fact, not even a member of the church. My church letter and membership still remained in the Second Reformed Church, which my mother had helped to establish and build when she came from the old country as a very young lady. The secretary of the board of deacons and elders in my church took note of this newspaper account and convened a meeting of the board for the purpose of dropping my membership. Before it was done they had alerted my twin brother to what they proposed to do, and he phoned me about the matter. I advised him to be quite sure to attend the meeting and to inform them that if they undertook to exclude me from the one and only church to which I belonged and from which my church letter had never been removed, I would file the necessary proceedings in the circuit court to enjoin such action. That is where the matter rested and my membership was never thereafter threatened.

Quite a number of newspapermen were curious about my relationship with Colonel Robert R. McCormick, editor, publisher, and owner of the *Chicago Tribune*. It was said that Colonel McCormick dominated the Republican political scene. This rumor was based on the close and intimate relationship between former United States Senator C. Wayland Brooks and the colonel. They were close but that did not mean that the *Tribune* or the colonel ever undertook to dominate or dictate.

When the decision was made that I would run for the Senate, I made it my business to arrange for an appointment with the colonel. At the appointed time I was in his outer office prepared to keep that appointment right on time. I shall never forget it.

His secretary said, "The colonel will see you now." Suddenly a door opened and I was quite sure that I observed correctly that the door had no doorknob by which it might be opened. It simply flew open and there in a huge, high-ceilinged room, so very tastefully decorated, was the colonel with hand outstretched. He bade me take a chair on the opposite side of the desk. It was a very brief meeting and I opened the conversation by saying simply, "Colonel, the news may have reached you that I have decided to seek a seat in the United States Senate. You have always been extremely helpful to the Republican party, and I felt it was only proper that you should hear the announcement from me rather than by a second-hand report. I have not come to solicit the support of the *Tribune.* That is a matter that you obviously must determine. I can only hope that my service in the House of Representatives over a sixteen-year period has been such as to merit your confidence and also the support of your people and beyond that, there is little more than I can say." He asked a few very brief questions and when I had answered, he arose and escorted me to the door. I noticed that with the side of his shoe he seemed to lightly kick a brass plate in the baseboard and the door opened and, of course, it intrigued me.

One other thing about that visit, however, intrigued me more. The colonel owned a huge, well-trained police dog. To me he seemed massive. He was in the colonel's office when I arrived. He came up as dogs will do and sniffed and frankly it frightened me until the colonel ordered him to go over and lie down. You will remember that in my college days, when I was in South Dakota selling home remedy books to farmers to make a little stake with which to go back to school, I was bitten by a police dog and never quite got over that experience. To this day I fear police dogs.

In every statewide political campaign, and for that matter in every local political campaign in Chicago or in Cook County, the question was invariably raised as to which candidate or candidates the so-called "West Side bloc" would support. This term was supposed to denote a syndicate or organization that allegedly prospered on vice, gambling, and corruption. Certainly some thought it to be a lineal descendant of the notorious Al Capone organization which flourished in the prohibition era and made bootlegging its principal industry. The West Side bloc, however, was something of an amorphous organization whose members, for the most part, were never named, though a few may have been elected to the Chicago City Council or the Cook County Board or to the Illinois legislature. I knew little or nothing about them, but I did know State Representative Peter Granata fairly well and used to see him in the course of the campaign in Cook County and sometimes on the street in downtown Chicago or at a political rally. He was always immaculately dressed and always very jovial.

Whenever I encountered him on the street I thought nothing about talking with him just as I might with any Chicago citizen. On one occasion such a chance encounter took place in front of the LaSalle Hotel. In the course of this visit I recall that he said, "If you are elected to the Senate, the Italian American group is certainly going to ask you for a favor."

"Pete," I said, "you and your group are entitled to ask me any legitimate favor. If it is a fair and proper request and I can honorably do it, I shall be as helpful as I can."

"It is just this and no more. We believe Italian Americans are entitled to recognition just as much as the Swedes or the Poles or any other group, and we would be prepared at the right time to suggest a name for consideration for a federal judgeship."

"Well, Pete, obviously such a thing will have to wait until we elect a Republican president. If we do, I shall be glad to entertain your suggestion. Do you have any particular person in mind?"

"I certainly do," he said, "I am thinking of Circuit Judge John Sbarbaro."

"If and when the time comes, refresh me on this matter and it will have consideration."

Ultimately that suggestion was made to me and I checked into the credentials of Judge Sbarbaro and found he was highly regarded. There was one impediment; he was sixty-seven years old. The general rule that prevailed was that an appointment to the federal bench when a person was over sixty years old was not considered very likely. Any consideration was precluded shortly thereafter when the judge was killed in an airplane accident. This was my sole experience with the so-called West Side bloc.

Election day wore on, and early in the evening there were some scattered returns, mainly from areas downstate, and they were quite favorable. But in mid-evening, results from the voting machines in Chicago were being reported to the city news desk for dissemination to all news media. When the clock indicated that it was about eleven o'clock, I was seventy-five thousand behind. I could see a look of agony and despair deepening on the face of my twin brother, who was with me. He took me off in a corner. I thought he was actually going to break down and cry. At last he managed to say, "I guess you're sunk."

Actually I was not feeling too happy at the moment, and yet I was absolutely certain that when the all votes were finally in I would be the winner. By way of comfort I said, "Wait until we get the returns from a few particular wards in Chicago. If I come close to an even break in those wards,

I'll know for sure that I shall win." I am not sure how much comfort it gave him, but at the moment it was the best I could do.

The night wore on and so did the morning, and by that time we had a fair idea that victory was won. When at long last the results were announced, they indicated that 3,609,614 Illinois voters had gone to the polls or voted by absentee ballot. It seemed a little incredible in view of the entrenched political machine in the city of Chicago, but the score sheet indicated that I had carried Cook County by 8,000 votes. The huge turnout of suburban voters in the county offset the vote in the fifty city wards. A rundown of the counties indicated that I had carried 82 of the 102 counties of the state and that the plurality was 294,354. I had received 54.1 per cent of the total vote.

So I was at last a senator.

EPILOGUE AND REFLECTIONS

T HE DATE WAS January 3, 1951. Under a constitutional provision it was the date for the Eighty-second Congress to convene since the previous Congress had not provided otherwise.

The other two Musketeers—Mrs. Dirksen and Miss Dirksen—sat in the first row of the members' gallery of the Senate. The occasion called for orchids and they wore them. I took a seat in the rear row of the Senate chamber on the Republican side. When the roll was called by the reading clerk, I shouted a lusty "Here!"

The vice-president was in the chair, prepared to administer the oath to new members. Certificates of election for the new senators were examined as attested by the various governors, and the names of the new senators were called alphabetically. When my name was called, my colleague, Senator Paul H. Douglas, escorted me to the rostrum. I held up my hand, repeated the oath, signed the book, and, finally, I could say that I was a United States senator.

Back at my temporary seat, I looked up at my two girls in the gallery and said to myself, there today are the two real reasons why I made it.

In political life one learns the meaning of fidelity and constancy of friends. Without those attachments life would be barren indeed and all too often hopes might be crushed. I could name ever so many whose loyalty was unshakable, but there are a few who should be mentioned because I have known them for long years. Such a list would have to include Ben Regan, one-time executive vice-president of International Food Service, Inc., and later a partner in the brokerage firm of Hornblower and Weeks; Joe T. Meek, executive director of the Illinois Federation of Retail Associations; Mark Van

Buskirk, director of the Illinois Dairy Products Association; and Robert Tieken, an attorney whom I later nominated for the office of United States district attorney in Chicago. There were also Ralph Scheu, who devoted himself so assiduously to the business of raising money for the campaign; Omer Poos from Hillsboro, Illinois, whom it was my pleasure to suggest for district judge on the Federal Judiciary; and John Meiszner, who captained the ethnic groups and later became collector of customs for Chicago and still later was appointed United States marshal for the Northern Judicial District. The group includes John Bishop, a quiet-spoken attorney who pursued what he thought were his own party responsibilities and did it in such a quiet and effective way; and William Stiehl, who later became the Republican county chairman of St. Claire County and who, together with his very capable wife, had so much to do in bringing about a reasonably favorable result in an area that most politicians thought was forever lost to the Republican party. There are many others I could name.

There was one other person whom I should mention in a very special way. His name was Morton Bodfish. He had been president of the United States Savings and Loan League, an organization made up of most of the savings and loan associations throughout the country. Later he became chairman of the board of the First Federal Savings and Loan Association in Chicago. Along with his other responsibilities, he was also at one time on the faculty of Northwestern University.

He called me one day and suggested that I drop in at his office for a visit. We were moving toward the end of the campaign. After some general discussion he said, "At this point how does it look to you?"

My answer was, "Morton, it's the old story. You're quite familiar with all the allegations that have been made over the years about vote frauds and vote stealing, and that any candidate on our ticket should know in advance that when he comes to the boundaries of Chicago that he will have a handicap that may run into thousands of votes. I do not know, as a matter of strict fact, about the extent of those practices, but I do know that if I can get a reasonably fair count on election day I'll win."

"That," he said, "was what I wanted to talk to you about. The United States League has member-associations all over Chicago. Generally speaking they are staffed with young and middle-aged men who are devoted to sound government. I believe I could get a substantial number of the fellows to turn out on election day and man the polls. They will stay right there until the polls close and the count begins. If you supply them with credentials as official watchers, they could remain in the polling place to make certain that there would be no cheating."

"When you speak of credentials," I said, "that offers no problem, but in all candor I wouldn't ask anybody to serve in this capacity without telling him that there are some inherent hazards. In some previous elections, poll watchers have been kidnapped, bound hand and foot, and thrown into a vacant apartment until the election has been assured one way or another. Then an anonymous telephone call to the police causes them to investigate. Usually the poll watcher has been found somewhat the worse for wear."

He assured me that he would begin an immediate recruitment of good, robust men who could be trusted and who had the courage and daring to see it through. Perhaps this one fact may have been as instrumental in victory as any one thing I could name.

Was it not Michelangelo who once remarked that trifles make perfection? May I dare presume that the outcome of a political campaign has on many occasions hung on what one might regard as a trifle? In hindsight, this one incident might not have been such a trifle after all.

Alexander County, Illinois, of which Cairo is the county seat, is the southernmost county in the state. Unbelievable as it may seem, this county is further south than most of Virginia, most of West Virginia, most of Kentucky, and most of Missouri. Naturally it would have something of a southern flavor and have a substantial number of black citizens. As I have said, it was the usual custom for statewide candidates to dip into Alexander County and the adjoining counties early in the campaign and never go back. Following the promise I had made in the primary campaign, I had divided my time between downstate and Chicago.

Republican County Chairman Jean Bode, lamented the fact that, in a way, they felt like political stepchildren. When she called me on the telephone and urged that I come to their area and help, I said, "Jean, what do you propose?"

"Well," she replied, "couldn't we have a dinner? I am sure if we had your assurance that you would come that it would be a complete sellout."

While this conversation was in progress, I was examining my calendar and we did agree upon a date for such a dinner to be held at the Cairo Hotel. How right she was about the sellout; the problem was what to do about the many people who demanded tickets for whom there was actually no room in the hotel's modest dining room.

I thought nothing more about the matter until a week before the scheduled dinner when I received an anonymous telephone call. It was from a man who refused to identify himself except to say that he was my friend and that he would vote for me. Then he said, "Dirksen, I don't suppose you know it but the Cairo Hotel, where your dinner is to be held, is segregated and they do not serve colored people. The liberal press already knows about this, and some of those newspapermen are already in Cairo staking out the situation to see what they can do to you after this dinner. They will advertise you all over the state as having been the sponsor of a dinner where not even the leaders of the Negro block could be served. You know better than I do that newspapers like the *St. Louis Post-Dispatch* and the *St. Louis Times* will make the most of this."

When he had finished, I said, "Whoever you are, I can only say a million thanks for alerting me."

I contacted Jean Bode and told her what had happened. Then I said, "I have a suggestion. Suppose we have a small dinner, with the officers of the county committee and the state and local candidates, and then hold the regular rally at the courthouse. We can easily defend this kind of arrangement. To be sure there will be some disappointed people but that invariably happens in every campaign. Suppose you discuss this with the hotel manager, and also make arrangements for the use of the courthouse for the rally that same night." This arrangement appealed to her; she quickly got the whole matter in hand and arranged for a dinner for only about twenty people. At the end of the dinner we all walked to the courthouse. The place was filled. Colored people sat on the left side of the center aisle facing the rostrum; the whites sat on the right side. This was still a matter of custom in Cairo. There was no furor, no demonstrations, and the only frustration was experienced by the ultraliberal press, which was there in force. In a campaign in which the results might have been close, trouble in Cairo could have had considerable impact.

It is interesting how quickly political passions can be aroused and equally interesting how quickly they can subside. Remembering my delightful visit with President Truman at the White House before I left Washington in 1948, I was interested when, in the last days of the campaign, the president agreed to a St. Louis speech on behalf of Senator Lucas. St. Louis was chosen for this purpose because it was just across the Mississippi River from Illinois, and there were radio, television, and press facilities there through which the president's speech could be adequately covered. That night President Truman paid his respects to me in language which came naturally to one who had been schooled in Kansas City ward politics. When he referred to me in the course of the speech, he called me "that Thing across the river." I fairly chortled to myself and thought, "It would take more than those words to win a victory," and I was right.

It was a long time afterward when I saw President Truman at a cocktail party sponsored by Mayor Daley of Chicago. The mayor had invited many Republicans, as was his custom. Virtually all of the invited guests were on hand when suddenly President Truman appeared through a side door. As he approached the crowd he saw me and said, "Dirksen, what have you in that glass?"

I said, "Mr. President, it's an old-fashioned."

Without hesitation he said, "Sounds good to me. I'll have one." He visited through the crowd.

When the opportunity presented itself, I engaged him in conversation and reminded him of what he had said to me when I quit Congress and, also, what he had called me in his one major speech on behalf of Senator Lucas. The president laughed quite heartily and simply said, "Dirksen, you know how those things are in a political campaign." And, of course, I did know.

It is often forgotten that in every sense, and particularly at the national level, we have party government. Quite often a voter may say that he is for the man and not for the party, but if "the man" means the elected candidate, he quickly finds when he takes his seat in Congress that he becomes a party man. He cannot escape it. To be sure, we have had a few independents but not many, and no matter how a man may vote, he fits in with some party program and structure.

It begins from the moment he is assigned a seat, particularly in the United States Senate where he must be assigned on his side of the aisle by a committee that handles such matters. We see this party structure unfold in the case of nominations made by the president to boards and commissions which have been created by the Congress. Invariably the statute states the number of members for such an agency and provides that no more than half plus one may come from the same political party.

One realizes the prevalence of the party structure also when newspapers record any given vote. It is inevitably tabulated as so many Democrats for, so many Republicans for, and so many Democrats against, so many Republicans against.

There will be sharp differences of opinion as to whether this is good or bad, but how would we fare if we did not have a party in power to be held accountable for the conduct of government and another party with the power to call it to account?

To be sure, there are liberal Republicans and liberal Democrats, and there are conservative Republicans and conservative Democrats. And there are moderates in the middle. The basic party structure still remains, however. It is still a two-party system under which we operate.

I recall rather vividly meeting a very active group of Republican women in the northern section of Illinois. They were full of energy, deeply interested in politics, and said very plainly that, although they bore the Republican label, they were for the man before they were for the party. Before my talks to this group, I indulged in equally plain talk. They seemed to be offended at that time. I was concerned not about myself but for a former senator whose name was on the ballot. I undertook to lay down what I considered to be the Republican gospel and to demonstrate that the party platform had more meaning than was usually attached to it, and that the party structure was a living organism.

There is a special point in all this. I have reserved it for this epilogue on the campaign of 1950. During the campaign I had observed the extraordinary number of young men and women who participated actively. When it was over I was the recipient of letters, from many such young people, from different parts of the country, in which they asked how to get into politics, how to become a congressman, how to become a senator. I had thought it was wonderful that they took such interest and particularly so since I had in my mind a series of questions which the Gallup poll had submitted to the country. The last of these questions was, "If you had a son or daughter would you like to see them aspire to a political career? If not, why not?" The response to that question by parents was almost unanimous: they did not want to see their sons and daughters venture into a political career, and the reason for it was that they felt that politics was corrupt. I felt this was unfortunate—a dismal misevaluation of American political life! I wanted to do something to change that image.

Those who wrote me were serious young men and women keenly interested in public service and public office. I made the distinction between public service and public office because we think of public office as elective, and because most of the letters indicated that it was the challenge of public office that intrigued them. I felt that those letters should not be ignored, nor should they be dealt with in a cavalier fashion.

In puzzling over this matter, I worked out a composite reply which I could send to those young people in its entirety, or from which I could extract some paragraphs that would be suitable for such a letter. The reply was as follows:

Dear Mr. Brown:

I was delighted to have your letter and to note that you are interested in a career in public office. Moreover, I was glad to note that at some point in the future you might aspire to a seat in the House of Representatives or the United States Senate. In our system of government virtually anyone may aspire and seek the highest office in the land. The very fact that in the Senate and in the House today are members who long ago were page boys in those same bodies should be proof enough that those goals are attainable.

Let me suggest that it might be well for you to acquaint yourself with the members of your local and county committee. You might help with the normal chores when the committee meets, such as running errands, manning the telephones, folding literature, and stuffing envelopes while listening in on the political conversations as candidates and others discuss issues, strategy, and many other matters.

I believe also that it might be quite useful and profitable for you to indulge in a bit of self-catechizing. Are you willing to sacrifice time, energy, money, and, in fact, almost everything in pursuit of a political goal? This is highly important because an elective political career calls for long hours and laborious work.

Are you at ease with people and is it easy for you to meet people in all walks of life? Public service is not a vacuum. The politician deals with people. It is essential that he meet them, that he like them, and that he understand them.

Can you stand heat and pressure? The very fact that you deal with people brings into play the divergencies of opinion, the conflicts of group interest which express themselves in the form of pressure. You may recall what President Truman once said, "If you can't take the heat, stay out of the kitchen."

Do you have the study habit? In the pursuit of public business, research, or in preparation for a speech or the analysis of a court decision or a legislative proposal, the study habit is indispensable.

Do you want a public career bad enough? The late Fannie Hurst, who by any standard was a highly successful author, once remarked that "a million people want to write but they do not want to do so hard enough." If you want to hard enough that urge becomes your sustaining source when adversity overtakes you. Are you patient? Public business is a huge, inert, diverse thing. It is a product of many miles and much thinking over a long period of time and does not move very fast. I am sure that your reading in both early and contemporary history will recall that dictators who rise to power through force and then undertake to rule by command and decree and display rank impatience do not last in a free representative society. Things do not move very fast nor very far at one time. Patience, therefore, becomes a veritable jewel.

Can you take defeat and bounce back? Defeat for public office is a common experience. I know how defeat can embitter. So often candidates feel certain that they have sufficient assurances from individuals and groups to make victory certain, and suddenly the victory turns to ashes.

How tolerant is your wife if you have one? Or your husband if you have one? If you are not married, the chances are that you will be in due course. You should remember that you do not run for public office—your family does. I recall instances where a son or wife or a brother ruined a promising political career for a reasonably young man with real talent for public affairs.

What will you give for what you get? Life is compensatory. Remember the formula they taught in high-school physics long ago that work out equals work in, and so it is in public life.

Do babies like you? It is quite a test, and I can assure you that babies are important.

Do old folks like you? There are a lot of them and they take their civic responsibilities seriously. How often a gracious and gentle hug for a person over sixty-five is like balm in Gilead.

Perhaps I should add one more thing. If you do undertake a venture of public office, the timing is important. What are the conditions which prevail? What are the circumstances and how do you fit into the overall picture? Was it not Shakespeare who wrote, "There is a tide in the affairs of men, which taken at the flood leads on to fortune; omitted, all the voyage of their lives is bound in miseries and in shallows."

I earnestly hope that this dissertation may be useful.

I can only trust and believe that this letter did not discourage aspirants, despite its frankness.

So you still want to be a senator? Why not?

INDEX